Spinoza's Epistemology through a Geometrical Lens

"Each chapter of *Spinoza's Epistemology through a Geometrical Lens* makes an important contribution to our understanding of Spinoza's philosophy. Homan develops a fascinating interpretation of Spinoza's views about the ontology of mathematics, which he applies in surprising and insightful ways to address a range of difficult interpretive and philosophical problems. The overarching picture is inspiring. Homan's Spinoza is a metaphysical realist, an optimist about the limits of human knowledge, and a friend to scientific inquiry."
—John Grey, *Department of Philosophy, Michigan State University, USA*

Matthew Homan

Spinoza's Epistemology through a Geometrical Lens

Matthew Homan
Philosophy and Religion
Christopher Newport University
Newport News, VA, USA

ISBN 978-3-030-76738-9   ISBN 978-3-030-76739-6   (eBook)
https://doi.org/10.1007/978-3-030-76739-6

© The Editor(s) (if applicable) and The Author(s), under exclusive licence to Springer Nature Switzerland AG 2021
This work is subject to copyright. All rights are solely and exclusively licensed by the Publisher, whether the whole or part of the material is concerned, specifically the rights of translation, reprinting, reuse of illustrations, recitation, broadcasting, reproduction on microfilms or in any other physical way, and transmission or information storage and retrieval, electronic adaptation, computer software, or by similar or dissimilar methodology now known or hereafter developed.
The use of general descriptive names, registered names, trademarks, service marks, etc. in this publication does not imply, even in the absence of a specific statement, that such names are exempt from the relevant protective laws and regulations and therefore free for general use.
The publisher, the authors and the editors are safe to assume that the advice and information in this book are believed to be true and accurate at the date of publication. Neither the publisher nor the authors or the editors give a warranty, expressed or implied, with respect to the material contained herein or for any errors or omissions that may have been made. The publisher remains neutral with regard to jurisdictional claims in published maps and institutional affiliations.

This Palgrave Macmillan imprint is published by the registered company Springer Nature Switzerland AG.
The registered company address is: Gewerbestrasse 11, 6330 Cham, Switzerland

[W]hen Spinoza speaks of intuitive knowledge and says: This kind of knowing proceeds from an adequate idea of the formal essence of certain attributes of God to the adequate knowledge of the essence of things, these few words give me the courage to devote my whole life to the examination of things...of whose formal essences I can hope to form an adequate idea.
—Johann Wolfgang von Goethe (1786)[1]

---

[1] *Briefwechsel zwischen Goethe und F. H. Jacobi*, ed. M. Jacobi (Leipzig: Wiedmann'sche Buchhandlung, 1846), 105–6.

Acknowledgments

I am grateful to a number of people who in one way or another helped me to bring this book project to fruition. Sanem Soyarslan, Karolina Hübner, and Christopher Martin graciously provided helpful feedback on chapter drafts. John Grey reviewed the manuscript for Palgrave and his judicious suggestions undoubtedly elicited improvements. Thanks to Edwin Curley and Brian McInnis for assistance on questions of text and translation; Graham Schweig for his advice; Eric Schliesser for his encouragement; and Phil Getz and Tikoji Rao for their editorial support. Many of the ideas expressed in this book can be traced back over ten years to my doctoral research, and I was fortunate to have Ursula Goldenbaum as my advisor during that germinal stage. She devoted countless hours to sharing her knowledge and insight with me, and to pointing me in the right direction. Her remarkable generosity as a teacher, mentor, and friend both then and since has been invaluable. My deepest thanks, finally, to Ashley Brewer, who cheerfully retrieves books for me from her library, supports everything I do, and fills my life with love and happiness.

Contents

1 **Introduction**   1
   1.1 *The Question of Mathematization*   6
   1.2 *Outline of Chapters*   15
   1.3 *A Note on Texts*   18
   References   19

2 **Mathematics and Methodology: Spinoza *Contra* Skepticism**   23
   2.1 *The Dogmatic Response*   25
   2.2 *Mathematical Ideas qua Epistemic Exemplars: Problems for the Dogmatic Interpretation*   30
   2.3 *Attaining the Idea of God: The Cartesian Response*   34
      2.3.1 *Textual Evidence for the Cartesian Interpretation*   37
   2.4 *The Cartesio-Dogmatic Response*   39
   2.5 *Objections and Replies*   42
   References   48

3 **Realism and Antirealism About Mathematical Entities**   51
   3.1 *Figures as Beings of Reason*   52
      3.1.1 *Figures as (Imaginative) Universals*   54
      3.1.2 *Figures as a Form of Measure*   58
      3.1.3 *Figures as Non-beings*   61
      3.1.4 *Genetically Conceived Figures*   63
   3.2 *Reductio ad Acosmism: The Case Against Antirealism*   66

	3.3	*Figure and Finite Bodies: The Case for Realism*	70
	3.3.1	*Descartes and the Ontological Status of Figures*	70
	3.3.2	*Spinoza's Theory of Corporeal Individuals and Figure*	73
	3.3.3	*What Are Figures in Spinoza?*	78
	3.4	*True Ideas of Number?*	82
		References	84
4	**Reason and Imagination in Spinozan Science**	87
	4.1	*Reason and Spinozan Science*	89
	4.1.1	*Common Notions as Foundations of Reason and Laws of Nature*	91
	4.2	*Imagination in Spinozan Science and Issues of Adequacy*	98
	4.2.1	*From the Historia Naturae to Common Notions*	100
	4.2.2	*Descending to Particulars*	106
	4.3	*Peculiar Common Notions*	111
		References	121
5	**Geometry and Spinozan Science**	123
	5.1	*Spinoza on the Geometry of Optical Lenses*	125
	5.2	*Response to an (other) Objection from Letter 12*	136
	5.2.1	*The Commensurability Response*	142
	5.3	*Letters 80–83 and the Incompleteness of Spinozan Science*	144
		References	149
6	**Spinoza's Notions of Essence**	153
	6.1	*Common Essence, Species Essence, and Individual Essence*	154
	6.2	*Formal Essence, Actual Essence, and Existence*	163
	6.2.1	*Formal Essences and Existence*	164
	6.2.2	*Actual Essences and Existence*	170
	6.2.3	*E2p8 Reconsidered*	175
		References	179
7	**Intuitive Knowledge: The Perfection of Reason**	181
	7.1	*Preliminary Analysis of the Principal Texts*	184
	7.2	*The Content of Intuitive Knowledge: The Common Essence Interpretation*	191

	7.3	*Beyond the Common Essence Interpretation*	197
		7.3.1 *A Geometrical Alternative to the Fourth Proportional Example: The Isoperimetric Problem*	198
		7.3.2 *The Isoperimetric Example and Spinoza's Definition of Intuitive Knowledge*	201
	7.4	*The Difference Between Reason and Intuitive Knowledge: A Method Interpretation*	208
		7.4.1 *Can* Conatus *Save the Content Interpretation?*	213
	7.5	Amor Dei Intellectualis *and the Supremacy of Intuitive Knowledge*	217
	7.6	*Intuitive Knowledge in Spinozan Science*	224
	References		224
8	**Conclusion**		227
	8.1	*Spinoza's Epistemic Outlook*	228
	8.2	*Spinoza Vis-à-Vis Descartes (and Galileo)*	232
	References		238
References			239
Index			249

Abbreviations

Works by Descartes

AT   *Oeuvres de Descartes*. 11 vols. Edited by C. Adam and P. Tannery. Paris: J. Vrin, 1996.

CSM   *The Philosophical Writings of Descartes*. Vols. 1–2. Translated and edited by John Cottingham, Robert Stoothoff, and Dugald Murdoch. Cambridge: Cambridge University Press, 1984–85.

CSMK   *The Philosophical Writings of Descartes*. Vol. 3. Translated and edited by John Cottingham, Robert Stoothoff, Dugald Murdoch, and Anthony Kenny. Cambridge: Cambridge University Press, 1991.

DM   *Discourse on Method, Optics, Geometry, and Meteorology*. Revised Edition. Translated by Paul J. Olscamp. Indianapolis, IN: Hackett Publishing Company, 2001.

Works by Spinoza

CM   *Cogitata Metaphysica* (*Metaphysical Thoughts*). Cited by part and chapter.

Curley   *The Collected Works of Spinoza*. 2 vols. Edited and Translated by Edwin Curley. Princeton, NJ: Princeton University Press, 1985, 2016. Cited by volume and page.

DPP   *Renati des Cartes Principiorum Philosophiae Pars I & Pars II* (*Descartes' Principles of Philosophy*)

E	*Ethics*
Ep.	Letters
G	*Spinoza Opera.* 4 vols. Edited by Carl Gebhardt. Heidelberg: Carl Winter, 1925. Cited by volume and page.
KV	*Korte Verhandeling van God de Mensch en deszelfs Welstand* (*Short Treatise on God, Man, and His Well-Being*). Cited by part, chapter, and paragraph number.
TIE	*Tractatus de Intellectus Emendatione* (*Treatise on the Emendation of the Intellect*). Cited by paragraph number.
TTP	*Tractatus Theologico-Politicus* (*Theological-Political Treatise*). Cited by chapter and paragraph number.

Translations of Spinoza are from Curley unless otherwise indicated. In citing Spinoza's *Ethics* (and the DPP), I use the following abbreviations: a = axiom, app = appendix, c = corollary, d = definition, defaff = definitions of the affects, dem = demonstration, lem = lemma, post = postulate, p = proposition, pref = preface, s = scholium. Thus, E2p40s2 stands for *Ethics*, Part 2, Proposition 40, Scholium 2.

List of Figures

Fig. 5.1 The figure depicts the reconvergence of light rays from an object (V, X, Y) via refraction in the eye's cornea and lens (L), and the observation (by P) of the image thereby formed at the back of the eye (R, S, T) from within an enclosed chamber (Z). (*Discourse on Method for Rightly Directing One's Reason and Searching for Truth in the Sciences, Together with the Optics, Meteorology, and Geometry, Which Are Essays in This Method.* Leiden: Maire, 1637) — 127

Fig. 5.2 The figure depicts Spinoza's contention that parallel rays entering a circular lens from any point are refracted so as to come together in a single point. (*Opera Posthuma.* J. Rieuwertsz, 1677, p. 532) — 128

CHAPTER 1

Introduction

Spinoza's philosophy has at its heart a hierarchical trio of kinds of knowledge (*cognitio*): imagination (*imaginatio*), reason (*ratio*), and intuitive knowledge (*scientia intuitiva*).[1] First and humblest, imagination consists

---

[1] *Cognitio* presents a difficult choice for the translator. While "knowledge" is the more common translation (and the one used by Curley), a number of commentators opt for "cognition." The latter tend to cite the fact that the first kind of *cognitio* is a cause of falsity (E2p41), whereas nothing worthy of the name "knowledge" should cause falsity. Since "cognition" is more epistemically neutral than "knowledge," it better encompasses the first as well as the second and third kinds of *cognitio* (both of which contain only true ideas). However, if we consider that the first kind of *cognitio*, for Spinoza, can be understood as a part or fragment of a *true* idea in God's intellect, then it makes sense, in my mind, to consider it as a kind of *knowledge*, albeit a partial or fragmentary kind of knowledge. This line of reasoning is reinforced when we consider such passages as E5p38dem: "The Mind's essence consists in *cognitione* (by E2p11); therefore, the more the Mind *cogniscit* things by the second and third kind of *cognitionis*, the greater the part of it that remains […]." As I see it, to translate *cognitio* and *cognoscere* here with the neutral "cognition" and "cognize" obscures the fact that the epistemic situation is not neutral. It is in our nature to *know*, and to the extent that we do not *know*, it is only because we are parts of God's infinite intellect, and thus *lack* knowledge. Whether our *cognitio* is inadequate (and thus a cause of falsity) or adequate (and thus true), then, it is a question of epistemically non-neutral *knowledge*, rather than neutral *cognition*. There is, however, another argument for translating *cognitio* as "cognition," namely, it offers an easy solution for respecting the difference between *cognitio* and *scientia*. If *cognitio* is rendered as "cognition," this leaves "knowledge" for *scientia*. I do not think this outweighs the disadvantages of the sterility of "cognition," however, so I will use "knowledge" for both *cognitio* and *scientia*, despite the problem with this procedure. Some

in the unexamined ideas and beliefs we accumulate about ourselves and surroundings just by virtue of being born into the world and interacting with its various denizens. We imagine that fire is hot, dogs bark, our decisions are free, the world is full of beauty, but not without ugliness, eventually we shall die, and other such things. It is not as easy to say what reason consists in, so a statement of its content must wait. What is certain is that it represents a major advance beyond the haphazard opinions of the imagination to genuine understanding. Nevertheless, Spinoza often treats reason as having primarily subordinate significance, a stepping stone to an even higher form of knowledge: intuitive knowledge.[2] At the pinnacle of the hierarchy, intuitive knowledge is claimed to yield insight into the essences of things, notably our own.

Each Spinozan cognitive state is also an affective one. This explains why summiting the ladder of knowledge comes with the promise of non-epistemic rewards as well: liberation from anger, fear, despair, and other destructive passions, as well as the enjoyment of the highest human blessedness and perfection, to name a few. The intrinsic connection that Spinoza sees between cognition and affection, and thus between knowledge and ethics, makes his theory of knowledge particularly attractive from a contemporary standpoint where epistemological and ethical issues are frequently siloed. Relative to its seventeenth-century context, too, Spinoza's epistemology is distinctive and distinctively compelling. Many of his contemporaries emphasized the material and technological fruits of knowledge. Descartes, for instance, memorably heralds the ascendance of modern, scientific humans as "the masters and possessors of Nature."[3] While Spinoza by no means despises scientific and technological progress, its ultimate value, for him, lies chiefly in conditioning a more intellectual *summum bonum*: "the knowledge of the union that the mind has with the whole of Nature" (TIE 13/G 2:8). This is far from a renunciation of worldly striving à la Pascal. Knowledge is power, for Spinoza, to be sure,

---

have used "science" for *scientia* to solve this problem. While this might work in certain contexts, rendering *scientia intuitiva* (Spinoza's third kind of *cognitio*) as "intuitive science" sounds tortured to my ear. See Curley 2:637–38 for further discussion.

[2] See KV 2.4.9/G 1:61; KV 2.26.6/G 1:109; E5p28/G 2:297. The notion of reason as a stepping stone, which receives strong emphasis in the *Short Treatise*, is much less apparent in the *Ethics*, signaling, as I will suggest later, an elevation in the status of reason from the early works to the *Ethics*. Nevertheless, Spinoza consistently stresses the superiority of the third kind of knowledge, and its status as the pinnacle of human knowing throughout his works.

[3] AT VI: 62.

but power conceived as psychological freedom, tranquility, and contentment.

These, then, are among the promises of Spinoza's epistemic program: knowledge of things as they truly are in themselves and the collateral achievement of human moral perfection. I have not even mentioned the prospective social benefits in the offing or Spinoza's eternity of mind doctrine. Suffice it to say that, with or without such additions, this all sounds very enticing. Can Spinoza actually deliver on any of these promises? This is a question that can be answered only by each student of Spinoza for themselves, but any serious assessment presupposes a careful study of Spinoza's epistemology. Remarkably, there have been very few books devoted to the topic.[4] In part, this may be explained by the deep embeddedness of Spinoza's theory of knowledge in his broader metaphysical system, which makes it something of a challenge (one this book will attempt to meet) to treat his epistemology in any depth without also expounding a detailed interpretation of his metaphysics. But this does not account for the existence of important, influential books on Spinoza's philosophy in general with little or nothing to say about the three kinds of knowledge.[5] The latter can only be explained (putting the predilections of commentators to the side) by the paucity and obscurity of what Spinoza says about the kinds of knowledge, especially the second and third kinds, despite their centrality to his philosophical project.

None of this means that Spinoza's epistemology is not worth studying in its own right. That the topic merits special focus is something that I hope will become increasingly apparent as we go along, if it is not so already. The endeavor faces significant challenges, however. The most significant are the two already indicated. First, it is necessary to respect the

---

[4] The only one of which I am aware, at least in English, is Parkinson 1954. A. Garrett 2003, which is more recent, should also be mentioned. Although it is devoted to Spinoza's method, there is significant overlap between methodology and epistemology in Spinoza, and Garrett's erudite study offers valuable insights into the latter. None of this is to say, of course, that there have not been many fine papers devoted to aspects of Spinoza's epistemology. I will have occasion to reference many of these over the course of this book.

[5] I have in mind, in particular, Bennett's *A Study of Spinoza's* Ethics (1984) and Della Rocca's *Spinoza* (2008). While addressing Spinoza's distinction between inadequate and adequate ideas, Della Rocca (2008) ignores the three kinds of knowledge altogether. Bennett, for his part, has some brief things to say about reason and imagination, but only condescends "reluctantly" to touch on intuitive knowledge in order to document its contribution to the "unmitigated and seemingly unmotivated disaster" that is, in Bennett's estimation, the second half of *Ethics* Part 5 (1984, 357).

embeddedness of Spinoza's theory of knowledge within the broader philosophical system, and the complex network of metaphysical underpinnings upon which a proper understanding of the epistemology rests, without losing sight of the epistemology to the metaphysics. Despite the connections to the metaphysics, as well as the ethics, which help to render Spinoza's epistemology especially compelling, the latter is more autonomous, nevertheless, in my view, than often thought. It will be relatively straightforward to meet this challenge, then, by supplying metaphysical background as the opportunity or need arises along the way of discussing the epistemological issues that are my concern.

Less straightforwardly, an interpretation of Spinoza's kinds of knowledge must be constructed with relatively scant, oftentimes seemingly contradictory textual materials. The primary problem is uncertainty regarding the nature and range of the content of Spinozan knowledge claims. It is not always apparent what knowledge is supposed to be *about* in Spinoza's system (beyond knowing that it must be about God, the one substance, one way or another). While this problem is formidable, it is not intractable, and I believe I have a way of mitigating the difficulty. A fruitful strategy, as I turn to explain, is to clarify the status of mathematical entities.[6]

The problem of uncertainty regarding the content of Spinozan knowledge claims is particularly acute in the case of mathematical content. Spinoza exhibits ambivalence about the epistemic status of mathematical ideas, as I will show, making it unclear whether knowledge of natural things includes mathematical knowledge or not. How this question is decided one way or another has far-reaching implications for the interpretation of Spinoza's epistemology and ontology. For this reason, my approach to Spinoza's epistemology will be based on an interpretation of the epistemic and ontological status of mathematical entities in Spinoza.

Generally speaking, the significance of mathematics for Spinoza's philosophy is well appreciated. The geometrical order in which Spinoza composed his masterwork, the *Ethics*, is the best-known and most outwardly striking way in which his philosophy bears the stamp of mathematical inspiration. Spinoza also frequently uses mathematical examples and analogies to illustrate key ideas and concepts of his philosophy. Notably, he compares the way in which things follow from God's infinite nature to the way in which it follows from the nature of a triangle that its three angles

---

[6] My article, "Geometrical Figures in Spinoza's Book of Nature" (Homan 2018b), is a forerunner of some of the interpretive ideas developed in greater detail here.

are equal to two right angles. In the early work, *Treatise on the Emendation of the Intellect*, moreover, Spinoza uses genetic ideas of mathematical objects to illustrate the formal properties of true ideas. For instance, he describes forming the concept of a sphere through the rotation of a semicircle around a center, explaining that he knows this is a true idea regardless of whether any sphere has ever been formed in this way.

Such mathematical examples and analogies have signaled to a number of commentators that mathematics does more in Spinoza than provide a model for presenting philosophy *ordine geometrico*. Spinozan reality seems itself to be ordered geometrically. For Spinoza, says Gueroult:

> Philosophy must take Geometry for its model, and will be true only if it manages to prove itself in the geometrical method. The geometrical method is, therefore, not just a borrowed garment, but Philosophy's inner spring, the necessary way in which it unfolds and advances as truth.[7]

More recently, Valtteri Viljanen argues that in Spinoza's "geometry-inspired ontology,"[8] "each and every genuine thing is an entity of power endowed with an internal structure akin to that of geometrical objects."[9] These interpretations emphasize what we might call the *formal* significance of mathematical examples.[10] They highlight the way in which mathematics provides a model for Spinoza's philosophy, leaving open the question whether mathematics itself features in its *content*.

It is indisputable that Spinoza uses mathematical examples to illustrate formal or structural aspects of his philosophy. As I will discuss in detail in Chap. 2, the sphere conceived as the rotation of a semicircle illustrates the form that an idea must take if it is to be a true idea. Spinoza also contrasts three ways of solving a mathematical problem to illustrate formal differences between the aforementioned three kinds of knowledge. This example is of no small value for understanding the kinds of knowledge and will be treated accordingly in what follows. In this study, however, I will primarily be interested in a different question regarding mathematics' significance and place in Spinoza's thought. In particular, do mathematical

---

[7] Gueroult 1974, 471, my translation.
[8] Viljanen 2011, 21.
[9] Viljanen 2011, 2.
[10] Viljanen stresses *formal* causation in his interpretation of Spinoza's ontology. When I speak of formal in this context, I do not refer to formal causation, but the form-content distinction.

entities feature in the *content* of Spinozan knowledge and reality? This question can be asked more specifically about geometrical entities—spheres, triangles, and circles—and also about numbers. Do geometrical figures feature in the content of Spinozan knowledge and reality? Do numbers? Spinoza famously resolves to treat human behavior "as if it were a question of lines, planes, or bodies."[11] What about lines, planes, and bodies themselves?[12] These questions provide a useful lens through which to interpret Spinoza's epistemology. So, at least, I hope to show.

1.1 The Question of Mathematization

In the case of Descartes, Spinoza's most important philosophical influence (and foil), the answer to the question concerning the reality of geometrical entities is most certainly, yes. Descartes stated as much explicitly: "I recognize no matter in corporeal things apart from that which the geometers call quantity, and take as the object of their demonstrations, i.e., that to which every kind of division, shape and motion is applicable."[13] Descartes' comment complements the following celebrated passage in Galileo's *Assayer*:

> Philosophy is written in this all-encompassing book that is constantly open before our eyes, that is the universe; but it cannot be understood unless one first learns to understand the language and knows the characters in which it is written. It is written in mathematical language, and its characters are triangles, circles, and other geometrical figures; without these it is humanly impossible to understand a word of it, and one wanders around pointlessly in a dark labyrinth.[14]

---

[11] E3pref/G 2:138. Curley renders "*de lineis, planis, aut de corporibus*" as "lines, planes, and bodies" (my emphasis). I have opted for the more literal translation of "*aut*" here.

[12] One of the questions to be taken up in this study (especially in Chap. 3) is whether Spinoza conceives bodies in geometrical terms or in some non-geometrical fashion. Spinoza's phrase, "lines, planes, or bodies," provides prima facie evidence for the geometrical interpretation that I will defend, since the association with "lines" and "planes" suggests that by "bodies" he means geometrical solids.

[13] CSM 1:247.

[14] Galileo 2008, 183.

The view of nature as constituted by mathematical entities, particularly, geometrical ones, as expressed in the passages just quoted, has come to be spoken of in terms of the *mathematization* of nature.[15]

The mathematization of nature is often used to describe what is thought by many to be among the most distinctive changes brought about by the scientific revolution over the course of the sixteenth and seventeenth centuries. Koyré writes,

> I believe that the intellectual attitude of classical science can be characterized by the following two changes, which are moreover intimately related: geometrization of space and dissolution of the Cosmos, that is to say the disappearance from within scientific reasoning of the Cosmos as a presupposition and the substitution for the concrete space of pre-Galilean physics of the abstract space of Euclidean geometry.[16]

The "grand narrative of mathematization"[17] has been criticized for oversimplification,[18] but I think it provides a useful heuristic for approaching Spinoza, nevertheless. Before I put the question of mathematization

---

[15] For a discussion of Descartes' project of mathematization, see Gaukroger 1980. See, especially, Gaukroger 1980, 123–35, for a useful comparative analysis of the respective Cartesian and Galilean projects of mathematization. Cf. Ariew 2016. Ariew argues against associating this passage with the mathematization thesis on the grounds that Descartes' physics is not founded on mathematics per se, but on the metaphysics of clear and distinct ideas; it is simply a coincidence, according to Ariew, that "mathematicians rely on some of the same clear and distinct ideas as natural philosophers do" (2016, 121). It is not clear to me, however, why it should matter to the validity of the mathematization thesis whether the overlap between physics and mathematics is coincidental or not. Even if it is due ultimately to a shared metaphysics of clarity and distinctness, the principles of physics end up being mathematical either way.

[16] Koyré 1978, 2–3.

[17] Gorham et al. 2016, 5.

[18] The charge of oversimplification is the guiding thesis of the recent volume of essays, *The Language of Nature: Reassessing the Mathematization of Natural Philosophy in the Seventeenth Century* (2016), edited by Gorham et al. The authors of the volume's introduction point out how the notion of mathematization glosses over important differences between types of mathematization. Intuitive geometrical models contrasted with less intuitive algebraic methods, for instance, and seventeenth-century figures debated the respective merits of both. While the idea of mathematization had a great deal of power in the seventeenth-century imagination, this was not always matched with the success of mathematization efforts in practice. A number of fields resisted mathematization while even in physics, many philosophers, such as Descartes, failed to articulate basic laws of nature in mathematical terms. Many prominent early moderns, moreover, such as Gassendi and Locke, who did much to advance

directly to our protagonist, let me say something about my understanding of the mathematization thesis itself. First, I understand it more specifically as a thesis about *geometrization*. The focus on geometry is evident in the passages from Descartes and Galileo (and Koyré) quoted above. I will have something to say about number later on, but my primary focus will be on figures.

Second, I see the mathematization thesis as consisting in the claim that all finite bodies in nature are geometrical inasmuch as they have some figure—whether circular, triangular, or what have you—just by virtue of being spatially extended. To accept this claim is to be a realist about mathematization. Very generally, mathematical realism affirms the mind-independent existence of mathematical entities. Within this general categorization, we can distinguish two strains. A stronger strain, typically associated with Plato (in particular, his doctrine of forms), holds that mathematical entities exist in and through themselves, independently of bodies.[19] To express this, I will sometimes attach a "per se" qualifier to talk of numbers or figures. (Thus, a sphere per se is a sphere conceived as existing in and through itself, independently of being physically instantiated by a body.) A weaker strain holds that mathematical entities exist independently of minds, but only insofar as they exist as the properties of bodies, not independently of the latter.[20] For the purposes of this study, I will assume that the stronger strain entails the weaker one, but not vice versa. Whether or not Descartes, for instance, believes that geometrical figures

---

"modern" thought, showed relatively little interest in mathematics. For further discussion of the oversimplification charge, see Gorham, Hill, and Slowik 2016, 1–28.

[19] For discussion of Platonism in contemporary philosophy of mathematics, see Balaguer 2009.

[20] Some philosophers of mathematics associate this form of non-Platonist realism with Aristotle. (See Franklin 2009.) Since Aristotle's philosophy of mathematics is a matter of scholarly dispute and since Aristotelianism is freighted with myriad connotations in the context of discussing early modern philosophy, I avoid this terminology here. I will touch upon Aristotle's philosophy of mathematics as background for considering Descartes' and Spinoza's in Chap. 3. "Psychologism" is considered by some philosophers of mathematics to be another form of non-Platonist realism. (See Balaguer 2009, 38.) Since psychologism is the view that mathematical entities exist as mental entities, this realist categorization is potentially misleading, since in this study the view that figures exist only as mental entities is categorized as a form of *antirealism*. My categorization hews more closely to the terminological landscape in the philosophical discussion of the problem of universals (which overlaps with, but is distinct from, the discussion of the ontology of mathematical entities in philosophy of mathematics).

exist independently of bodies, he believes at minimum that bodies must have one kind of shape or another. Since my main question is whether natural bodies have mathematical properties, and, as a corollary, whether mathematics contributes to the knowledge of natural bodies, when I speak about mathematical realism (without qualification), I mean to encompass the weak no less than the strong strain. In the case of both Descartes and Galileo, scholars have debated the extent to which they might be interpreted as Platonists (in the sense outlined above).[21] I will not have anything to say on this question here.[22] It suffices for my purposes that Descartes and Galileo are both at least *weak* mathematical realists.

The umbrella of weak mathematical realism is broad enough to encompass even anti-rationalist philosophers, such as Gassendi and Hobbes.[23] To be sure, there are differences between Gassendi and Hobbes, on the one hand, and Descartes, on the other, in regard to philosophy of mathematics, as witnessed by Gassendi's and Hobbes' respective objections to Descartes' *Meditations*.[24] Both philosophers object, on similar grounds, to Descartes' claim in Meditation Five to know the true and immutable nature of a triangle regardless of whether any triangle exists mind-independently in nature or has ever so existed. What they take issue with is the notion that triangles have natures independent of physical instantiation. Hobbes argues, "A triangle in the mind arises from a triangle we have seen, or else it is constructed out of things we have seen."[25] Gassendi similarly writes, "It is the intellect alone which, after seeing material triangles, has formed this nature and made it a common nature."[26] As these quotations show, both Gassendi and Hobbes hold that the notion of a triangle comes from encounters with material triangles (or similar things from which the notion is constructed) and thus cannot exist, as Descartes claims, regardless of whether any triangle exists mind-independently in nature.

---

[21] For discussion (and criticism) of Platonist readings of Galileo, see Palmerino 2016. For discussion of Platonist readings of Descartes, see Nolan 1997.

[22] I touch on the question of Descartes' Platonism in Chap. 3.

[23] In dubbing Hobbes an anti-rationalist, I mean to highlight primarily his hostility to innate ideas, as exhibited in his objections to Descartes' *Meditations*. (The same goes for Gassendi, too.)

[24] This is not to say, of course, that there are no differences between Gassendi and Hobbes, too. See n. 27.

[25] CSM 2:135.

[26] CSM 2: 223.

It would be a mistake to assume, however, that Gassendi's and Hobbes' rejection of Descartes' true and immutable natures doctrine entails mathematical antirealism *tout court*. Although Gassendi and Hobbes are known for their respective commitments to "nominalism" about universals (like "triangle"),[27] this does not entail a rejection of the weak mathematical realism outlined above, but only of the stronger (Platonist) strain. Whether or not there are such things as mathematical universals (existing independently of minds and bodies), there may well be *particular* mathematical entities (or at least material things with particular mathematical properties), as shown by Hobbes' and Gassendi's respective talk of "a triangle we have seen" and "material triangles" in the above quotations.

Another potential mistake that we must guard against is thinking that limits on our *knowledge* of the mathematical properties of physical things say anything in and of itself about the *existence* of such mathematical properties. If there is one thing on which all the "modern" philosophers agree, it is surely that sensation cannot be innocently taken as a reliable guide to the true nature of the physical world. Since it is widely agreed that sensation must be relied upon to gain knowledge of physical nature, at least with respect to its particular details, it is also widely agreed that knowledge of the particular details of physical nature poses a serious epistemic challenge. This is true for Descartes and Galileo no less than for Gassendi and Hobbes (and, as we will see, Spinoza). Since Gassendi and Hobbes believe that sensation is the *only* access we have to physical reality, they tend to be more pessimistic about our prospects for mathematical knowledge of nature than Descartes, who believes that some things about the physical world are knowable a priori. Once again, however, this difference does not

---

[27] A difference between Gassendi and Hobbes is that whereas Gassendi appears to recognize the existence of general *concepts*, Hobbes generally appears not to do so. Gassendi's talk of a common nature formed in the intellect in the passage quoted in the previous paragraph exhibits this recognition. The view that universals exist only as concepts in the mind is often called "conceptualism." In this case, "nominalism" would represent the stronger view that universals do not even exist as concepts. This terminological division can be seen in, for instance, Di Bella and Schmaltz 2017, 4–7. According to this terminology, then, Gassendi, along with many other early modern philosophers (including, arguably, Descartes), is a conceptualist while Hobbes is a nominalist. Usage of these terms is quite inconsistent, however. LoLordo (2017) depicts Gassendi as recognizing universal concepts, but characterizes him as a nominalist. Leibniz (1989, 128), notably, characterizes the mainstream early modern view as "nominalist," reserving the term "super-nominalist" for Hobbes. I am following Leibniz and LoLordo in using "nominalist" here in the broad sense that encompasses "conceptualism."

affect the basic question concerning the mind-independent *existence* of mathematical entities (or properties).

Let me add a further related clarification that is part terminological and part substantive. It is not uncommon for scholars to use the labels "constructivist" and "instrumentalist" in contrast with "realist" when discussing views of mathematization and mathematical entities.[28] In my view, a natural way to interpret the notions of mathematical constructivism and instrumentalism is entirely neutral with regard to the question of the mind-independent existence of mathematical entities. Instrumentalism suggests that mathematical calculations can be used to make predictions, while constructivism suggests that mathematical conceptions can be artificially crafted, like linguistic conventions, for human use and convenience. Hobbes, for instance, describes constructing the conception of a circle through a rotating line.[29] (Likely influenced by Hobbes, Spinoza uses the same example, as I will discuss later on.) For Hobbes, since this conception provides a cause of the circle, it allows for the deduction (or prediction) of effects. It should be clear, however, that the fact that this conception is artificially constructed and can be used (instrumentally) for deductive and predictive purposes says nothing about whether circles exist in nature that correspond to the conception or not. It is true that both "constructivism" and "instrumentalism" may carry antirealist connotations, but this is because they are often associated with independent reasons for rejecting the mind-independent existence of mathematical entities. (When this is the case, though, it is important to remember, the rejection is, at least in the seventeenth century, more clearly of the strong, Platonist, mathematical realism discussed above, not necessarily the weaker kind.) In the case of neither notion, however, is this association necessary. Hence, I find it potentially confusing to use these notions in contrast with realism and will instead deploy the starker "antirealism" for this purpose.

---

[28] Sepkoski's monograph *Nominalism and Constructivism in Seventeenth-Century Mathematical Philosophy* (2007) is notable for its association of the term "constructivism" with the nominalism (and antirealism) of such figures as Gassendi, Hobbes, and Berkeley. Sepkoski defines constructivism in explicitly antirealist terms as "the belief that mathematical objects are not mind-independent entities or abstractions from physical reality, but rather are artificial 'constructions' produced by the mind that serve as tools in mathematical demonstration" (2007, 129). For usage of the term "constructivism" in relation to Spinoza, see Hübner 2016, 59. Gorham et al., by contrast, deploy the term "instrumentalism" in contrast with "realism" in discussing attitudes toward mathematization (2016, 3).

[29] See Hobbes 2005, 6.

While I will at times have occasion to speak of constructivism or mathematical construction, I will take these terms to be neutral as to the question of the mind-independent existence of mathematical entities, for the reasons just given.

From the foregoing sketch, I think it is safe to say that while seventeenth-century thinking about mathematization was far from monolithic, there were also some common points of agreement, even among otherwise quite disparate figures. This agreement centered around the idea that material things are extended and that extended matter has the properties of shape, size, and mobility. Even among figures generally pessimistic about the prospects for successfully applying mathematics to the study of natural phenomena, there is broad, implicit consensus that a material world exists outside the mind with the properties mentioned. Thus, the mathematization of nature, in at least a weak sense, can be considered something of a received (if not universally agreed upon) opinion among the generation of moderns that directly preceded Spinoza.[30]

Against this backdrop, let us turn to Spinoza. Should he be seen as a mathematical realist as well? An affirmative answer to this question was long taken more or less for granted, as is perhaps unsurprising, given what has just been said. This tendency is succinctly represented by Jonathan Bennett's remark, "Being a child of his time, Spinoza [...] assumed space to be Euclidean and infinite in all directions."[31] However, some recent scholars have cast doubt on Spinoza's acceptance of the mathematization thesis, arguing that numbers and figures are, for him, nothing more than mental abstractions or "beings of reason." According to Eric Schliesser, for instance, "Spinoza sided with those who criticized the aspirations of the physico-mathematicians such as Galileo, Huygens, Wallis, and Wren who thought the application of mathematics to nature was the way to

---

[30] Francis Bacon is perhaps an exception here, though even in his case, recent scholars have found him friendlier to mathematics and quantification than traditionally thought. See Jalobeanu 2016.

[31] Bennett 1984, 21. See also Curley 1988, 33; Allison 1987, 25; Lecrivain 1986, 15–24; and Lachterman 1978, 75–80. In defending an alignment of Spinoza with the modern mechanistic philosophy of Descartes and Hobbes, Lachterman (1978, 76–7) takes himself to be departing from the previous, romantic, and idealist interpretations of Spinoza, which downplayed or ignored the scientific dimensions of his thought. In this light, I certainly do not suggest that the interpretation of Spinoza as a realist about mathematics was *always* standard.

make progress."[32] Reflecting this scholarly trend, the editors of a recent volume on mathematization in the seventeenth century allege that Spinoza has a "metaphysical program that is quite unfriendly to mathematization."[33] If numbers and figures are beings of reason, then Spinoza's book of nature is not written in mathematical language like Galileo's, Spinoza's material universe is not geometrical like Descartes', and mathematics can be no help in understanding nature. If this is right, it means that Spinoza broke even more dramatically from Descartes than usually thought.

Is it right? An answer to this question will be developed over the course of the book, but some stage-setting remarks are in order. One thing is clear (and will become clearer below): Spinoza's comments on mathematical entities are deeply ambivalent. As a result, the question of mathematization in Spinoza poses a genuine interpretive conundrum, and it is to the credit of recent antirealist interpretations of Spinoza that they have forced argument on the issue. As I suggested above, since the ambivalence about mathematical entities creates ambiguities that vex the interpretation of Spinoza's epistemology, clarifying the status of mathematical entities holds out hope of interpretive remedy. To interpret Spinoza's persistent treatment of mathematical entities as beings of reason to mean that Spinozan nature is not mathematical (per the antirealist interpretation) is certainly one way of clarifying the status of mathematical entities in Spinoza. However, the antirealist interpretation generates a dilemma. If Spinoza rejects mathematical entities (and properties) as part of his physical ontology, then, given that he affirms the existence of finite bodies, what, for him, are such things like?[34] They cannot be spheres or spherical, trapezoids

---

[32] Schliesser 2014, 2. Other recent interpreters who have raised doubts about ascribing the mathematization thesis to Spinoza include Melamed 2000; Peterman 2015; and Manning 2016. A less recent detractor is Deleuze 1990, 21–2, 278.

[33] Gorham et al. 2016, 6. It should be noted, however, that the paper on Spinoza included in the volume (Goldenbaum 2016) takes the standard view of Spinoza as a realist about mathematization for granted. See Goldenbaum 2016, 277.

[34] I assume that Spinoza *has* a physical ontology, and, thus, that Spinoza is not an idealist. I recognize that some commentators have read Spinoza as an idealist, and thus my assumption that he is not might be deemed question-begging. To this charge I would say the following. First, although I accept that there are viable grounds for an idealist reading of Spinoza (notably, Spinoza's definition of attribute in E1d4), it is nevertheless the case that the vast majority of textual evidence tends in the opposite direction. I have in mind Spinoza's affirmation of a seemingly self-sufficient attribute of extension and his ubiquitous talk of extended bodies and their motions. Second, although I will not engage directly with the arguments for the idealist reading (i.e., I will not discuss the controversy surrounding E1d4

or trapezoidal. Either he has (or holds out for) a positive, non-mathematized conception of finite bodies, or he disclaims the possibility of knowing anything about them (beyond the most general metaphysical knowledge, such as, for instance, that they are modes of extension, defined by capacities for motion and rest).

Neither horn of this interpretive dilemma is without difficulty. The second, skeptical reading comports with Spinoza's skepticism about sensory cognition, upon which knowledge of particular finite bodies would have to rely. Such skepticism was a point of widespread consensus among seventeenth-century moderns, as noted above, but it did not lead everyone to deny the possibility of knowledge of particulars. Recognition of the inaccuracy of naïve experience instead prompted attention to scientific methodology. While it is possible that Spinoza thought our knowledge of concrete particulars was restricted to the most general metaphysical claims, his own attention to scientific methodology indicates otherwise. If Spinoza did think knowledge of particulars could provide at least the target for a scientific program, we are pushed to the other interpretive alternative: that Spinoza envisioned a non-mathematized scientific knowledge of bodies. The problem with this is that it is far from clear what such a non-mathematized conception of finite bodies might look like, for Spinoza, especially in light of the already intimated predominance of mathematization in the early modern imagination. Both antirealist interpretive options tend toward mystification of the Spinozan natural world. Recall Galileo's remark that without geometry "one wanders around pointlessly in a dark labyrinth."

Perhaps Spinozan nature is a dark labyrinth. Before we acquiesce to this conclusion, however, it is worth exploring the possibilities for a mathematical realist interpretation. In my opinion, a realist interpretation of geometrical figures in Spinoza is much more plausible than has been appreciated in the recent literature. Spinoza's treatment of mathematical

at any length), I will present arguments on behalf of geometrical figures as the determinations of finite bodies in Chap. 3. Inasmuch as these arguments help make the case for the realist reading of physical nature in Spinoza, my interpretation does not beg the question. Admittedly, Spinoza's affirmation of finite bodies is not without well-known problems, even if mind-independent physical reality is assumed. I touch on some of these issues in Chap. 3. For an overview of idealist readings of Spinoza, see Newlands 2011. For a recent defense of a realist reading of the attributes, see Melamed 2018, 90–5. See also, my paper, Homan 2016, in which I argue for the parity of thought and extension qua attributes, thereby countering a major motivation for the idealist reading.

entities as beings of reason must be dealt with, but I think this can be done within a realist interpretive framework. In short, I will argue that even if geometrical figures per se are beings of reason, they exist mind-independently nevertheless as the determinations of finite bodies. In the taxonomy sketched above, Spinoza is a weak mathematical realist (at least with regard to geometrical figures).

Like its antirealist counterpart, the realist interpretation serves to clarify an important question concerning the scope and content of Spinozan knowledge of the physical world. But the realist interpretation has a significant advantage: in delivering a positive verdict for geometrical figures, it licenses the development of mathematical examples for illustrating Spinozan knowledge claims. This is a highly valuable result, especially in the case of interpreting Spinoza's second and third kinds of knowledge, where the objects of these modes of knowing, and the content of Spinoza's definitions of them, are far from clear. The result also helps to illuminate related interpretive matters regarding Spinoza's philosophy of science, including his conception of scientific method.

1.2 Outline of Chapters

This, then, is the overarching strategy of the book. I will develop the case for attributing a realist view of mathematization to Spinoza. Then, on this basis, I will use Spinoza's mathematical examples to help illuminate the content of Spinozan knowledge claims. Doing so will help to answer a number of interpretive conundrums in Spinoza's epistemology. I do not pretend to provide a comprehensive exploration of every nook and cranny of Spinoza's epistemology.[35] Nor will I be steered by contemporary

---

[35] It is perhaps futile to attempt to list the epistemological issues I will *not* take up, since there are indefinitely many that could be identified, but I want to mention three notable omissions. (1) One interesting question outside the scope of this study pertains to Spinoza's theory of error as privation: what happens to an imaginative, inadequate conception of X when we come to achieve an intellectual, adequate understanding of X? Is the former radically transformed (perhaps *eliminated*) or do we go on experiencing the world as we did prior to gaining adequate understanding, albeit with the *addition* of adequate ideas? For a thought-provoking discussion of this question, see Cook 1998. (2) Another issue is the question of whether Spinoza's theory of epistemic justification is foundationalist or coherentist. Since God is the epistemic foundation in Spinoza's system, and since God is, in a sense, everything, it would not be wrong to say that to know anything one must know everything. Nevertheless, in my view, it is God as foundation that is doing the epistemic work, not God as everything. While I do not argue for this point explicitly, what I say in Chap. 2 should help

epistemological concerns. Instead, I intend to follow a thread from Spinoza's early engagement with skepticism in the TIE to the culmination of his epistemology in *Ethics* Part 5 and the link between intuitive knowledge and the highest human blessedness. The thread will be guided by the question of mathematization and issue in an interpretation of the major elements of Spinoza's epistemology, especially the hierarchical trio of kinds of knowledge.

I begin, in Chap. 2, with Spinoza's response to skepticism. I argue that a due consideration of the nature of true mathematical ideas and the use to which Spinoza puts them against skeptical disputation suggest that his philosophical methodology is more Cartesian than has often been appreciated. The discussion of this chapter allows me to introduce a number of the major concepts and themes that scaffold the discussion of ensuing chapters, in particular, the distinction between intrinsic and extrinsic features of ideas, the key epistemic notions of adequacy and truth, the foundational role of God in Spinoza's system, and the question of the reality of mathematical objects.

In Chap. 3, I address the question of the ontological status of mathematical entities, particularly geometrical figures (though I also touch on numbers). I discuss the status of mathematical entities as beings of reason and mount a case against mathematical antirealism. Despite the fact that geometrical figures per se are beings of reason, I argue for a realist interpretation of geometrical figures as the determinations of finite bodies. Advancing this argument requires me to examine Spinoza's discussions of

---

to motivate, and partially justify, my view, if only indirectly. For discussion of this issue and defense of a coherentist reading, see Steinberg 1998. (3) Finally, I do not explicitly take up the question of Spinoza's commitment to the principle of sufficient reason. The PSR is emphasized in Michael Della Rocca's highly influential interpretation of Spinoza (especially in Della Rocca, 2008) and, as a result, has recently been much discussed by Spinoza scholars. (For critical discussions of Della Rocca's PSR-focused reading of Spinoza, see Laerke 2011, Garber 2015, and Lin 2019, 164–81.) There is no doubt that the PSR is relevant to Spinoza's epistemology. As I will emphasize and discuss in more detail below, to know X, for Spinoza, is to know the cause of X. Inasmuch as this suggests a commitment to the PSR, the PSR looms large over any study of Spinoza's epistemology. For Della Rocca, however, the PSR is an Ur-principle that governs all aspects of Spinoza's system, thus transcending epistemological matters (at least as narrowly conceived). Indeed, perhaps somewhat ironically, one of the few areas of Spinoza's philosophy that Della Rocca has relatively little to say about are the three kinds of knowledge themselves (especially the second and third kinds). To take up the PSR as understood by Della Rocca in any systematic manner, then, calls for a very different kind of study than what is proposed here.

physical individuals in the *Ethics* and elsewhere. In addition to marshaling textual evidence for my interpretation, I address some questions regarding the property ontology of geometrical figures.

Chapters 4 and 5 are focused on Spinoza's scientific methodology and philosophy of science. They follow up an implication of the findings of Chap. 3: if figures feature among the determinations of finite bodies, then geometry, as the science of figure, should have a role to play in the scientific investigation of finite bodies. In Chap. 4, I provide an interpretation of Spinoza's scientific method and discuss the interaction of reason and imagination in Spinozan science. I address a number of interpretive issues pertaining to reason especially, including the nature, origin, and adequacy of common notions. I argue for a hypothetico-deductive interpretation of Spinoza's scientific method, stressing the role of hypotheses in bridging the epistemic gap between nature's most general laws and singular things.

Chapter 5 is devoted, in part, to developing an example of Spinozan science in practice and exhibiting the role of geometry therein. In this regard, I offer a reading of Spinoza's epistolary writings on optics and his treatment of a question of optimal lens shape. I also address a further objection to my realist interpretation of geometrical figures stemming from Letter 12, as well as the difficulty raised by the incompleteness of Spinoza's thinking about physics for any interpretation of Spinozan science.

The topic of Chap. 6 is Spinoza's notion (or, more accurately, notion*s*) of essence. This is the most metaphysical discussion of the book. It provides the necessary background for approaching Spinoza's conception of intuitive knowledge, which he characterizes in terms of knowledge of the essences of things. I argue for a spectrum interpretation of essences in Spinoza, distinguishing between common essences at the level of attribute and infinite mode at one extreme, individual essences at the level of finite individuals at the other extreme, and species essences in the middle (which, I argue, exist only as beings of reason). I also address the sense in which the essences of finite things exist non-durationally and are themselves finite (as opposed to infinite modes).

Chapter 7 attempts finally to make sense of Spinoza's obscure conception of intuitive knowledge. I stake out a number of interpretive claims on this issue. First, I argue that adequate knowledge of the singular essences of things is impossible for finite intellects, which means that intuitive knowledge can only aspire to adequate knowledge of common essences or species essences of things. Second, with the help of a geometrical example that is modeled on, but more suggestive than, Spinoza's fourth proportional example, I argue for a "method interpretation" of the distinction between reason and intuitive knowledge. According to a method interpretation, in general, the second and third kinds of knowledge do not differ in terms of their respective knowledge contents, but only in their respective methods of arriving at the same knowledge content. According to my particular version of the method interpretation, intuitive knowledge is best understood as the perfection of reason. This means that the extent to which intuitive knowledge and reason are seen as different kinds of knowledge or merely different grades of a single kind is a question more of emphasis than substance. The burden of any method interpretation is to explain why Spinoza puts such an emphasis on the superiority of intuitive knowledge, linking it alone to the intellectual love of God and the highest human blessedness. I argue that my method interpretation offers an especially cogent explanation of this superiority in terms of affective differences between the kinds of knowledge. At the end of the chapter, I discuss the role that intuitive knowledge might play in Spinozan science.

In the final, concluding chapter, I reflect upon the portrait of Spinoza's epistemology that emerges over the course of the book, defend its sanguine, Cartesian cast, and highlight, in closing, an important epistemological contrast between Spinoza and Descartes.

1.3   A Note on Texts

Before getting underway, let me add a remark about my use of Spinoza's texts in developing my interpretation. Since this is not a study of any particular text, but of Spinoza's epistemological thinking in general, I intend to make full use of the writings comprising Spinoza's corpus insofar as they are relevant to the matters in question. While this is generally standard practice and unproblematic, the authority of a few texts is sometimes the subject of scholarly doubts. This is true, in particular, in the case of the TIE and Spinoza's geometric exposition of *Descartes' Principles of Philosophy*, both of which, especially the former, will feature prominently in my interpretation. Doubts about the authority of the TIE attach to the fact that it was an early work (perhaps Spinoza's first) that Spinoza never completed. Whether or not Spinoza ever seriously intended to go back and finish the TIE after having initially set it aside, however, it seems to have continued to satisfy him "in the main," as Curley acknowledges,[36] throughout his life, as evidenced by occasional, scattered references in later writings. Of course, there are points of philosophical substance on which Spinoza's thinking evolved or changed from the TIE to later works. In such cases (one or two of which I will discuss below), I will generally defer to the authority of later works, especially the *Ethics*. Insofar as the TIE is not contradicted by later doctrine, however, I will feel free to conscript it into my interpretation. The extent to which this proves illuminating will, I hope, amply justify the practice.

Being an exposition of Descartes' philosophy, not his own, Spinoza's DPP raises a different set of issues. In using it, I will look not just for lack of contradiction, but explicit confirmation, by explicit doctrine elsewhere in Spinoza's oeuvre. When such confirmation is available, I will use the DPP as a welcome supplement to other texts. Although the *Cogitata Metaphysica* (Spinoza's appendix to the DPP) seems to represent Spinoza's own views to a greater extent than the main text of the DPP, I will adopt a similar, cautious approach to this text as well.

References

Allison, Henry E. 1987. *Benedict de Spinoza: An Introduction*. Revised Edition. New Haven: Yale University Press.

Ariew, Roger. 2016. "The Mathematization of Nature in Descartes and the First Cartesians." In *The Language of Nature: Reassessing the Mathematization of Natural Philosophy in the Seventeenth Century*, edited by Geoffrey Gorham et al., 112–134. Minneapolis, MN: University of Minnesota Press.

Balaguer, Mark. 2009. "Realism and Antirealism in Mathematics." In *Philosophy of Mathematics*, edited by Andrew D. Irvine, 35–102. Burlington, MA: North Holland.

Bennett, Jonathan. 1984. *A Study of Spinoza's* Ethics. Indianapolis, IN: Hackett.

Cook, J. Thomas. 1998. "Spinoza and the Plasticity of Mind." *Studia Spinozana* 14:111–36.

Curley, Edwin. 1988. *Behind the Geometrical Method: A Reading of Spinoza's* Ethics. Princeton, NJ: Princeton University Press.

Deleuze, Gilles. 1990. *Expressionism in Philosophy: Spinoza*. Translated by Martin Joughin. New York: Zone Books.

Della Rocca, Michael. 2008. *Spinoza*. New York, NY: Routledge.

---

[36] Curley 1: 5.

Di Bella, Stephano, and Schmaltz, Tad M. 2017. "Introduction to Universals in Modern Philosophy." In *The Problem of Universals in Early Modern Philosophy*, edited by Stephano di Bella and Tad M. Schmaltz, 1–13. New York, NY: Oxford University Press.

Franklin, James. 2009. "Aristotelian Realism." In *Philosophy of Mathematics*, edited by Andrew D. Irvine, 103–156. Burlington, MA: North Holland.

Galileo, Galilei. 2008. *The Essential Galileo*. Translated by Maurice A. Finocchiaro. Indianapolis, IN: Hackett Publishing Company.

Garber, Daniel. 2015. "Superheroes in the History of Philosophy: Spinoza, Super-Rationalist." *Journal of the History of Philosophy* 53(3): 507–21.

Garrett, Aaron V. 2003. *Meaning in Spinoza's Method*. Cambridge, UK: Cambridge University Press.

Gaukroger, Stephen. 1980. "Descartes' Project for a Mathematical Physics." In *Descartes: Philosophy, Mathematics and Physics*, edited by Stephen Gaukroger, 97–140. Sussex, U.K.: Harvester Press.

Goldenbaum, Ursula. 2016. "The Geometrical Method as the New Standard of Truth, Based on the Mathematization of Nature." In *The Language of Nature: Reassessing the Mathematization of Nature in the Seventeenth Century*, edited by Geoffrey Gorham et al., 274–307. Minneapolis, MN: University of Minnesota Press.

Gorham, Geoffrey, Hill, Benjamin, and Slowik, Edward. 2016. "Introduction." In *The Language of Nature: Reassessing the Mathematization of Natural Philosophy in the Seventeenth Century*, edited by Geoffrey Gorham et al., 1–28. Minneapolis, MN: University of Minnesota Press.

Gueroult, Martial. 1974. *Spinoza II: L'Âme (Éthique, II)*. Paris: Aubier-Montaigne.

Hobbes, Thomas. 2005. *The English Works of Thomas Hobbes of Malmesbury*. Vol. 1. Translated by William Molesworth. London: John Bonn, 1839. Replica edition, Elbiron Classics.

Homan, Matthew. 2016. "On the Alleged Exceptional Nature of Thought in Spinoza." *Journal of Philosophical Research* 41: 1–16.

———. 2018b. "Geometrical Figures in Spinoza's Book of Nature." *Journal of the History of Philosophy*. 56(3): 455–476.

Hübner, Karolina. 2016. "Spinoza on Essences, Universals, and Beings of Reason." *Pacific Philosophical Quarterly* 97: 58–88.

Jalobeanu, Dana. 2016. "'The Marriage of Physics with Mathematics': Francis Bacon on Measurement, Mathematics, and the Construction of a Mathematical Physics." In *The Language of Nature: Reassessing the Mathematization of Natural Philosophy in the Seventeenth Century*, edited by Geoffrey Gorham et al., 51–80. Minneapolis, MN: University of Minnesota Press.

Koyré, Alexandre. 1978. *Galileo Studies*. Translated by John Mepham. Atlantic Highlands, NJ: Humanities Press.

Lachterman, David R. 1978. "The Physics of Spinoza's *Ethics*." In *Spinoza: New Perspectives*, edited by Robert W. Shahan and J. I. Biro, 71–112. Norman: University of Oklahoma Press.

Laerke, Mogens. 2011. "Spinoza's Cosmological Argument in the *Ethics*." *Journal of the History of Philosophy* 49(4): 439–462.
Lecrivain, André. 1986. "Spinoza and Cartesian Mechanics." In *Spinoza and the Sciences*, edited by Marjorie Grene and Debra Nails, 15–60. Dordrecht: D. Reidel.
Leibniz, Gottfried. 1989. *Philosophical Papers and Letters*. Edited and translated by Leroy E. Loemker. Dordrecht: Kluwer Academic Publishers.
Lin, Martin. 2019. *Being and Reason: An Essay on Spinoza's Metaphysics*. New York, NY: Oxford University Press.
LoLordo, Antonia. 2017. "Gassendi on the Problem of Universals." In *The Problem of Universals in Early Modern Philosophy*, edited by Stephano di Bella and Tad M. Schmaltz, 13–40. New York, NY: Oxford University Press.
Manning, Richard. 2016. "Spinoza's Physical Theory," *The Stanford Encyclopedia of Philosophy*. Edward N. Zalta (ed.), URL = https://plato.stanford.edu/archives/win2016/entries/spinoza-physics/.
Melamed, Yitzhak Y. 2000. "On the Exact Science of Nonbeings: Spinoza's View of Mathematics." *Iyyun, The Jerusalem Philosophical Quarterly* 49: 3–22.
———. 2018. "The Building Blocks of Spinoza's Metaphysics: Substance, Attributes, and Modes." In *The Oxford Handbook of Spinoza*, edited by Michael Della Rocca, 84–113. New York, NY: Oxford University Press.
Newlands, Samuel. 2011. "More Recent Idealist Readings of Spinoza." *Philosophy Compass* 6(2): 109–19.
Nolan, Lawrence. 1997. "The Ontological Status of Cartesian Natures." *Pacific Philosophical Quarterly* 78: 169–194.
Palmerino, Carla Rita. 2016. "Reading the Book of Nature: The Ontological and Epistemological Underpinnings of Galileo's Mathematical Realism." In *The Language of Nature: Reassessing the Mathematization of Natural Philosophy in the Seventeenth Century*, edited by Geoffrey Gorham et al., 29–50. Minneapolis, MN: University of Minnesota Press.
Parkinson, G.H.R. 1954. *Spinoza's Theory of Knowledge*. London: Oxford University Press.
Peterman, Alison. 2015. "Spinoza on Extension." *Philosopher's Imprint* 15: 1–23.
Schliesser, Eric. 2014. "Spinoza and the Philosophy of Science: Mathematics, Motion, and Being." In *The Oxford Handbook of Spinoza*, edited by Michael Della Rocca. DOI: https://doi.org/10.1093/oxfordhb/9780195335828.013.020.
Sepkoski, David. 2007. *Nominalism and Constructivism in Seventeenth-Century Mathematical Philosophy*. New York, NY: Routledge.
Steinberg, Diane. 1998. "Method and the Structure of Knowledge in Spinoza." *Pacific Philosophical Quarterly* 79: 152–69.
Viljanen, Valtteri. 2011. *Spinoza's Geometry of Power*. Cambridge, UK: Cambridge University Press.

CHAPTER 2

Mathematics and Methodology: Spinoza *Contra* Skepticism

Mathematical ideas have a vital role to play at the logical beginning of Spinoza's philosophy, in establishing the viability of his rationalist system against skepticism (by which I mean radical, all-knowledge-denying skepticism of the Pyrrhonian sort). Simple mathematical ideas display the formal features of true ideas, while failing to be true in the full sense. They show how to ground the system, while not themselves sufficing to do so. This ambivalent epistemic status of mathematical ideas will form a major theme of this study. Its significance for explaining Spinoza's response to skepticism has generally been overlooked. The latter is widely thought to run roughly as follows: "True ideas signal their own truth. So, in order to remove any skeptical doubts about our capacity for knowledge, all we need is a true idea; we do not need any guarantee of truth beyond the apprehension of the idea itself. But we do have a true idea, etc." This contra-skeptical response is dismissive and un-Cartesian. Dismissive, because, in renouncing any need for an external sign of truth, Spinoza rejects the very premise of the skeptical challenge—that it is possible for an idea to appear true, even on the closest inspection, but in fact be false. Un-Cartesian, since Descartes concedes just the possibility that Spinoza rejects. I take issue with this standard reading.[1] As I will argue, due

---

[1] Examples of the dismissive, un-Cartesian interpretation of Spinoza's response to skepticism include Bolton 1985; D. Garrett 1990; Mason 1993; Wilson 1996; Della Rocca 1994, 2007, 2008; Perler 2017. An interpretation that paints a more Cartesian portrait of Spinoza's

consideration of mathematical ideas bedevils the dismissive, un-Cartesian interpretation of Spinoza's response to skepticism, which, for reasons to be explained below, I call the "dogmatic response." In my view, Spinoza is more indulgent of the skeptic's concerns (even if unsympathetic) and, indeed, more Cartesian in his response to them than generally appreciated.

Admittedly, the dogmatic response plays an important role in Spinoza's response to skepticism, and there is truth to interpretations that stress it. (For brevity's sake, I will sometimes refer to such interpretations as "dogmatic interpretations" without meaning that the interpretations themselves are dogmatic. My own interpretation incorporates elements of the dogmatic interpretation.) However, the dogmatic response cannot be all there is to Spinoza's response to skepticism, since there are ideas—most conspicuously, genetic, or causally constructed mathematical ideas—that have the intrinsic features of true ideas, but are not true in the sense of corresponding with a real object in nature. Spinoza recognizes this, describing such ideas as abstractions that exhibit only "the form of truth" (TIE 105/G 2:38). Not only do we have such ideas, but they are the most plausible candidates for the "given true idea" with which Spinoza claims the method, and, indeed, philosophy as a whole, must begin (TIE 38/G 2:16). Thus, Spinoza must show that his system does not traffic in abstractions, but is grounded in an idea that is true in the fullest sense. He does this by way of the idea of God. Given its overt parallels with Descartes' well-known appeal to God to counter skepticism, I call it the "Cartesian response." Ultimately, the dogmatic and Cartesian responses are interdependent, functioning as elements of a single contra-skeptical stratagem. Let us call it the "Cartesio-dogmatic response."

Exploring the ambivalent epistemic status of mathematical ideas in the context of Spinoza's response to skepticism provides an opportunity to introduce many of the concepts that will feature prominently in subsequent chapters, especially Spinoza's notion of adequate ideas, and to construct the theoretical framework within which the rest of the discussion will unfold. Fixing the role of God in grounding the system of knowledge, moreover, allows me to sketch the elementary metaphysical framework of Spinoza's philosophy. Finally, the chapter provides a first glimpse at the

---

response to skepticism is Doney 1975. See also Schneider 2016. Schneider's focus is not on Spinoza's response to skepticism, but his argument for a Cartesian-friendly interpretation of Spinoza's epistemological foundations is complementary, in part, with the Cartesian-friendly interpretation of Spinoza's response to skepticism that I defend in this chapter.

interpretive dividends to be gained through critical scrutiny of Spinoza's use of mathematical examples. I will begin by laying out the basis for the dogmatic interpretation of Spinoza's response to skepticism. It offers a useful backdrop against which to consider the methodological significance of the mathematical ideas that Spinoza puts forward as epistemic exemplars.

2.1 The Dogmatic Response

Spinoza's most sustained engagement with skepticism occurs in the *Treatise on the Emendation of the Intellect*, his early and unfinished methodological work. (As we will see, his discussion of skepticism is intertwined with discussion of philosophical method.) In TIE 30, Spinoza sets out to find "the Way and Method" for attaining knowledge, and immediately anticipates a skeptical objection:

> To do this, the first thing we must consider is that there is no infinite regress here. That is, to find the best Method of seeking the truth, there is no need of another Method to seek the Method of seeking the truth, or of a third Method to seek the second, and so on, to infinity. For in that way we would never arrive at knowledge of the truth, or indeed at any knowledge. (TIE 30/G 2:13)

The skeptical objection that he anticipates here is a form of the classic problem of the criterion.[2] The problem is that you have to have criteria for distinguishing the true from the false, if you make claims to truth. But how do you know that the criteria are legitimate? You would seem to need second-order criteria to guarantee the first-order criteria, and third-order criteria to guarantee the second-order criteria, and so on, leading to an infinite regress. Here Spinoza frames the problem in terms of a regress of methods. In response, he goes on to give his well-known tools analogy. A hammer is needed to forge iron. One might think that in order to make a hammer, you first need a hammer with which to make it, and another hammer to have made that hammer, and so on. Reasoning in this way, one might conclude that human beings have no power to forge iron (TIE 31/G 2:13–14). The answer to this sophistical line of reasoning, Spinoza

---

[2] For a discussion of the issue as it emerged in the Hellenistic period, see Striker 1990. For discussions of the criterion problem in more recent epistemology, see Chisholm 1973 and Williams 1999. See Schneider 2016 for critical discussion of Chisholm's reading of Spinoza. For a defense of Chisholm's reading, see Delahunty 1985, 15–24.

explains, is to recognize that humans did not have to begin with hammers. They could begin with simpler tools with which they were born, such as hands. If we are simply born with hands, which are a kind of tool, we do not get ensnared in a regress of having needed tools with which to build tools and so on. By analogy, we have certain inborn intellectual tools that we can use to build up a system of knowledge without having needed other intellectual tools with which to fashion the initial intellectual tools. We do not need a method for arriving at a true idea, a method for finding that method, and so on, if "we have a true idea" (TIE 33/G 2:14) at the outset. So, the solution to the regress of methods objection is to recognize our possession of innate resources.

At this point, the skeptic rejoins: but how do you know that your alleged inborn true idea is in fact true? There must be a sign that the idea is true, and in order to be certain that the sign is the right sign, there is a need for another sign, and so on. We are back to the problem of the criterion with its attendant regress. So, how does Spinoza answer this more dogged version? How is he certain that an idea that he thinks is true in fact *is* true? Spinoza's initial answer appeals to the relationship between an idea and its object. He says, "A true idea (for we have a true idea) is something different from its object. For a circle is one thing and an idea of the circle another – the idea of the circle is not something which has a circumference and a center, as the circle does" (TIE 33/G 2:14). He also gives another example: "Peter, for example, is something real; but a true idea of Peter is an objective essence of Peter, and something real in itself, and altogether different from Peter himself" (TIE 34/G 2:14). To have an idea of Peter, to know Peter, then, Spinoza goes on to explain, is something different from having an idea of an idea of Peter, from knowing an idea of Peter. Finally, he reasons: "From this it is clear that certainty is nothing but the objective essence itself, i.e., the mode by which we are aware of the formal essence [i.e., the essence of the object of the idea] is certainty itself. And from this, again, it is clear that, for the certainty of truth, no other sign is needed than having a true idea" (TIE 35/G 2:15).

So, no sign is needed to be certain that one has a true idea beyond the true idea itself. This, ultimately, is his answer to the regress objection. But how is Spinoza's reasoning supposed to work here? How does he get from his initial distinction between idea and object (illustrated by the examples of the circle and Peter) to the claim that certainty "requires no sign," as he puts it in the next paragraph (TIE 36/G 2:15)? I take it that Spinoza's assertion that a true idea is something different from its object means that the object of an idea is not itself *in* or *of* the idea. An idea inherently has a relationship—specifically, a relationship of representation—with something outside of it. This is perhaps most obvious in the case of ideas of bodies, since bodies are extended, whereas the ideas of them are not—ideas of circles do not have a circumference, as Spinoza says. But the idea-object relation need not be an idea-body relation. It can also obtain between one idea and another idea. A true idea of Peter is "something real in itself," which can be the object of a second-order idea. Whether it is an idea of an idea or an idea of a body, the idea transcends itself in having an object, and this guarantees, for Spinoza, contact with something real—whether that reality is corporeal or mental. The upshot of this is to rule out a skeptical scenario whereby I have an ostensibly true idea of Peter, say, with all of the intrinsic features of a true idea (more on these in a moment), yet Peter exists *only* in my idea, and thus I am not in fact making contact with anything real—anything outside of the idea itself—in having my ostensibly true idea of Peter. Hence, as Spinoza says, certainty just is the awareness of the essence of an object. When we perceive the essence of an object, there is no question of not *actually* making contact with the object, since perceiving the object *is* to make contact with it. From this, Spinoza concludes that no external guarantee of the certainty of a true idea is needed beyond having and apprehending the true idea itself. In this way, the skeptical regress problem never gets off the ground, or so the argument seems to go.

If this is the correct interpretation of Spinoza's response to skepticism—I will argue it is not—it is somewhat surprising in that it is predicated upon a metaphysical point, in particular, a point about the nature of ideas. This is surprising since there appears to be no reason why a skeptic would accede to a metaphysical claim about the nature of ideas when precisely what is at issue is the prospect of knowing anything at all. (This is especially the case since the metaphysical claim is plainly contentious. The view that ideas are themselves objects of thought, and thus that the mind does *not* inherently make contact with external things, at least not with physical things, just by virtue of having ideas was a live option in the seventeenth century.[3]) In other words, it seems that Spinoza's metaphysical gambit flagrantly begs the question.

Michael Della Rocca has developed a leading interpretation of Spinoza's antiskepticism that leans on the metaphysical point just sketched and has

---
[3] See McRae 1965.

something to say about the charge of question-begging.[4] Before considering it, I need first to explain Spinoza's distinction between "intrinsic" and "extrinsic" features of ideas (see E2d4/G 2:85), which I have invoked already and which is crucial to the matter at hand. By an "extrinsic" feature of ideas, Spinoza means the agreement (or disagreement) of ideas with their object. This agreement (or disagreement) determines the truth (or falsity) of ideas. "Intrinsic" features, by contrast, are those that the idea has in itself, without relation to its object. Descartes' clarity and distinctness provide good examples of intrinsic features of true ideas. Indeed, in his early texts Spinoza primarily uses these Cartesian terms in speaking of ideas with exemplary intrinsic qualities, although the official term later becomes "adequate" (*adaequatus*). In the *Ethics*, Spinoza defines an adequate idea as one which "insofar as it is considered in itself, without relation to an object, has all the properties, or intrinsic denominations of a true idea" (E2d4/G 2:85). Della Rocca refers to Spinoza's "intrinsic" features as "representational" and to his "extrinsic" features as "epistemic." In this idiom, clarity and distinctness are exemplary "representational" features of ideas. Della Rocca's representational/epistemic language provides a useful gloss on Spinoza's intrinsic/extrinsic distinction, and I will use both sets of terms interchangeably in what follows.

Della Rocca sees the skeptical possibility that an idea could have all the representational features of truth and yet still be false as involving a "primitive bifurcation"[5] between the representational (or intrinsic) and epistemic (or extrinsic) features of ideas. He believes that Spinoza rejects the primitive bifurcation as a "brute fact" in violation of the principle of sufficient reason.[6] With regard to the charge of question-begging, Della Rocca holds that Spinoza is no worse off than the skeptic. That is, Spinoza denies primitive bifurcation of representational and epistemic features, whereas the skeptic affirms it. The two are at an impasse, but Spinoza's denial is no less plausible (or more question-begging) than the skeptic's affirmation.[7]

Putting to the side the issue of question-begging for the moment, I think there are two problems with interpreting Spinoza's response to

[4] Della Rocca 2008, 127–34, 2007, 1994. See also Perler 2017. Perler argues à la Della Rocca that Spinoza's antiskepticism is based in metaphysical assumptions (in particular, holism, anti-dualism, and naturalism).
[5] Della Rocca 2007, 859; see also Della Rocca 2008, 130–1.
[6] Della Rocca 2007, 864; see also, Della Rocca 2008, 130–1.
[7] Della Rocca 1994, 39–40; see also Della Rocca 2007, 872–3.

skepticism as a denial of bifurcation between representational and epistemic features of ideas on basic metaphysical grounds. First, Spinoza's metaphysics is rooted in the nature of God. Even if Della Rocca is right that Spinozan metaphysics is at the most basic level driven by the principle of sufficient reason (a question I will not take up here), the metaphysical point about the nature of ideas must still go through God. That is, if ideas in the human mind can be said inherently to make contact with reality, then it is insofar as the human mind is "a part of a thinking being," as Spinoza says in TIE 73 (G 2:28), by which he means, "part of God's intellect." (I come back to this point below.) But at this stage of the TIE, the knowledge of God has not been reached yet. The order here is important from a methodological perspective, as I will explain more fully below, since Spinoza says repeatedly that the method is only perfect when it arrives at knowledge of a perfect being. This suggests that the method does not begin with metaphysical assumptions about God, or, *a fortiori*, the nature of ideas. (It suggests, furthermore, that the view of Spinoza's epistemology as a secondary outgrowth of the metaphysics is too simplistic.)

The second problem with the foregoing interpretation is that it ignores the problem posed by mathematical ideas, which exhibit the disconnect between representational and epistemic features that Della Rocca takes Spinoza to reject without qualification. Before turning to such mathematical ideas in the next section, I want to return briefly to the issue of question-begging. It will allow me to clarify a terminological point.

Della Rocca thinks that Spinoza and the skeptic are on equal footing with regard to the issue of question-begging. The skeptic believes that the default position is ignorance and that claims to knowledge must be justified. Della Rocca's Spinoza believes, by contrast, that the default position is knowledge. Are these starting points in fact equal? Is knowledge just as likely a default as ignorance? I have my doubts, though I will not develop them here, since, even if default knowledge were just as likely as default ignorance, there would be, nevertheless, an impasse, and breaking the impasse one way or the other appears to require a dogmatic assertion.[8] At least, this would presumably be the position of the skeptic content to

---

[8] Cf. Perler 2017, 237. Perler claims, "Spinoza is in a default position," on the grounds that the skeptic must make assumptions, such as, that a bifurcation between representational and epistemic features (or between mental and bodily states, as Perler frames the issue) is possible. I do not see how this puts Spinoza in a default position, since Spinoza makes his own assumptions of holism, anti-dualism, and so on, on Perler's reading.

repose in the "standoff of equipollence."[9] If this is right, then to claim knowledge as the default position, as the above response to skepticism does, can justifiably be considered a "dogmatic response" to skepticism. In using the term "dogmatic" I refer narrowly to the presumption of the sort just considered (on metaphysical grounds or otherwise) that impasse between skeptic and antiskeptic breaks *de jure* in favor of the latter. While the dogmatic response has an important role to play in Spinoza's response to skepticism, as I will show in subsequent sections, it functions as one piece of a larger architectonic.

2.2 Mathematical Ideas qua Epistemic Exemplars: Problems for the Dogmatic Interpretation

Let us follow a little further Spinoza's development of his conception of method in the TIE. Recall that he has already addressed concern about a regress. There is no need for a method to find the right method because we start off on the right track with our inborn intellectual tools. If the method should teach us how to form true ideas (and avoid false ones), then all we have to do is reflect upon the true ideas that we already have and use them as a guide. Hence, Spinoza says, "Method is nothing but a reflexive knowledge, or an idea of an idea [....] So that Method will be good which shows how the mind is to be directed according to the standard of a given true idea" (TIE 38/G 2:15–16). So far, this accords with the dogmatic interpretation discussed above. But when we inquire more closely into the "given true idea" that is supposed to provide us with a standard, problems for the dogmatic response emerge. What is the "given true idea" that provides the touchstone of the method? What are some examples? In the previous section, we saw that Spinoza uses two examples, an idea of a circle and an idea of Peter. Are these both "given true ideas"?

It is implausible that a true idea of a human individual (such as I take "Peter" to be) would be a candidate for an entry-level true idea. Even after studying Spinoza's mature philosophy it is unclear whether a true idea of an individual human being is even possible for finite minds (given its apparent complexity) or what such an idea, if possible, would be like. (I take up these questions in later chapters.) A much more plausible candidate is the idea of the circle and other similarly simple mathematical notions. Spinoza never specifies examples or parameters of the "given true

---

[9] Barnes 2000, xxi.

idea," and perhaps for good reason—he may have thought that many different kinds of idea could do the job.[10] Nevertheless, there is evidence that Spinoza deemed mathematical ideas particularly well suited. There is, for one thing, Spinoza's historical conjecture in the Appendix to *Ethics* Part 1 that human beings would still be stuck in the cave of animistic, teleological thinking had they not at some point come to realize that mathematics provides a more adequate model of truth (G 2:79). There are also the important mathematical examples that Spinoza uses in the TIE to illustrate the properties of true ideas.

He says that we can form an idea of a sphere, for instance, by contemplating the object formed by the rotation of a semicircle around its center (TIE 72/G 2:27). He also describes an idea of a circle formed by the rotation of a line around a fixed end (TIE 96/G 2:35). In both cases, Spinoza presents the ideas as examples of true ideas and uses them to illustrate how properly to form true ideas. The genetic ideas of the sphere and the circle represent true ideas that we know to be true, as Spinoza says, by "an intrinsic denomination" (TIE 69/G 2:26). They thus exemplify the sorts of ideas that Spinoza said require no other sign of their truth beyond their own intrinsic nature (TIE 35), in addition to fitting the *Ethics*' definition of adequate ideas as possessing the "intrinsic denominations" of true ideas.

If these mathematical ideas serve as exemplary "given true ideas," however—and I believe they do—this raises a problem for the dogmatic response to the skeptic. By Spinoza's own admission, they are not in fact true in the sense of corresponding to an object in nature. In the case of the sphere, he says that the idea "has no object in nature" and that "we may know that no sphere in nature was ever produced in this way" (TIE 72/G 2:27). For its part, Spinoza describes the circle as "an abstract thing" and as a "being of reason," contrasting it with "Physical and real beings" (TIE 95/G 2:35). If Spinoza understands truth to consist in the agreement between an idea

---

[10] For a recent discussion of the interpretive issues raised by Spinoza's "given true idea," see Nelson 2015. Nelson is dubious, as am I, that the given true idea can be the idea of God itself (as some interpreters have suggested), and he assigns to the idea of God a crucial grounding role, as I do (see Sect. 2.3 of this chapter). However, Nelson thinks that any idea (true or false) can serve as the given idea, since any idea provides material for thinking about God (and thus leads to an idea of God). I have a different understanding of the sense in which the given true idea serves as a standard. On my reading, it is important that the given idea is a true idea (prior to any idea of God), since it is the *form* of the true idea that guides the intellect to a properly formed (i.e., true) idea of God. So even if the given idea is not a mathematical idea, it has to be true, or at least true *in form*, in the manner discussed below.

and a real object in nature, then there is a significant sense in which these exemplary mathematical ideas are *not* true, after all.[11]

There is good evidence that Spinoza does understand truth to consist in the agreement between an idea and a real object in nature. He says that the ultimate goal is for the intellect to "reproduce the connection of Nature" (*Naturae concatenationem referre*) (TIE 95/G 2:35) and speaks similarly elsewhere of intending for the mind to reproduce the "likeness of nature" (*Naturae exemplar*) (TIE 42/G 2:17). The conception of truth as correspondence is further reinforced when we consider that Spinoza ultimately (i.e., once the idea of God is reached) conceives of truth in terms of God's idea of things (TIE 73/G 2:28; E2p11c/G 2:94–5), which, by Spinoza's parallelism doctrine, completely represents the *concatenatio Naturae*. The extent to which our own ideas are true is measured, then, by the extent to which they are the same as God's, that is, the extent to which they reproduce Nature. I will call ideas that are true in this full sense of corresponding to (or reproducing) a real object in nature *robustly* true ideas. Since Spinoza says that the ideas of the sphere and the circle do not reproduce nature, then they are not robustly true.

I suggest that we consider the genetic mathematical ideas as true in one sense but not in another. We have already seen in what sense the ideas are not true. In what sense are they true? In the *Ethics*, Spinoza says, "A true idea must agree with its object" (E1a6/G 2:47). The genetic mathematical ideas are true in the sense that they do agree with their objects. The sense in which this is the case is brought out by Spinoza's contrast between conceiving a sphere through the rotation of a semicircle, on the one hand, and conceiving the rotation of a semicircle on its own (without being joined either to the concept of the sphere or to a cause determining its motion), on the other (TIE 72/G 2:27). In the second instance, the motion goes beyond the concept of the semicircle itself inasmuch as it is not contained in the latter. The thought contains either too much (Spinoza says that the simple thought of a semicircle or of motion on its own would be unproblematic) or not enough (i.e., it is not joined to the concept of the sphere or to a cause determining the motion). Either way, the thought

---

[11] For discussion of Spinoza's views regarding abstractions, especially in his early writings, see Newlands 2015. Newlands (2015, 263) helpfully distinguishes between good and bad abstractions in Spinoza, but in claiming that Spinoza consistently rejected abstractions as confused in the earlier works (only recognizing "good abstractions" in later ones), Newlands appears to overlook the genetic mathematical ideas of the TIE, which are both abstract and clear and distinct.

of a moving semicircle on its own does not agree with itself. When the thought of a moving semicircle is joined to the concept of a sphere, as in the exemplary case, by contrast, now the total thought does agree with itself, since the moving semicircle generates the sphere (and is thus contained by the concept of the latter).

This internal agreement must be bought, however, at the price of stipulation. The motion of the semicircle is explained only by virtue of being stipulated for the sake of conceiving the sphere. As Spinoza says about the latter, "its object depends on our power of thinking." The cause of the sphere is one that we "feign…at will."[12] It is for this reason that the objects of the genetic mathematical ideas are not real objects. Because their objects are stipulated, they do not "make contact" with an object external to them (to invoke the metaphorical phrase I used above).

Genetic mathematical ideas are true, then, in the sense of agreeing with their objects, but untrue insofar as their objects are not real objects. Spinoza in fact provides language that nicely captures the ambivalent truth of the genetic mathematical ideas. He speaks of such ideas as exhibiting "the form of the true" (TIE 69/G 2:26), "the form of the true thought" (TIE 71/G 2:26), and "the form of truth" (TIE 105/G 2:38). We can say, then, that the genetic mathematical ideas are true *in form*, but not true *robustly*. To be true in form is to exhibit the sort of internal agreement exhibited by the genetic mathematical ideas. To be true robustly is to be true in form *and* correspond to a real object external to the idea. This distinction between true-in-form and robustly true ideas plays an important role in my interpretation of Spinoza's epistemology and will be invoked accordingly in the chapters to come.

At present, matters stand as follows. We saw that Spinoza responds to the skeptic by pointing to ideas that reveal their own truth and need no additional guarantee of their truth. But if all he has in mind are ideas true *in form*, then the skeptic is still justified in demanding some guarantee that the ideas are true in the full sense of corresponding to nature, that is, that

---

[12] Spinoza's language of "feigning" here can make it sound as if these mathematical ideas, which I have spoken of as "abstractions" (following Spinoza), are also kinds of fiction. This is potentially misleading, since Spinoza speaks of fictions separately in TIE 52–65, and it is clear from the discussion there that fictions are very different from the genetic mathematical ideas. The difference is that fictions, Spinoza says, "cannot be clear and distinct, but only confused" (TIE 63/G 2:24), whereas the genetic mathematical ideas are clear and distinct. For this reason, I speak of the genetic mathematical ideas as "abstractions." I return to the issue of fictions and their connection to the TIE's mathematical ideas in the next chapter.

they are *robustly* true. In other words, the notion of true-in-form ideas cannot be all there is to Spinoza's response to the skeptic. As I now turn to show, it is not.

2.3 Attaining the Idea of God: The Cartesian Response

"Since the truth, therefore, requires no sign," Spinoza writes,

> but it suffices, in order to remove all doubt, to have the objective essences of things, or, what is the same, ideas, it follows that the true Method is not to seek a sign of truth after the acquisition of ideas, but the true Method is the way that truth itself, or the objective essences of things, or the ideas (all those signify the same) should be sought in the proper order. (TIE 36/G 2:15)

We have already seen that the dogmatic response emphasizes the denials in this and related passages: the truth requires *no sign*; the true Method is *not* to seek a sign of truth after the acquisition of ideas. I now want to highlight the positive culmination of the statement, namely, that the true method consists in seeking true ideas *in the proper order*. While it is not immediately clear what Spinoza means by this from the passage just quoted, he elsewhere reveals his meaning. He says at several points that the method will be "most perfect" when the mind reflects on and has a true idea of the most perfect Being (TIE 38–39/G 2:16; TIE 49/G 2:19). At one point he says, "in the beginning we must take the greatest care that we arrive at knowledge of such a Being as quickly as possible" (TIE 49/G 2:19). At two other points (both of which will be worth quoting), he says something similar about "the source and origin of Nature." Addressing a concern about the deception that arises from conceiving things too abstractly and "confusing Nature with abstractions" (G 2:28), Spinoza writes:

> But we shall not need to fear any such deception, if we proceed as far as we can in a manner that is not abstract, and begin as soon as possible from the first elements, i.e., from the source and origin of Nature. (TIE 75/G 2:29)

This passage echoes an earlier statement (the first part of which I quoted above):

> for our mind to reproduce completely the likeness of Nature, it must bring all of its ideas forth from that idea which represents the source and origin of the whole of Nature, so that that idea is also the source of the other ideas. (TIE 42/G 2:17)

There is no doubt that Spinoza is talking about God when he refers both here to the origin of Nature and elsewhere to the most perfect being. Thus, proceeding "in proper order" means arriving at the knowledge of God, thereby perfecting (or completing) the method. The last two passages I quoted help to explain *why* arriving at an idea of God perfects the Method. Both passages indicate that the knowledge of God serves in a *grounding* capacity.

When I say that knowledge of God serves in a grounding capacity, this means a few things. First, it means that, in the case of our idea of God, the intrinsic (or representational) indicators of truth entail extrinsic truth as correspondence. That is, when we arrive at the idea of God we can be sure that we do not traffic in abstractions ("we shall not need to fear any such deception"), but rather possess an idea that corresponds to a real object in nature (i.e., is true robustly). Second, it means that we can be sure that ideas that are derived from the idea of God are themselves grounded in the first sense, or true robustly. (The idea of God "is also the source of other ideas.") It is in this second sense that we can speak of the knowledge of God as grounding a system of knowledge. Third, God is ground in being the "source and origin of the whole of Nature," that is, the cause of all things.

What is it about the idea of God that permits it to serve in this remarkable grounding capacity? Spinoza appears to address this question in TIE 76 as follows:

> But as for knowledge of the origin of Nature [i.e., God], we need not have any fear of confusing it with abstractions. For when things are conceived abstractly (as all universals are), they always have a wider extension in our intellect than their particulars can really have in nature. [...] But since [...] the origin of Nature can neither be conceived abstractly, or universally, nor be extended more widely in the intellect than it really is, and since it has no likeness to changeable things, we need fear no confusion concerning its idea, provided that we have the standard of truth (which we have already shown). For it is a unique and infinite being, beyond which there is no being. (TIE 76/G 2:29)

The thought seems to be that we can*not* have an abstract idea of God because an abstract idea is one in which the intellect extends more widely than its object, but it is not possible, in the case of God, for the intellect to extend more widely than its object. This is, presumably, because God encompasses everything that can be thought (clearly and distinctly)—"it is a unique and infinite being, beyond which there is no being."

Spinoza's reasoning here is unclear and seems question-begging. It seems that we can only be sure that our idea of God does not extend more widely than its object if God exists, but God's existence has not been established yet. What is needed at this point is a proof of God's existence. Of course, for Spinoza, as for Descartes, the idea of God is itself a fast lane to establishing God's existence. What may, ultimately, be fundamentally special about the idea of God (in comparison with other ideas, including mathematical ones) is that it uniquely provides a basis for demonstrating the existence of its object a priori. (This, in turn, may explain why the idea of God resists abstraction better than Spinoza's own explanation in TIE 76.) The details of Spinoza's proof (or proofs) of God's existence are beyond the scope of this study.[13] For present intents and purposes, attaining a clear and distinct idea of God is tantamount to establishing God's existence. Whatever the case may be regarding what precisely enables the idea of God to function in a special grounding capacity, I hope to have established that, for Spinoza, it does so function.

I now want to take stock of the ground covered thus far. Prior to proving God's existence, it is possible that our ideas are akin to the mathematical exemplars discussed above: true in form, but not robustly. This means that we may *doubt* the robust truth of our ideas prior to arriving at knowledge of God, which, as we have seen, cannot be thought abstractly (or be merely true in form), but must correspond with its object (or be true robustly). This means, further, that, in completing the Method, the attainment of knowledge of God also completes Spinoza's answer to the skeptic. If God does indeed play this role in Spinoza's response to skepticism, then a distinctly Cartesian dynamic comes into focus (*pace* the standard interpretation of the response as dismissive and *un*-Cartesian): we begin with ideas that have, like the mathematical exemplars, all the intrinsic characteristics of true ideas, but whose actual correspondence with real objects in nature is dubitable. On the basis of these first true ideas (which provide our first tools, per Spinoza's metaphor), we proceed as quickly as possible

---

[13] For an influential analysis of the *Ethics*' versions of the proofs, see D. Garrett 1979.

to attain knowledge of God.[14] Upon attaining knowledge of God, we have touched ground (or made contact), as it were, have no further doubts about the truth of our ideas, and the skeptic is answered.[15] There is reason to think that Spinoza proceeded in such a Cartesian manner knowingly and deliberately, as I will now argue.

2.3.1 Textual Evidence for the Cartesian Interpretation

In his brief discussion of the "doubtful idea" in TIE 77–80, Spinoza says that doubt does not arise through any given idea per se, but rather "through another idea which is not so clear and distinct that we can infer from it something certain about the thing concerning which there is doubt" (TIE 78/G 2:29–30). As Spinoza explains, doubt regarding one's perception of the size of the sun does not arise from the perception of the sun itself, but from the separate consideration that the senses sometimes deceive. From this, he infers: "only so long as we have no clear and distinct idea of God, can we call true ideas in doubt by supposing that perhaps some deceiving God exists, who misleads us even in the things most certain" (TIE 79/G 2:30). It is significant here that Spinoza concedes the possibility of doubting true ideas. This is something that makes no sense on dogmatic interpretations of Spinoza's response to skepticism, where the very notion of doubting ostensibly true ideas is rejected, but does make sense if we understand Spinoza to be referring to ideas true in form, as I have proposed.

---

[14] Mathematical ideas appear to play an instrumental role as exemplars in establishing knowledge of God. In both TIE 79 and the Prolegomenon to *Descartes' Principles of Philosophy*, Spinoza commends the knowledge of God for its analogy to our knowledge of the interior angles of the triangle.

[15] Cf. Primus 2017. According to Primus, the understanding of God qua one substance ensures the agreement of our clear and distinct ideas with formally real *ideata*. She also believes that achieving the understanding of God is necessary to avoid dogmatism. On these points, I am in agreement. She also sees the distinction between ideas true in form and robustly true ideas as tracking the difference between the knowledge yielded by reason (the second kind of knowledge) and *scientia intutiva* (the third kind of knowledge). In my view (as I explain in Chap. 7), reason and intuitive knowledge are different ways of apprehending the same knowledge content (with the same epistemic status), so, in this regard, my interpretation differs. As I will explain further in the next chapter, I use the notion of *entia rationis* (as well as the notion of "heuristics," and later, "hypotheses") (rather than *ratio*) to categorize ideas that are merely true in form, but not robustly true.

Spinoza discusses the same deceiving God doubt in the Prolegomenon to *Descartes' Principles of Philosophy*, citing mathematical truths as examples of the sort of true idea that can be doubted so long as one has a confused, rather than clear and distinct, idea of God's nature. In both the DPP and the TIE, Spinoza argues for the same resolution to the doubt: the deceiving God doubt is removed by forming a clear and distinct idea of God. As he says in the DPP: "When we have formed such an idea [of God], that reason for doubting Mathematical truths will be removed" (DPP Prolegomenon/G 1:148). The fact that Spinoza's discussion of the deceiving God doubt in the DPP fits so closely with the analogous discussion in TIE 77–80 justifies using it to piece together Spinoza's own thinking (and not just his version of Descartes').

Spinoza believes, then, that apprehending the existence of God is the key to silencing skeptical doubts. Descartes' influence here is unmistakable, but this does not mean that Spinoza's handling of skepticism is the same as Descartes'. For one thing, his antiskeptical rhetoric is more hostile, at times, than anything one finds in Descartes,[16] but there are important substantive differences too. I will discuss Spinoza's distinctive handling of the problem of the Cartesian circle shortly. Another important difference worth noting here concerns the step that follows the proof of the existence of a non-deceiving (or non-abstract) God. For Descartes, after having proven the existence of a benevolent creator, it remains only to point out that since God created our mental faculties we need no longer entertain the doubt that they systematically deceive us. (Of course, this brings up the problem of error, leading to Meditation Four's appeal to free will, which Spinoza strenuously repudiates.) Spinoza's God, by contrast, is not a benevolent creator, but the substance of the universe. This is, undoubtedly, the most profound and consequential difference between Descartes' and Spinoza's respective philosophies. It means that Spinoza cannot invoke God's benevolence in settling skeptical concerns. Instead, he must appeal to the participation of the human mind in the infinite intellect.

Consider Spinoza's demonstration in the *Ethics* of the proposition, "Every idea that in us is absolute, or adequate and perfect, is true" (E2p34):

---

[16] I have in mind, in particular, a passage in the TIE that culminates with Spinoza denouncing certain kinds of skeptic as "automata, completely lacking a mind" (TIE 48/G 2:18).

Dem.: When we say that there is in us an adequate and perfect idea, we are saying nothing but that (by 2p11c) there is an adequate and perfect idea in God insofar as he constitutes the essence of our Mind, and consequently (by 2p32) we are saying nothing but that such an idea is true, q.e.d. (G 2:116)

E2p11c, referenced in this passage, makes explicit for the first time in the *Ethics* that the human mind is a part of the infinite intellect of God, proceeding to explain on this basis that ideas in the human mind are identical with ideas in God's infinite intellect. E2p32, the other reference in E2p34dem, is as follows:

All ideas, insofar as they are related to God, are true.
Dem.: For all ideas which are in God agree entirely with their objects (by 2p7c), and so (by 1a6) they are all true, q.e.d.

The foregoing trio of propositions in the *Ethics* shows again how God plays a grounding role in Spinoza's epistemology, and it is only insofar as the human mind participates in the divine intellect that their truth is guaranteed. The fact that Spinoza's claim in E2p34 that all adequate ideas are true needs to be demonstrated provides further evidence that the relationship between the intrinsic or representational features of ideas (i.e., clarity and distinctness, or, as in E2p34, adequacy and perfection) and their extrinsic or epistemic features must be argued for and cannot be assumed from the outset. The fact that the demonstration, moreover, appeals to the mind's participation in the divine intellect supports my contention that the argument for the extrinsic agreement of intrinsically felicitous ideas must pass through God.

2.4 The Cartesio-Dogmatic Response

As anyone familiar with Descartes' attempt to overcome skepticism knows, there is ample room for doubting that the Cartesian gambit can succeed. The problem is that it appears question-begging to trust the proof of God's existence while one is entertaining the deceiving God doubt. After all, couldn't the proof of God's existence itself be a trick of the deceiver? Fully cognizant of the problem of the Cartesian circle, Spinoza rejects this concern. For Spinoza, we only doubt God's veracity while *lacking* a clear and distinct idea of God's nature. Once we come to enjoy a clear and distinct idea of God's nature (and his attendant, essential existence), the doubt disappears. It does not matter *how* we arrive at the clear and distinct idea of God and his existence, so long as we get there.[17]

But could the skeptic not simply invoke the distinction between the representational properties of the clear and distinct idea of God's existence and the epistemic status of this idea in casting doubt on the success of any alleged apprehension of God's existence, just as in the case of the exemplary mathematical ideas? That is, could our idea of God not appear true while being, in fact, false? For Spinoza, as we have seen, the difference between the mathematical ideas and the idea of God is that only the former admits of abstractness. The idea of God, by virtue of its nature, must match its object—it cannot extend further than it (or fail to correspond to it in any other way)—and so reveals its own robust truth. The answer to the skeptic, then, is, no: thanks to its unique qualifications, the idea of God could not merely seem true, while actually being false.

This, I think, is where things come to a head between Spinoza and the skeptic. (Things come to a head at a similar point between the skeptic and Descartes, too, as I will discuss momentarily.) The skeptic will refuse to accept that the idea of God reveals its truth—what guarantee is there, after all, that the idea, for all that it might seem true, is, in fact, true (or even clear and distinct, for that matter)? Spinoza, for his part, will invoke the dogmatic response: the truth of the idea of God is self-verifying. The ground of all things is, as it were, self-grounding. No external guarantee is required. It is not merely true in form; it is true in the full sense of corresponding with a real object in nature, namely, the cause of all things. Once we have arrived at this ultimate ground, all ideas derived in relation to that ground, inherit its robust truth qua correspondence.

That Spinoza would respond to skepticism about the truth of the idea of God by invoking the dogmatic response in the way I have just suggested is implied, I take it, by everything I have said up to this point. It is implied, in particular, by the several passages I quoted in the first part of Sect. 2.3, where Spinoza makes it clear that a true idea of God provides the foundation for everything else, and attaining a true idea of God brings the method to fruition. A further consideration can be adduced as well. As Spinoza warns in the *Theological-Political Treatise* (and concedes in the Prolegomenon to the DPP), if we could not be certain of God's existence, "we could never be certain of anything" (TTP 6.17/G 3:84; TTP 6.26/G 3:86). Faced with a choice between accepting the truth of the idea of God

---

[17] DPP Prolegomenon/G 1:148–9.

and total skepticism, Spinoza opts for the former on the presumptive grounds that the latter option is unacceptable. Popkin calls this "the argument from catastrophe,"[18] but I think we can just as well see it as an aspect of the dogmatic response, which, as I said, functions by deciding *de jure* any impasse between skepticism and antiskepticism in favor of the latter.

Let me summarize what I have said so far about the dogmatic and Cartesian responses, and explain how I see it all as coalescing. The dogmatic response cannot work on its own for reasons that Spinoza himself brings out: it is possible for an idea to have the form of truth, and yet fail to be true robustly. This, I showed, is the case with the genetic ideas of the sphere and circle that Spinoza discusses in the TIE. Thus, skeptical doubts stemming from a distinction between the representational features of an idea and its epistemic status cannot be defused by insisting, as the dogmatic response attempts to do, that no such distinction obtains. The failure of the dogmatic response on its own provides a good explanation for the presence of the Cartesian response in Spinoza's writings, since the Cartesian response addresses precisely those skeptical doubts that the dogmatic response fails to silence. (That such an explanation is lacking in dogmatic interpretations of Spinoza's response to skepticism strikes me as a significant limitation of those interpretations.[19]) As we have seen, however, the Cartesian response has its own shortcomings. Without the dogmatic response to rebuff skeptical doubts about the truth of the idea of God qua ground, the wheel of the Cartesian circle spins to the skeptic's delight. The dogmatic response preempts this scenario. Thus, the dogmatic and Cartesian responses are interdependent and are best seen as aspects of a single response, which I am calling the "Cartesio-dogmatic response." The response is dogmatic insofar as, in the end, the system is based and predicated upon a self-verifying idea, one whose truth is its own sign, or for which no (external) sign is required. The response is Cartesian insofar as there is only one idea that is uniquely qualified to be self-verifying in the requisite way, to wit, the idea of God's nature and existence.

One final point regarding the hyphenated moniker, "Cartesio-dogmatic": in tacking "dogmatic" onto "Cartesian," it might seem as if I

[18] Popkin 2003, 249.
[19] Della Rocca (2007, 32) sees the discussion of skepticism in TIE 79 (the Cartesian response) as inconsistent with the initial discussion from TIE 30–49 (the dogmatic response). Cf. Doney (1975), who sees the two discussions as divergent on the grounds that Spinoza addresses merely verbal skepticism in the former and genuine skepticism in the latter. Bolton (1985) ignores the latter discussion altogether.

mean to imply that Descartes' response to skepticism contains nothing of the dogmatic response. I do not mean to imply this. After all, Descartes is no more inclined to let the wheel of the Cartesian circle spin than Spinoza. It needs to be put to a stop at some point, and I do not see how this can be done without some version of a dogmatic response to the skeptic. At some point, that is, the rationalist must insist, "this is simply self-evident." Curiously enough, however, Descartes seems rather reluctant to advert to this insistence openly in defusing the circularity charge. Instead, he finesses his distinction between truths whose demonstration he *currently* perceives clearly and distinctly and ones whose demonstration he only *remembers* having perceived as such at some point prior.[20] Spinoza eschews such subtleties and is forthright, as we have seen, in his explicit articulation and deployment of the dogmatic response contra skepticism—perhaps a result of having learned the lesson of Descartes' entanglement in the problem of the circle. In the end, this difference may be more tonal and tactical than substantive and strategic.[21] As I hope to have shown, there is a significant extent to which Descartes' and Spinoza's responses to skepticism are structurally isomorphic (despite profound and consequential differences concerning the nature of God).

2.5 Objections and Replies

I can think of three potential objections to the Cartesio-dogmatic interpretation outlined here that warrant discussion. I will start with one that is comparatively tricky to answer. One might object to the central argument of this chapter by denying that intrinsic and extrinsic features of truth do in fact come apart in the case of genetic mathematical ideas, as I have argued, or in the case of any other ideas that exhibit "the form of truth." In particular, one could argue that all ideas true in form do correspond with real objects in nature, contrary to what I have maintained.[22]

---

[20] CSM 2: 100, 104, 171. See also my discussion of the Cartesian circle in Homan 2018.

[21] This does not mean that there are not neighboring strategic differences between Descartes and Spinoza regarding, for instance, the deployment of skepticism as a *means* to gain certainty. Spinoza does not actively deploy hyperbolic doubt in the way that Descartes does to achieve epistemic objectives. For an interesting explanation for why this might be the case, see Steinberg 1993. See also Garrett 1990, 19–21.

[22] In theory, one could alternatively object that genetic mathematical ideas in fact do *not* exhibit all the intrinsic features of truth, as I have claimed, and thus pose no greater skeptical problem than obscure and confused ideas. I say "in theory" because it is not clear how this

This would mean that the genetic idea of the sphere, for instance, does in fact correspond with a real sphere in nature. If this objection succeeds, then the dogmatic interpretation would appear to be vindicated.

Don Garrett defends a dogmatic interpretation of Spinoza's response to skepticism that addresses the issue of true-in-form ideas head-on (something other dogmatic interpretations fail to do, as far as I can tell). Garrett suggests that what might seem like an idea true merely in form (or what he refers to as a true idea of a "non-existent possible"[23]) is in fact a true idea of an object that exists as a formal essence comprehended in God's attributes. Garrett's interpretation invokes E2p8, which reads, "The ideas of singular things, or of modes, that do not exist must be comprehended in God's infinite idea in the same way as the formal essences of singular things, or modes, are contained in God's attributes" (G 2:90). In demonstrating this proposition, Spinoza explains that when he speaks of things "that do not exist," he means things that do not exist in duration, leaving open a kind of non-durational existence as a formal essence. Garrett uses Spinoza's example of the architect who has an adequate idea of a house that has not been built, arguing that the fact that the house is never actually built (and thus does not exist in duration) "does not violate the correspondence requirement, because the architect's idea is strictly of the formal essence of the house, and that formal essence does exist as a pervasive feature (in fact, as an 'infinite mode') of extension."[24] If Garrett's interpretation works for the architect's idea of the building, then it should also work for the genetically conceived sphere, which Garrett does not discuss, but which Spinoza deploys in the same context and for the same purpose as the architect's idea. On Garrett's interpretation, then, when Spinoza says in TIE 72 with regard to the genetically conceived sphere, "no sphere in nature was ever produced in this way," he is not denying correspondence with a real object. While the sphere may not exist in duration, it is comprehended as a formal essence in the attribute of extension. In particular, it exists as the infinite mode of extension.

In Chap. 6, I will present arguments against Garrett's interpretation of the formal essences of singular things as infinite modes. In my view, the

---

objection would work in practice, since I do not know what intrinsic features the mathematical ideas might lack. As we have seen, the only intrinsic features Spinoza mentions in any obvious sense are clarity and distinctness, and Spinoza explicitly says that the mathematical ideas exhibit those.

[23] Garrett 1990, 35.
[24] Garrett 1990, 36.

formal essences of singular things are finite. Taking this for granted at present, is it possible that the true genetic idea of a sphere corresponds not to a sphere existing in duration, but to a formal essence conceived as finite? I do not think so. Singular things, according to Spinoza, are finite individuals with determinate existence (E2d7)—horses, human beings, stars, and so on.[25] If the formal essences of such things do not exist in duration, they provide the definition of an individual that must be able to exist in duration at some point in time. (I will argue for this point in Chap. 6.) Are spheres singular things able to exist in duration? If we take "sphere" to mean a mathematical abstraction, I think not. Spinoza is clear that such things are beings of reason with no object in nature—durational or otherwise. A sphere per se (i.e., considered as existing in and through itself, not as a property of a material thing) cannot come into durational existence at any point in time. Thus, it does not have a formal essence comprehended in the attribute of extension, and my interpretation of genetic mathematical conceptions as true in form, but not robustly, avoids the Garrett-inspired objection I have just presented.

Perhaps one might point to a spherical object, such as a soap bubble, instead. That is a much better candidate for being a singular thing capable of durational existence with a formal essence comprehended in the attribute of extension (i.e., one of Garrett's non-existent possibles), but it is also quite a bit more complicated than the abstract mathematical idea. Can the rotating semicircle serve as an adequate thought of the soap bubble,

[25] The relationship between Spinoza's terms "singular thing" (*res singularis*) and "individual" (*individuum*) raises some difficult interpretive issues. Spinoza defines an "individual" in terms of a fixed ratio of motion and rest (E2p13d) among bodies, and "singular things" as "things that are finite and have a determinate existence" (E2d7). The latter definition is extremely vague, though in specifying that singular things must be finite, this differentiates them from individuals in one respect, inasmuch as the latter can be infinite as well as finite (as I will discuss in Chap. 3). What complicates matters considerably is that Spinoza's definition of singular things in E2d7 proceeds with a clause couched in terms of individuals: "And if a number of Individuals so concur in one action that together they are all the cause of one effect, I consider them all, to that extent, as one singular thing." It may or may not be the case that something can be a singular thing without also being an individual, so my gloss of "singular thing" as a finite individual is not uncontestable. Nevertheless, there is sufficient overlap between Spinoza's notions of a singular thing and a *finite* individual (and sufficient lack of clarity about any difference between them), in my view, to justify making this stipulation for the purposes of the present study. When discussing physical individuation, I will generally refer to Spinoza's definition of "individual," since it is more relevant to the subject matter of this study. I discuss Spinoza's definition of "individual" in Chap. 3. For further discussion of these terms and the question of their interrelation, see Melamed 2013, 72–79.

or of any other spherical object? Assuredly, understanding spheres can provide a useful heuristic for understanding *some* things about soap bubbles, but this is not sufficient to constitute the essence of the soap bubble understood as the definition of a singular thing. I will return to the complex issue of the essences of things in Chap. 6.

Putting the issue of essences to the side for now, there is an independent reason to prefer my interpretation over Garrett's (or another dogmatic interpretation like Garrett's), and it is one I have mentioned before. Garrett's interpretation, as with other dogmatic interpretations, offers no explanation for the presence of explicitly Cartesian aspects of Spinoza's discussion of skepticism in the TIE and elsewhere. The interpretation offered here, by contrast, makes sense of the two central elements that are clearly present in Spinoza's response to skepticism—the Cartesian and the dogmatic. It does so, moreover, in a way that coherently explains their interrelation.

Turning now to a second line of criticism, one might object to the fact that my argument is founded primarily on the *Treatise on the Emendation of the Intellect*, an early, unfinished work. It might be thought that Spinoza abandoned many of the positions staked out there, particularly the Cartesian ones, as he grew out of Descartes' shadow. Although Spinoza does not engage the skeptic explicitly in the *Ethics* as he does in the TIE, one might urge that the entire system elaborated in the later work obviates radical skepticism. Spinoza's famous doctrine of parallelism, in particular, might seem to preclude the gap between representational and epistemic features that I said obtains in the case of genetic mathematical ideas, and thereby the whole skeptical problematic fueled by the gap. Spinoza even uses a geometrical figure to illustrate the parallelism doctrine, stating, "a circle existing in nature and the idea of the existing circle…are one and the same thing" (G 2:90/E2p7s), just explained under two attributes (i.e., extension and thought, respectively).[26] It must be admitted that Spinoza does not explicitly base the proof of E2p7 ("The order and connection of ideas is the same as the order and connection of things") on any theological premises. The bewilderingly terse demonstration appeals only to E1a4, the so-called causal axiom ("The knowledge of an effect depends on, and

---

[26] Cf. the statement quoted earlier from TIE 33: "a circle is one thing and an idea of a circle another" (G 2:14). The combination of Spinoza's idea-object dualism (and attribute pluralism) with his substance monism means that the idea of the circle and the circle (existing in nature) are both different *and* the same. I discuss this further in Homan 2014.

involves, the knowledge of its cause"). This might seem to vindicate Dominik Perler's version of the dogmatic interpretation, according to which Spinoza assumes very basic and sweeping antiskeptical doctrines, such as anti-dualism, naturalism, and holism, at the very outset.[27] Whereas in the TIE, Spinoza had felt the need to address skeptical concerns in a quasi-Cartesian manner, by the time of the *Ethics* Spinoza has changed tack, simply presupposing a theoretical framework immune to radical skepticism.

If we take a proposition such as E2p7 in isolation, it can indeed seem as if Spinoza must be taking basic antiskeptical doctrines, such as those just mentioned, for granted. If we adopt a broader view of what is going on the *Ethics*, however, it seems clear that Spinoza does no such thing. Notwithstanding E2p7's puzzling demonstration (which is widely deemed to be underwrought[28]), it is surely true that almost everything in the *Ethics* depends upon Spinoza's conception of God as the one substance. But the existence of God as the one substance is argued for at the very beginning as the sine qua non of the system. It is not taken for granted. This is what we should expect given the Cartesio-dogmatic interpretation I've laid out here.

There is one final point to make regarding the *Ethics* and the issue of skepticism. Although I said that Spinoza does not engage the skeptic explicitly in the *Ethics* as in the TIE, there is one notable passage relevant to the skeptical problematic. E2p43s is often quoted as evidence of Spinoza's dogmatic response to skepticism. However, a careful reading of this text reveals the Cartesian aspect of Spinoza's response as well. When Spinoza says, in E2p43s (in the vein of the dogmatic response), "truth is its own standard," he immediately adds, "it is as necessary that the mind's clear and distinct ideas are true as that God's ideas are" (G2:124), indicating (in the vein of the Cartesian response) that it is only *after* having established God qua epistemic ground that we know our clear and distinct ideas are true. A note that Spinoza added to TTP 6, moreover, provides explicit confirmation of this point. Having discussed the means of clearly and distinctly apprehending God's existence a priori, he adds: "If we do that, it becomes evident to us: first, that God exists necessarily and is everywhere; next, that whatever we conceive involves in itself the nature of God and is conceived through it; *and finally, that everything we*

---

[27] Perler 2017, 12.
[28] See Della Rocca 2008, 91–2; Bennett 1984, 127–8.

conceive adequately is true" (G 3:253, emphasis added). Per the final (italicized) clause, it is only *after* having proven God's existence that we can be assured that our adequate ideas are true, or, in other words, that ideas with the intrinsic features of truth actually also correspond extrinsically with a genuine object in nature.[29]

To be sure, antiskeptical passages can be found in Spinoza's later writings that deploy the dogmatic response without hint of the Cartesian.[30] But there is no reason to think that such passages conflict with the Cartesio-dogmatic interpretation, since the dogmatic aspect of the response serves aptly as shorthand for the total response. After all, the Cartesian response depends ultimately on the dogmatic one.

This last point raises a final objection, however. If the Cartesian response depends ultimately on the dogmatic one, is the dogmatic response not Spinoza's ultimate response to skepticism? Are proponents of a dogmatic interpretation not right, then, after all? Responding to this objection affords me an opportunity to reiterate the central claims of this chapter. In the first place, according to the dogmatic interpretation, Spinoza rules out the possibility of any disconnect between the representational and epistemic features of ideas ab initio. I have argued, by contrast, that Spinoza is not in a position to rule out this disconnect at the outset, since the genetic mathematical ideas that he highlights for their exemplary representational features, and which first provide us with a standard of truth (thus initiating the method), are not robustly true, but, as Spinoza himself puts it, exhibit only the "form of truth." Spinoza does rule out the disconnect in question eventually, but only *after* having grounded the truth of ideas in the

---

[29] See also TTP 4:10, which further confirms the lasting relevance of the Cartesian response in Spinoza's thinking about skeptical doubt: "because nothing can either be or be conceived without God, and because we can doubt everything so long as we have no clear and distinct idea of God, all our knowledge, and the certainty which really removes all doubt, depends only on the knowledge of God" (G 3:59–60).

[30] There is, for instance, the following statement from Letter 76 to Burgh:

> I do not presume that I have discovered the best Philosophy; but I know that I understand the true one. Moreover, if you ask how I know this, I will reply: in the same way you know that the three Angles of a Triangle are equal to two right angles. No one will deny that this is enough, not if his brain is healthy and he is not dreaming of unclean spirits, who inspire in us false ideas which are like the true. For the true is the indicator both of itself and of the false. (G 4:320a)

knowledge of God (and the related participation of the human mind in the divine intellect) in which the method culminates. So, my interpretation of Spinoza's response to skepticism is very different from the dogmatic one in locating the denial of any disconnect between representational and epistemic features at the end of the method, and not at the beginning. Spinoza's response to skepticism is, as a result, less dogmatic than it might otherwise have been.

The ambivalent epistemic status of genetic mathematical ideas highlighted in this chapter helps to frame the discussion going forward. On the one hand, simple mathematical ideas are perfectly clear and distinct, exemplifying the form that true ideas should have. On the other hand, they are not actually true in the sense of corresponding to an object in nature. This ambivalence reflects a tension. The goal is to have true ideas, but it is also to have ideas of real things, not abstractions. For reasons that will emerge over the course of subsequent chapters, it is not possible to have *robustly* true ideas of finite particulars due to the need to rely on distortive sensory experience for our knowledge of particulars. As a result, the true ideas of finite particulars of which we are capable must remain at a level of abstraction. True abstract ideas, or what we can also call true beings of reason, represent both a concession to our limitations as well as an epistemic asset. It will be important to remember that while true abstract ideas are beings of reason, they are also true, at least in form, and thereby provide an adequate framework for understanding, albeit a hypothetical one.

References

Barnes, Jonathan. 2000. "Introduction." In Outlines of Scepticism by Sextus Empiricus, edited by Julia Annas and Jonathan Barnes, xi–xxxi. Cambridge, UK: Cambridge University Press.
Bennett, Jonathan. 1984. *A Study of Spinoza's* Ethics. Indianapolis, IN: Hackett.
Bolton, Martha. 1985. "Spinoza on Cartesian Doubt." *Noûs* 19: 379–395.
Chisholm, Roderick. 1973. *The Problem of the Criterion*. Milwaukee, WI: Marquette University Press.
Delahunty, R. J. 1985. *Spinoza*. London: Routledge & Kegan Paul.
Della Rocca, Michael. 1994. "Mental Content and Skepticism in Descartes and Spinoza." *Studia Spinozana* 10: 19–42.
———. 2007. "Spinoza and the Metaphysics of Skepticism." *Mind* 116: 851-74
———. 2008. *Spinoza*. New York, NY: Routledge.
Doney, Willis. 1975. "Spinoza on Philosophical Skepticism." In *Spinoza: Essays in Interpretation*, edited by Eugene Freeman and Maurice Mandelbaum, 139-57. La Salle, Il: Open Court.

Garrett, Don. 1979. "Spinoza's 'Ontological' Argument." *Philosophical Review* 88(2): 198–223.
———. 1990. "Truth, Method and Correspondence in Spinoza and Leibniz." *Studia Spinozana* 6: 13–43.
Homan, Matthew. 2014. "Spinoza and the Problem of Mental Representation." *International Philosophical Quarterly* 54: 75–87.
———. 2018. "Memory Aids and the Cartesian Circle." *British Journal for the History of Philosophy* 26: 1064–1083.
Mason, Richard V. 1993. "Ignoring the Demon? Spinoza's Way with Doubt." *Journal of the History of Philosophy* 31: 545–64.
McRae, Robert. 1965. "'Idea' as a Philosophical Term in the Seventeenth Century." *Journal of the History of Ideas* 26: 175–90.
Melamed, Yitzhak Y. 2013. *Spinoza's Metaphysics: Substance and Thought.* Oxford, UK: Oxford University Press.
Nelson, Alan. 2015. "The Problem of True Ideas in Spinoza's *Treatise on the Emendation of the Intellect.*" In *The Young Spinoza: A Metaphysician in the Making*, edited by Yitzhak Y. Melamed, 52–65. Oxford, UK: Oxford University Press.
Newlands, Samuel. 2015. "Spinoza's Early Anti-Abstractionism." In *The Young Spinoza: A Metaphysician in the Making*, edited by Yitzhak Y. Melamed, 255–71. Oxford, UK: Oxford University Press.
Perler, Dominik. 2017. "Spinoza on Skepticism." In *The Oxford Handbook of Spinoza*, edited by Michael Della Rocca, 220–39. Oxford University Press.
Popkin, Richard. 2003. *The History of Scepticism from Savonarola to Bayle.* Oxford, UK: Oxford University Press.
Primus, Kristin. 2017. "*Scientia Intuitiva* in the *Ethics.*" In *Spinoza's Ethics: A Critical Guide*, edited by Yitzhak Y. Melamed. Cambridge, UK: Cambridge University Press.
Schneider, Daniel. 2016. "Spinoza's Epistemological Methodism." *Journal of the History of Philosophy* 54: 573–599.
Steinberg, Diane. 1993. "Spinoza, Method, and Doubt." *History of Philosophy Quarterly* 10: 211–24.
Striker, Gisela. 1990. "The Problem of the Criterion." In *Epistemology* (Companions to Ancient Thought 1), edited by S. Everson, 143–160. Cambridge, UK: Cambridge University Press.
Williams, Michael. 1999. "Skepticism." In *The Blackwell Guide to Epistemology*, edited by John Greco and Ernest Sosa, 35–69. Oxford, UK: Blackwell Publishers.
Wilson, Margaret D. 1996. "Spinoza's theory of knowledge." In *The Cambridge Companion to Spinoza*, edited by Don Garrett, 89–141. Cambridge, UK: Cambridge University Press.

CHAPTER 3

Realism and Antirealism About Mathematical Entities

One of the major themes of the last chapter was the ambivalent status of certain mathematical entities in Spinoza's discussion of methodology and skepticism in the TIE. Genetic conceptions of geometrical figures have no object in nature and yet are said to be true conceptions. This generates an ambivalence when we consider that truth, for Spinoza, implies correspondence with a natural object. Which is it, then, do genetically conceived figures have objects in nature or not? We can ask this question about mathematical entities in general, including both numbers and figures (both genetically conceived and otherwise). What is the ontological status of mathematical entities in Spinoza? Do they have any extra-mental existence? If not, why not? If so, in what sense? I said in Chap. 1 that how we answer this question has important ramifications for how we interpret key areas of Spinoza's epistemology. In particular, we need to get clear on the status of mathematical entities before we can turn to Spinoza's philosophy of science and the kinds of knowledge. That is the goal of this chapter.

I will argue for a version of realism regarding geometrical figures in Spinoza. This goes against the recent trend in the Spinoza literature, which has generally favored antirealist interpretations of mathematical entities, including geometrical figures. Antirealism about figures is the denial that figures have any existence outside the mind. Per realism, by contrast, figures do exist outside the mind. The distinction just articulated is admittedly very broad. Realism and antirealism both come in a variety of stripes and I will introduce further distinctions and qualifications going

© The Author(s), under exclusive license to Springer Nature
Switzerland AG 2021
M. Homan, *Spinoza's Epistemology through a Geometrical Lens*,
https://doi.org/10.1007/978-3-030-76739-6_3

forward. To anticipate one, I deny that Spinoza is a Platonist about mathematical entities, including figures. Geometrical figures, I will argue, exist (insofar as they exist *outside* the mind) *in* bodies, not in themselves or independently of bodies. As is often the case with Spinoza, however, there are limits to the fineness of grain possible in interpreting his views, given the relative lack of detail that Spinoza himself provides on the topic and the ambiguity in what he does say. Despite this caveat, I will argue that it is possible to zero in on a few interpretive options that have in common the affirmation of figures as the (objective) determinations of finite bodies.

The chapter has four sections. In the first, I explain Spinoza's notion of beings of reason and discuss the ways in which figures can be regarded as such. The thesis that figures are beings of reason and nothing more provides the basis for the antirealist interpretation: if figures are beings of reason (and nothing more), then, since the latter necessarily lack extra-mental existence, figures too must lack extra-mental existence. I present a refutation of this antirealist line of argument in the second section of the chapter. In the third section, I outline what I take to be the correct, realist interpretation of figures as the determinations of finite bodies and attempt to articulate in as much detail as possible what I understand figures to be ontologically speaking. Finally, I address briefly the question of numbers.

3.1 Figures as Beings of Reason

We saw that Spinoza regarded figures as beings of reason in his early work, the TIE. He espouses the same view as late as 1676 (Ep. 83), suggesting that this is not a matter on which his opinion changed. We also said that ideas of figures have no object in nature or lack extra-mental existence. It is now time to get clearer on what it means for figures, or anything else, to be beings of reason. What is a being of reason? In what sense do beings of reason have no object in nature or lack extra-mental existence? In what sense are figures beings of reason? Answering these questions is a prerequisite for settling the question of the ontological status of figures, the main task of this chapter.

Let me begin with a terminological point. "Being of reason" (*ens rationis*) is not the only term that Spinoza uses when speaking of mental entities lacking extra-mental objects. He also uses "abstraction" (*abstractum*), "being of imagination" (*ens imaginationis*), and "aid to the imagination" (*auxilium imaginationis*). Although he uses these terms more or less interchangeably, they have different connotations, and this can potentially create some confusion, especially given the terminological links to the first and second kinds of knowledge, imagination, and reason, respectively. Spinoza seems, for the most part, happier with the term "being of imagination" (or "aid to the imagination"), since, as we will see, he treats beings of reason primarily as creatures of the imagination. He uses the term "being of *reason*," I presume, in deference to its history of scholastic usage. I will argue below that there is a sense in which some beings of reason are actually better seen as creatures *of reason* (i.e., an adequate form of knowledge) than *of imagination* (i.e., an inadequate form of knowledge). Until otherwise noted, however, I will generally follow Spinoza's lead in treating the different terms as more or less interchangeable.

Spinoza's most extended, and illuminating, discussion of beings of reason occurs in the first chapter of the CM (a polemic, at least, in part, against certain scholastic conceptions of *entia rationis*).[1] Spinoza there defines a being of reason as "nothing but a mode of thinking," which has no object that can exist (or that exists necessarily) (CM 1.1/G 1:233–4). In addition to beings of reason, Spinoza identifies two other categories of non-being in the CM: chimeras and fictions. Chimeras, being internally contradictory, cannot even be thought, and so are mere verbal beings. Beings of reason, by contrast, can at least be thought. (This rules out the possibility that Spinoza is an extreme nominalist about figures. Unlike chimeras, they are not just names.)[2] The contrast between fictions and

---

[1] Spinoza targets specifically those who divide being into real being and being of reason as well as those who say that a being of reason is not a mere nothing. It is not entirely clear whom Spinoza has in mind, though the clearest candidates would appear to be those thinkers that Suárez characterizes in *Metaphysical Disputation* 54 as believing that beings of reason "somehow agree with real beings in the character of being" on the grounds that beings of reason, like real beings, are "said to be" (Suárez 1995, 60). For instance, since we say that someone *is* blind, then blindness, a being of reason, must have some manner of being. Spinoza explicitly criticizes this basis for dividing being into real being and being of reason, saying, "I do not wonder that Philosophers preoccupied with words, or grammar, should fall into such errors. For they judge the things from the words, not the words from the things" (CM 1.1/G 1:235). In the notes to his translation of *Metaphysical Disputation* 54, John P. Doyle cites Cajetan, Capreolus, Deca, Ferrara, and Soncinas as belonging to this category (Suárez 1995, 60, n.14). Since Suárez himself says that beings of reason do not belong to the genus of being, he would presumably be immune to Spinoza's main criticism (Suárez 1995, 60–64). Cf. Curley 1:301, n. 2.

[2] Spinoza at one point says that beings of reason "can not in any way be classed as ideas" (CM 1.1/G 1:234), but this is misleading. In this context, Spinoza seems to be using "idea" in a restricted sense to mean a mode of thinking with a real object in nature. Elsewhere, Spinoza says that any mode of thinking is an idea (E2a3), and I take this to be his more

beings of reason is harder to pin down, and Spinoza is not always careful to distinguish them clearly and consistently. As I will argue below, the genetically conceived figures of the TIE exhibit characteristics of fictions as well as beings of reason. Roughly and provisionally, fictions involve the combination of multiple terms, whereas beings of reason, as modes of thinking *about* a given object, lack this kind of explicit conjoining of distinct objects into a single idea (such as the fiction of a golden mountain, which conjoins the ideas of gold plus mountain).

Spinoza distinguishes three kinds of beings of reason in the CM: (1) modes of thinking for *retaining* things, which encompasses class concepts, such as genus and species; (2) modes of thinking for *explaining* things, in particular time, number, and measure (for explaining duration, discrete quantity, and continuous quantity, respectively); and (3) modes of thinking for imagining non-beings as beings. This tripartition provides a helpful framework for thinking about the different ways in which something might be a being of reason. It will be helpful, in particular, in determining the sense in which figures count as beings of reason. An argument can be made for fitting figures into each of the three categories. I will consider them in order, discussing in each case the basis for fitting figure into the category in question, and the sense in which this suggests that figures lack extra-mental existence. Afterward, I will discuss the challenge of fitting the genetically conceived figures of the TIE into the CM's taxonomy of beings of reason, and thus, of making sense of their designation as beings of reason.

3.1.1 Figures as (Imaginative) Universals

The first category of beings of reason includes modes of thinking used to help us retain things more easily. In light of Spinoza's examples, namely, genus and species, it seems clear that he is talking about universals. His most extensive discussion of the formation of universals occurs in E2p40s1. He describes there a mechanistic process via the workings of the imagination that happens automatically, without intention. This differentiates it somewhat from the discussion in the CM, where the universals seem to be chosen purposefully for mnemonic value. But I do not think this difference is ultimately consequential for present purposes. If figures are beings

---

consistent usage. Since beings of reason are modes of thinking, then they are ideas, albeit without real objects.

of reason in this category, then ideas of figures will be formed according to the mechanism described in the *Ethics*, whether the idea is consciously deemed useful from a mnemonic standpoint or not. To understand the account of universal formation given in the *Ethics*, it will be necessary to preface some remarks regarding the workings of the imagination in general. (This will also serve to prepare some of the groundwork for our discussion of Spinozan science in the next chapter.)

Imaginatio (i.e., the first kind of knowledge) is Spinoza's term for (roughly) what we nowadays refer to as sensory experience.[3] It bears only passing analogy to what we today understand by "imagination," though clear sense can be made of talk of "images" in this context, as I will explain. Thus, I will use "sensation" (and "sensory") along with the straightforward transliteration "imagination" (and "imaginative") in discussing Spinoza's *imaginatio*. The first thing to say is that, in Spinoza's view, every sensory experience (or image) corresponds to an affection of the body.[4] The body is affected by virtue of its interactions with external bodies. It is easiest to think of affections as literal impressions made in the material of the body. (This is how Spinoza himself talks.[5]) Think, for instance, of the sun's rays altering the nerves in your eye. The state of the eye that results from the impact of the sun's rays would be an example of a bodily affection. Just like a footprint in the sand is a kind of image of the foot that made it, so the impressions or affections of the body are images of the external objects that brought them about. The human mind, according to Spinoza, is the mental correlate of the human body. This means that whatever happens in physical form in the human body also happens in mental form in the human mind. There is no causal interaction between one attribute and another (in this case, thought and extension). Rather (per E2p7,

---

[3] Spinoza's *imaginatio* includes experience by way of the five senses, as well as memory and our capacity for dreams and other fictive sensory experiences (including what we more narrowly understand as the purview of the imagination today). If we take "sensation" nowadays to refer narrowly to the deliverances of the five senses, then Spinoza's *imaginatio* is clearly broader. But I think our more contemporary notion of "sensation" admits of a broader construal that encompasses memory and dreams insofar as the latter have a sensory component. On a broad construal of sensation, then, Spinoza's *imaginatio* is a similar concept. Spinoza defines the imagination, or the first kind of knowledge, in E2p40s2/G 2:122, but he first explains image formation in E2p17s/G 2:105–6.

[4] In explaining his use of the term *imago*, Spinoza states, "to retain the customary words, the affections of the human Body whose ideas represent external bodies as present to us, we shall call images of things [*rerum imagines*]" (E2p17s/G 2:106).

[5] See E2p17dem2/G 2:105.

Spinoza's parallelism doctrine), each has the same order and connection of causes. So, when the body has a physical image of the sun as a result of being affected by the sun's rays, the mind has a correlative mental image. Hence, when we are affected by external things, and have ideas of such affections, we are said to imagine.

The second important point is that an image has more to do with the nature of one's own body than it does with the nature of the external body that caused the image (E2p16c2/G 2:104). Take the footprint again. The same foot moved in the same way makes a very different "image" in sand than in packed dirt or grass. Each material reflects the image of the foot according to its own nature. Thus, the image that the sun's rays make in my eye is determined by the nature of my eye and will be different from the image that the same rays might make in the eye of a very different kind of creature. While I imagine the sun as yellow, round, and 200 feet away, a Martian might imagine the sun as black, square, and 5 feet away.

Turning to the epistemic component of Spinoza's account of sensory experience (or imagination), we can see that our imaginative perceptions are inadequate (i.e., they are *not* adequate, in the sense of "adequate" discussed in the last chapter), since they reflect not the nature of the external object itself, but primarily the nature of our own bodies. Spinoza describes them as "mutilated and confused" (E2p29c/G 2:114). Whether or not this was intended, I think the terms "mutilated" and "confused" usefully highlight two distinguishable aspects of the inadequacy of sensory ideas. The ideas are mutilated, in the sense of truncated, insofar as they are based on the idea of the effects of the thing on the body absent any ideas of the cause. They are confused, in the sense of muddled, insofar as the effects of the external thing on the body are determined by both the body's own nature and the nature of the external body (without any certainty as to which nature determines what part of the effect). In this sense, mutilation is more basic than confusion. It is *because* we do not know the causes of our bodily affections that we cannot distinguish our body's contributions from the contributions of the external bodies, and thus perceive the affections confusedly.[6] I will not pursue this suggestion any further,

---

[6] Cf. Della Rocca 1996, 57–64. According to Della Rocca's reading, a sensory idea is confused because it is literally *of* both the (proximate) cause of the bodily affection and the bodily affection itself (qua effect). As I have argued elsewhere (Homan 2014, 82), since the mind is the idea of its body *alone*, and since the cause of the bodily affection is external to the body, I do not think Della Rocca's literal interpretation can be quite right.

however. Whatever the precise explanation of the inadequacy of our sensory ideas, the important point for present purposes is *that* they are inadequate.

A few additional points are needed to explain how universals can be formed on the basis of the imagination. First, the body has the capacity to be affected by something whether or not the cause of the affection remains present or not (E2p17c/G 2:105). The sand is impressed in the shape of a foot both when the foot is present in the indentation and after the foot is removed. The impression remains, moreover, until it is wiped out by another impression (say, one formed by waves raking the beach). Second, the body can be affected by many things at the same time (bearing in mind that the latter do not all need to be present for the affections to endure) (E2p18/G 2:106). Third, the mind has a limited capacity to distinctly imagine multiple things at the same time. Once this limit is exceeded, the images blur together, and the resulting confused agglomeration forms a universal (E2p40s1/G 2:120–1). Since the ear cannot distinctly register each individual sound made by the crashing of the waves in the ocean, it hears a single diffuse sound that is actually the confusion of the individual constituent sounds. Likewise, when the body is overwhelmed by a cacophony of disparate affections, and is able to register no clear distinctions between them, the mind has an idea only of what they all have in common, and so forms the idea of a "being" or "thing." Such an idea is maximally confused. Universals, such as "dog," result from lesser degrees of confusion. In this case, the body is able to discriminate dogs from non-dogs, but confuses the distinctions between the dogs themselves, engendering ideas of what they all have in common. As discussed above, each individual will perceive this common feature according to the nature of its own body. So, one will form the notion of a dog as a barking animal, while another (perhaps) will form the notion of a tail-wagger.

Let me, finally, relate this discussion of imaginative universals to figures. Spinoza does not speak of figures in E2p40s1, but it is not hard to see how the account could be adapted to describe the formation of ideas of figures.[7] If I am exposed to many different kinds of circular things—tires, clocks, hula hoops, and so on—it is possible that my capacity to distinguish their differences will be superseded, and I will be left with a confused idea of what they have in common, to wit, circularity. This commonality

---

[7] Cf. Melamed's discussion of how the account of abstraction in E2p40s1 can be adapted to explain the formation of our ideas of numbers (Melamed 2000, 12–13).

will reflect my own nature more than the nature of the external objects themselves. Hence, my idea of circularity will be a being of imagination no less than "barking animal."

In the Appendix to *Ethics* Part 1, Spinoza warns against conflating the affections of the imagination with "things," and states,

> all the notions by which ordinary people are accustomed to explain nature are only modes of imagining, and do not indicate the nature of anything, only the constitution of the imagination. And because they have names, as if they were notions of beings existing outside the imagination, I call them beings, not of reason, but of imagination. (G 2:82–3)

This passage makes it clear that Spinoza does not believe that the beings of imagination in question have any extra-mental existence. Although Spinoza's target in E1app are evaluative terms such as good and evil, beauty and ugliness, because his condemnation of such terms is based on their dependence on "the constitution of the imagination," the critique extends to the imaginative universals we have been discussing, which also depend on the constitution of the perceiver. Thus, if it turns out that ideas of figures are best seen as imaginative universals, that is, beings of reason of the first category (and nothing more), then they are *mere* modes of thinking (sans extra-mental existence) due to their relativity to the constitution of the imagination by means of which they are formed.

Given what we said about the genetically conceived ideas of the TIE in the previous chapter, however, it is perhaps already apparent that even if we do form many, or even most, of our ideas of figures according to the imaginative mechanism outlined above, the latter is not our *only* way of forming ideas of figures; and so the analysis of figures as imaginative universals must prove inconclusive with regard to the question of their extra-mental existence. I will return to this point in Sect. 3.2, after we have had a chance to further discuss the genetically conceived figures of the TIE, and the other kinds of beings of reason of the CM.

3.1.2 Figures as a Form of Measure

Spinoza says that the second category of beings of reason includes modes of thinking by which we *explain* (*explicemus*) a thing "by determining it through comparison with another" (CM 1.1/G 1:234). He singles out time, number, and measure as the modes of thinking by which we explain things, in particular, duration, discrete quantity, and continuous quantity, respectively. In Letter 12, Spinoza discusses the same trio of time, number, and measure. He says there that these modes of thinking (which he also calls modes of imagining) are used to determine (*determinare*) their respective objects so that we may more easily imagine them. To take the case of number, I presume that in saying that we use number to explain or determine discrete quantity, Spinoza has in mind subsuming a group of things under a numerical category. So, rather than referring vaguely to the mice living behind the cupboard, I can refer more precisely to the *seven* mice living behind the cupboard. This enables me to distinguish those mice from the *five* that lived there last winter. Using the notions "seven" and "five" enables me to imagine the groups of mice more easily. Counting seven as opposed to five mice also seems to be a case of determining one group through comparison with another.

If this is right, then we can similarly understand time to explain or determine duration by using units or measures of time to divide up duration into comparative segments. Hence, we use minutes and hours to determine one length of time as much shorter (or longer) than another.[8] It is easier to grasp a period of time in terms of minutes or hours than it would be without such categories. In this regard, we can understand why Spinoza refers to time, measure, and number as *aids* of imagination.

Before turning to measure, I want to say something about what makes such determinations as number and time beings of reason (or imagination), lacking extra-mental reality. The case of time is, at least as I have portrayed it, relatively straightforward. Units of time, such as minutes and hours, are arbitrary. There are not in fact sixty extra-mental entities that correspond to the minutes in an hour. Minutes exist, then, only in how we choose to consider the make-up of an hour. (The same can be said, mutatis mutandis, about hours and days.) The case of number is not quite as straightforward. While it seems easy to see why there are not sixty extra-mental things corresponding to the minutes in an hour, aren't there in fact seven mice living behind the cupboard? In my view, there are indeed (or certainly could be, at any rate) seven mice living behind the cupboard (though, of course, we must consider them as modes, not substances, lest we flout Spinoza's monism). However, considering them *qua* seven adds nothing to their being. They do not exist, in other words, *as* seven things. Each is simply itself (to court tautology). Seven is not a real property of

---

[8] Cf. Descartes' similar analysis of time in CSM 1:212.

any extra-mental thing. (We might think here of Frege's point that 1000 cannot be a property either of each individual leaf on a tree or of the foliage in general.[9]) Seven is just a way that we can consider them, a mental category under which we subsume them. Seven is, in that case, just a mode of thinking (or imagining) the individuals.

Let us turn now to measure. I've suggested the way in which time and number are used to determine indeterminate stretches of duration and indeterminate masses of discrete quantity, respectively. In what way does measure determine indeterminate regions of continuous quantity? It is the contention of some interpreters that measure must function by organizing indeterminate regions of continuous quantity into geometrical figures. Thus, Yitzhak Melamed argues,

> Spinoza distinguishes between measure and number by noting that the former is continuous, while the latter is discrete. But what sort of things can be continuous? I see no other candidates apart from duration and extension. Since continuous duration is named by Spinoza 'time' and is criticized separately, there is no other thing that the criticism of measure could be addressed to, apart from geometrical figures, as abstractions of extended things.[10]

A point in favor of Melamed's interpretation is the fact that Spinoza does indeed define figure or shape in terms of determination (and, recall, measure is a way of *determining* continuous quantity). In Letter 50, Spinoza describes figure as "nothing but a determination" (G 4:240b). If figures are beings of reason, like number and time, this means of course that such determinations do not exist outside of the mind, but are just ways in which *we* determine quantity (or extension) in thought.

But there is an alternative interpretation of measure that is at least as plausible as Melamed's. On this reading, there is a closer analogy between time and measure. Just as time consists in the application of arbitrary units of measure, such as minutes and hours, to divide up duration, so "measure" consists in the application of arbitrary units, such as meters and miles, to divide up continuous quantity. Just as there are not actually 60 distinct entities corresponding to the minutes in an hour, so there are not 26.2 distinct things that correspond to the miles in a marathon. Instead,

---

[9] Frege 1980, 28. Unlike Frege, however, I do not see any evidence that Spinoza is committed to securing realism about numbers (by affirming a third realm, for instance). I return to this issue in the last section of this chapter.

[10] Melamed 2000, 14. See also Schliesser 2014, 17.

there is just the duration (in the case of the hour) or the continuous quantity (in the case of the marathon). This is consistent with continuous quantity being parceled geometrically. The base of a given triangle might be thought of as 100 centimeters or as 1 meter. It is *this* that is arbitrary, and hence merely a mode of thinking—not the triangle itself.

This alternative interpretation of measure in terms of *units* of measure, rather than figure, is preferable, in my view, for a few reasons. First, it is supported by the closer analogy with time, as just depicted. Second, it is easier to make sense of the idea that there are not really 26.2 real parts of a marathon than it is to make sense of the idea that planets are not really spherical (at least roughly). This is because the former is obviously arbitrary—the marathon can just as easily be considered as made up of 42.2 kilometers—in a way that the latter is not.

Finally, there is some precedent for this alternative interpretation in Hobbes' analysis of quantity in *De Corpore*. Hobbes understands quantity in terms of what answers the question *how much?* (or how long? or how big? etc.). He gives as examples, "the journey is a hundred miles; the field is a hundred acres; the bulk is a hundred cubical feet," explaining that in this way "the magnitude of the thing may be comprehended in the mind. Quantity, therefore, cannot otherwise be defined, than to be *a dimension determined*, or *a dimension, whose limits are set out, either by their place, or by some comparison*."[11] Hobbes' understanding of quantity as something *determined* so that it may be comprehended in the mind echoes Spinoza's talk of determining quantity in Letter 12 for the sake of more easily imagining it, and tends to corroborate the interpretation of measure in terms of units of measure rather than in terms of geometrical figures.

3.1.3 Figures as Non-beings

The CM's third category of beings of reason includes modes of thinking by which "we imagine nonentities positively, as beings" (CM 1.1/G 1:234). As examples, Spinoza cites "blindness, extremity or limit, term, darkness, etc." It is not difficult to see why Spinoza regards such notions as beings of reason. When we speak of the darkness descending, for instance, we reify (metaphorically, of course) something which does not itself have positive existence, namely, darkness. It would be more accurate to say that the light is receding (or, perhaps better, that the earth is

---

[11] Hobbes 2005, 139.

turning). Similarly, the extremity or limit of the table, for instance, is not itself something positive. Rather, it is where the table meets what is not-table.

In this light, the following passage from Letter 50 suggests that figures belong in this third category of beings of reason:

> whoever says that he conceives a shape (*figuram*) indicates nothing by this except that he conceives a determinate thing, and how it is determinate. So this determination does not pertain to the thing according to its being, but on the contrary, it is its non-being. Therefore, because the shape is nothing but a determination, and a determination is a negation, as they say, it can't be anything but a negation. (Ep. 50/G 4:240b)

If shape is determination, determination is negation, and therefore shape is nothing but negation, as Spinoza says here, then ideas of shapes look like ways of imagining non-entities as beings. In particular, shapes would seem to constitute kinds of extremity or limit. When we say that some table is circular, or that its surface forms a circle, we are referring to the boundary where the table edge meets the space that surrounds the table. This edge determines the table vis-à-vis surrounding space, but this determination is not itself part of the table. Figures are made up of points, lines, and planes, all of which notions can be construed, like the perimeter of the table, as modes of thinking by which we conceive non-beings as beings. In this way, Spinoza's analysis of shape in Letter 50 in terms of determination and negation fits nicely with his analysis of extremity or limit in the CM and provides a good case for seeing shape as a being of reason. If shape is a being of reason (and nothing more), moreover, as we know, it has no extra-mental reality.[12] In the next section, I will reject this antirealist inference on the grounds that it throws bodies out with the bath water, so to speak, and leads to acosmism. Before I give this rebuttal, however, we need to consider the genetically conceived figures of the TIE in relation to Spinoza's discussion of beings of reason and fictions in the CM. Because

---

[12] Somewhat surprisingly, Letter 50 is not discussed in the antirealist literature from what I can tell. (I do not see references to it in Melamed (2000), Schliesser (2014), or Peterman (2015).) Far more emphasis is placed, in general, on Spinoza's critique of time, number, and measure in Letter 12. Nevertheless, Schliesser (2014) deploys the remark, "Being finite is really, in part, a negation" (E1p8s1), as an epigraph to his article, and Melamed describes mathematics as a "science of non-beings" (2000, 20), suggesting a similar line of argument to the one outlined in this subsection.

they are ostensibly true and non-imaginative, they present the toughest case for the antirealist.

3.1.4 Genetically Conceived Figures

If figures can be seen as universals in the first category of beings of reason, then they are formed through the imagination. It is their origin in the imagination that explains why their objects are not real. Spinoza says in Letter 12, moreover, that time, number, and measure are beings of the imagination. The third category of beings of reason in the CM, finally, are explicitly defined as modes of imagining. The beings of reason in the CM, then, are beings of *imagination*. The genetically conceived figures of the TIE, by contrast, do not appear to be creatures of imagination. They appear, instead, to be born of the intellect. What, then, are we to make of the latter? Are they modes of thinking sans extra-mental existence, after all?

Let us, first, try to get clearer on the sense in which the genetically conceived figures of the TIE are intellectual, rather than imaginative. The distinction between intellect and imagination is a major theme of the TIE, and, indeed, of Spinoza's philosophy, in general. Spinoza characterizes intellectual conceptions as arising "from the very power of the mind," and imaginative ones as stemming from external causes, where the mind "has the nature of something acted on" (TIE 84/G 2:32). This comports with what we said about the mechanism of the imagination above. We might add to this Spinoza's comment in the *Ethics* that ideas of the imagination are "like conclusions without premises" (E2p28dem/G 2:113). They are ideas of effects, absent causes. (This, I suggested, is how we should understand Spinoza's description of them as mutilated.) This implies that ideas of the intellect are like conclusions *with* premises, or, in other words, ideas of effects in terms of their causes. We read, in the TIE: "really, knowledge of the effect is nothing but acquiring a more perfect knowledge of its cause" (TIE 92/G 2:34); and, in the *Ethics*: "The knowledge of an effect depends on, and involves, the knowledge of its cause" (E1a4/G 2:46).[13]

---

[13] E1a4, the so-called causal axiom, has both normative, epistemic force (one *must* know the causes of things in order to have knowledge, as is the emphasis of the similar passage in TIE 92) and descriptive, metaphysical force (it simply *is* the case that all knowledge depends on knowledge of causes, and involves the latter). This leads to an interpretive difficulty that has exercised scholars inasmuch as it seems to imply that all knowledge is adequate. After all, to know something adequately is to know it *per causam*, but, as a matter of fact, all knowledge *is* knowledge *per causam*. But how can this be, since Spinoza recognizes inadequate

In the last chapter, I spoke of the truth of genetic conceptions of figures in terms of internal agreement. We can now flesh out that account in terms of cause and effect. Conceiving an effect in terms of its cause is precisely what the genetic conceptions of the TIE promise, of course. As Spinoza explains in reference to the genetic definition of a circle as the figure produced by a line rotated around a fixed end, what makes this definition adequate is the fact that knowing the cause of a thing permits the deduction of all of its properties. (In this way the idea is ensured to agree with its object.) This guarantee that one's conception is complete (as opposed to the mutilation of the imagination's ideas), or at least potentially complete, in implicating all the thing's properties, plausibly provides the "intrinsic denominations of a true idea," thereby satisfying Spinoza's definition of adequacy in E2d4.[14]

knowledge, which he compares to conclusions without premises (E2p29s), ideas of effects without ideas of their causes? The fact that Spinoza invokes the causal axiom in arguing that the mind perceives external bodies insofar as external bodies cause the body to be affected in different ways (E2p16dem, c1) complicates matters further, since in this context Spinoza is discussing inadequate sensory perception. Wilson (1991) stresses E2p16 in critiquing Gueroult's position that the axiom applies only to adequate knowledge (Gueroult 1968, 95–8). But I think E2p16 can be interpreted in a way that is consistent with Gueroult's interpretation, and the general problem raised by the causal axiom can be allayed, if we recall what I said above (n. 1 in Chap. 1) in explanation of my decision to translate *cognitio* as "knowledge." That is, in a sense all knowledge *is* adequate, since inadequate knowledge is privative, and to have inadequate knowledge is to constitute a part of a whole, adequate understanding, that is, God's understanding, which provides the standard for what constitutes knowledge. As I read E2p16, when my body is affected by an external body, my mind has an idea *only* of my body *qua* affected. So, my mind *lacks* the idea of the bodily affection's cause, but nevertheless involves an idea of the cause to the extent that my body bears the literal impress of the cause. The result of the idea of the affection absent its cause is a confused idea of an external body. (See my paper, Homan 2014, for further discussion of the mechanics of mental representation involved here, as well as Chap. 4.) All of this is, it seems to me, consistent with the notion of inadequate knowledge as privative, and thus does not require a special extension of the axiom to inadequate knowledge. Cf. Morrison 2015.

[14] Cf. Marshall 2008, 56–62. Marshall identifies two requirements for an adequate idea: (1) the idea must be wholly (not only partially) contained in the human mind; and (2) the idea must also include an adequate idea of the object's cause. I think the brief account I have given of adequacy in light of Spinoza's genetic definitions is consistent with Marshall's. Genetic definitions are only genetic insofar as they include an adequate cause of their object. Moreover, I have argued, on the basis of that cause, all the properties of the thing can be deduced, which guarantees that the object is wholly contained in the idea, thereby satisfying Marshall's first requirement. Cf. Descartes, CSM 2:155. Descartes denies that we can ever be sure that our idea of an object is complete in the sense of containing all the properties that are in the thing. On this basis, Descartes denies that we can ever have adequate knowledge.

The fact that internal agreement is ensured through genetic conception does not change what we said before—the former is bought at the price of stipulation. It is the cause, of course, that is stipulated in this case. This produces a true conception, albeit one true only in form. Recall Spinoza's admission that in the case of the genetically conceived figures, the cause is one we "feign at will" (*fingo* ad libitum) (TIE 72/G 2:27). The language of *feigning* in this context suggests fiction. As noted above, Spinoza is careful to distinguish fictions and beings of reason in the CM. The difference was that while the former consists in the connection of multiple terms, the latter does not. But in the case of the genetically conceived figures of the TIE, there is quite clearly a connection of multiple terms. The genetic conception of the sphere joins the idea of a semicircle to the idea of motion around a center. Similarly, the genetic conception of the circle joins the idea of a line to that of motion around a point.

Does this mean that the genetically conceived figures of the TIE should be considered fictions? The oxymoronic notion of a true fiction is no less at odds with what Spinoza says about fictions than the notion of a true being of reason is at odds with what he says about beings of reason. Spinoza is clear in his discussion of fictions in both the TIE and the CM that they are confused creatures of the imagination. He is at pains in the CM to make clear that fictions "cannot be clearly and distinctly perceived" and are formed "without any guidance from reason."

There is, moreover, a sound basis for linking the genetically conceived figures of the TIE with the beings of reason of the CM. Even if the figures of the TIE are creatures of the intellect, not the imagination, this does not mean that they don't exhibit features of beings of reason. They are constructed from points, lines, and planes, after all. Such abstractions are best regarded as beings of reason of the third category. They are all extremities. A plane is the superficial extremity of a solid (three-dimensional) object. A line is the extremity of a plane. A point is the extremity of a line. In each case, to conceive the extremity positively as a being is to conceive a nonentity as a being. Such a conception is a being of reason of the third kind. So, it does not matter whether the figure is conceived through a cause, like the genetic conceptions of the TIE, or passively, without a cause, like the images of the CM. In either case, the conception has as its content, points, lines, and planes, and so, is a being of reason in that respect.

I discuss this discrepancy between Spinoza and Descartes on the subject of adequate knowledge in the concluding chapter.

What, then, are we to make of the genetically conceived figures of the TIE? On the one hand, they are like beings of reason insofar as they are constructed out of non-entities conceived as entities. They are also like fictions insofar as they are constructed "at will" by the connection of two otherwise unconnected ideas. On the other hand, while all other beings of reason and fictions seem to be creatures of the imagination, the genetically conceived figures are of intellect born. Indeed, unlike their imaginative counterparts, they are aptly named beings *of reason*. While all other beings of reason and fictions cannot be clearly and distinctly perceived, the genetically conceived figures of the TIE are clear and distinct ideas *par excellence*. While all other beings of reason and fictions are neither true nor false (having no real object), the genetically conceived figures of the TIE exemplify the form of truth in completely reproducing the essence of their objects.

The genetically conceived figures of the TIE, then, defy straightforward categorization. In the context of Spinozan dualisms of imagination and reason, fantasy and reality, the genetically conceived figures of the TIE appear to be in a limbo straddling the sharp division.[15] This, as I will argue in subsequent chapters, makes them ideally suited to mediate the division. In doing so they will have a central part to play in advancing a coherent account of Spinoza's epistemology.

3.2   *Reductio ad Acosmism*: The Case Against Antirealism

In the last section, it was established that there are a variety of lights in which to see figures as beings of reason. On this basis, the case for antirealism about figures appears cut and dried. What it means to be a being of reason (or imagination) is to exist as nothing more than a mode of thinking. In other words, it means that beings of reason have no existence outside of the human mind. Figures, as we have seen, are beings of reason. Therefore, figures have no existence outside of the human mind.

---

[15] Cf. Gueroult 1968, 422. Gueroult distinguishes between imaginative and intellectual conceptions of figure, but concedes that even the intellectual conception involves elements of the imagination, and so the distinction does not hold: "However, as the geometrical essence can be conceived only by the delimitation of indeterminate extension by means of figure taken in its first sense, the two senses of the word *figure* tend to run together, and the result is an equivocation" (my translation).

Things are not quite as straightforward as this. The success of the antirealist case depends on the sense in which figures are understood to be beings of reason. It matters, that is, whether figures are regarded as imaginative universals, forms of measure, or non-beings. I already raised doubts about the second option (figures as forms of measure). As for the first (figures as imaginative universals), the argument cannot be that we form ideas of figures through the imagination, and products of the imagination, reflecting one's own nature more than the nature of the object, do not properly represent extra-mental reality. Even if the imagination were our only way of accessing figures, that fact alone would not suffice to entail the non-existence of figures outside of the mind. It would merely put limits on our ability to gain knowledge of figures. To show that figures have no existence outside of the imagination, it needs to be demonstrated that figures are *inherently* creatures of the imagination.

Spinoza seems clearly to countenance intellectual conceptions of figures, as we have seen. This would seem to rule out the possibility of figures as inherently imaginative. However, we saw that the intellectually conceived figures of the TIE are strange beasts, exhibiting features of true ideas, as well as of fictions and beings of reason. Although the genetically conceived figures are true *in form*, they have as their content lines and planes, or, in other words, the sorts of extremity that constitute beings of reason of the third kind. It might be argued that the latter, the content of the genetic figures, is inherently imaginative. After all, as we said above, extremities or limits or determinations (to use the language from Letter 50)—such as geometrical figures are made of—do not exist in themselves; they exist only as imagined in the mind. This means that however the genetically conceived figures of the TIE may be creatures of the intellect in their formal construction, their content is inherently imaginative, and this inherently imaginative component means that their objects cannot, even in principle, have any extra-mental existence.

The foregoing is the strongest line of argument for antirealism about figures, in my view. It provides an explanation for why figures cannot exist outside the mind that addresses the toughest case for the antirealist, namely the true-in-form figures of the TIE. Nevertheless, I think it is susceptible to a fatal *reductio*.

The antirealist argument just considered depends upon the following line of reasoning, taken from Letter 50: figure is nothing but determination, and determination is negation; therefore, figure is nothing but negation, or, in other words, non-being. (I linked this up with the CM by interpreting figural determination here as a kind of limit or extremity, thus fitting figures for the third category of beings of reason.) Consider now how this line of reasoning can be redirected to target the reality of finite bodies, instead of figures. If determinations are non-beings, it might be argued, then that makes bodies non-beings as well. After all, Spinoza defines bodies in terms of determination as "a mode that in a certain and determinate way expresses God's essence insofar as he is considered as an extended thing" (E2d1/G 2:84). More generally, Spinoza defines finitude in terms of limitation (E1d2/G 2:45), inferring on this basis that "being finite is really, in part, negation" (E1p8dem/G 2:49).

A first pass at the *reductio*, then, is as follows: if figures are non-beings because they are determinations, then bodies are non-beings, too, because they are defined in terms of determinations. It might be objected that this *reductio* trades on an equivocation: *being* a determination is not the same thing as *having* determination. Figures *are* determinations—nothing more—that is why they can justly be considered non-beings. Bodies, by contrast, are not themselves determinations; they have limits, but they are not the limits themselves. So, bodies are on firmer ontological footing. I think there is something to this objection: figures and bodies are, indeed, on different ontological footing. I will build this into my own interpretation of the ontology of figures below. But the objection misses the bigger picture. If determination *itself* does not exist, since it is negation, then finite bodies cannot exist either, since they are essentially determined: if they weren't, they'd be infinite (which is certainly incompatible with being finite).

For the *reductio* to work, it needs to be absurd (as a reading of Spinoza) to think that finite bodies do not exist on the grounds that they are determined. Is it absurd? At least some readers of Spinoza have thought not. Hegel famously charged Spinoza with "acosmism"—the view that the world of finite things does not really exist, since only the infinite, that is, God, exists—on the grounds that Spinoza understood finitude in terms of determination and determination in terms of negation.[16] The worry that finite bodies in some deep sense do not really exist is a serious one for Spinoza interpretation. A basic feature of Spinoza's philosophy (and one of its most challenging) is that finite modes—tables, trees, human minds, and so on—do not have their own independent existence. Only one thing has independent, substantial existence in Spinoza's philosophy, namely,

[16] See Hegel 1995, 281.

God, an absolutely infinite being consisting of an infinity of infinite attributes. Finite modes exist, at bottom, only as ways in which God exists. Given this picture, it would seem that finite beings do *not* exist qua finite, and so there is nothing in which the being of a finite, determinate thing consists qua finite, determinate thing. Rather, finite beings exist only qua infinite, and their being consists in the attributes which express the essence of the one infinite substance. But to say that finite beings exist only qua infinite is just another way of saying that they do not really exist at all.

It is relatively clear, however, that Spinoza himself thought finite modes (including bodies) *do* exist—and not just as figments of our imagination, but as real things. A variety of evidence might be marshaled in support of this proposition, but perhaps the clearest is the fact that Spinoza thought intuitive knowledge yields adequate understanding of the essences of singular (i.e., finite) things (a contention that will be our focus in Chap. 7).[17] As an interpretation of Spinoza's *intentions*, then, the case for acosmism is not very strong. Proving that Spinoza was *entitled* to affirm the existence of finite things given the logic of his more basic commitments is a very different matter. Attempting to vindicate Spinoza's affirmation of the existence of finite things would take us quite far afield.[18] Fortunately, such a venture is unnecessary. My current aim is to address the arguments for antirealism about figures, not the arguments for acosmism. Since most interpreters of Spinoza, including most antirealists, do not wish to maintain that Spinoza is an acosmist, the *reductio* works as an ad hominem directed against them (at least insofar as they advance the antirealist argument I have presented here as the strongest[19]): *unless* we wish to embrace acosmism, we must affirm the reality of figures, since the argument for the non-being of figures implies also the non-being of finite bodies. Call this argument the *reductio ad acosmism*. I will have more to say about figure and finite bodies when I present the positive case for realism about figures in the next section.

---

[17] For other evidence that Spinoza believed in the existence of finite modes, see Melamed 2010, 89–91.

[18] For discussion of the merits of various strategies for defending the reality of finite things in Spinoza, see Hübner 2015. See also Lin 2019, 128–32.

[19] See n. 12.

3.3 FIGURE AND FINITE BODIES: THE CASE FOR REALISM

I just argued that if we accept that finite bodies exist in Spinoza's ontology, then we must also accept that figures exist as well. This is because finite bodies are defined by their determinations, and figures are among the determinations of finite bodies. This provides the basis for a realist interpretation of figures in Spinoza: figures exist as the determinations of finite bodies; in other words, they exist as the properties of bodies, *in re*. But how can this be squared with Spinoza's indisputable commitment to regarding figures as beings of reason? After all, to say that something is a being of reason is precisely to deny that it has any existence outside of the mind. So, if figures are beings of reason, how can they also exist as objective, mind-independent properties of finite bodies, as I am now claiming? There is a relatively straightforward way of resolving this apparent tension. The resolution turns on a distinction between figures understood in abstraction from bodies, or what I will call figures per se, on the one hand, and figures understood as the determinations of bodies, on the other. Whereas figures per se are beings of reason, figures as the determinations of finite bodies have extra-mental existence. I take it that the first part of this statement has already been established by what we have said in this chapter. The *reductio ad acosmism* of the antirealist argument just outlined helps to establish the second part, albeit only in an indirect, provisional manner. It is necessary now to build a positive case for the reality of figure. It will be helpful to begin by examining Descartes' views on figures, since they provide a useful guide for understanding Spinoza's.

3.3.1 Descartes and the Ontological Status of Figures

As is well known, Descartes understands the basic nature of the physical world in terms of extension. By extension is meant extension in length, breadth, and depth, or, in other words, spatial dimensionality. Bodies are just extended things. Finite bodies—the only type we are capable of comprehending, according to Descartes—have spatial limits. The latter determine the body as having one shape or another. That corporeal substance, or body, is characterized by size, motion, and, what is most relevant for present purposes, *shape* (as opposed to other properties, such as color) is a constant refrain in Descartes' corpus.[20] Shape, then, follows naturally from

---

[20] See CSM 2:44/AT VII:63; CSM 1:89/AT XI:26; CSM 1:217; AT VIIIA:33.

a conception of body in terms of spatial extension and the finitude of body. It is in this light that Descartes remarks, "my entire physics is nothing but geometry."[21]

Nevertheless, Descartes recognizes the capacity of geometers to consider lines, planes, and other geometrical objects, abstracted from bodies. In the *Rules for the Direction of the Mind*, he says, "when we are concerned with a figure, we should bear in mind that we are dealing with an extended subject, conceived simply with respect to its having a shape."[22] That is, to think of a figure is to think of the shape of some body, while ignoring all of the aspects of the body (such as its motion and size) besides the shape (albeit, as Descartes also adds, "not denying" the other aspects). In the *Principles*, Descartes says, "number, when it is considered simply in the abstract or in general, and *not in any created things*, is merely a mode of thinking; and the same applies to all the other *universals*, as we call them."[23] As the ensuing discussion makes clear, Descartes understands figures to count among the other universals mentioned here. He is saying, then, that when geometers consider figures per se (i.e., not insofar as they are in bodies), the figures are only modes of thinking. The figures are *considered* in themselves, we might say, but they do not *exist* in themselves.

Aristotle notably believed that geometrical entities, such as lines and surfaces, exist in natural bodies, but are "separable" by the mathematician. Geometry, Aristotle explains, "investigates natural lines but not *qua* natural."[24] In other words, in geometry, lines are not considered as (*qua*) features of natural bodies, they are considered in themselves, as if they were self-subsistent entities.[25] In this sense, the view of the relation between figures and bodies that I am attributing to Descartes is Aristotelian. In both cases, geometrical entities exist *in* bodies, but can be abstracted in

---

[21] CSMK: 119.
[22] CSM 1:61.
[23] CSM 1:212, first italics mine.
[24] Aristotle 1984, vol. 1, 331.
[25] Exactly how to understand mathematical objects and their relation to the sensible things from which they are abstracted in Aristotle are open questions. One issue is whether sensible things can instantiate the exact mathematical objects studied by mathematicians. If not, then an account of abstraction needs to be provided to explain the discrepancy. For such an account, which highlights the role of intelligible (as opposed to sensible) matter in mathematical thinking, see Mueller 1970. For a contrasting account, according to which mathematically exact properties *are* instantiated in sensible things (and can thus be abstracted, as it were, more directly from the latter), see Lear 1982.

thought by selectively attending to one aspect of bodies, such as their surface, while ignoring others.[26]

Like Aristotle, Descartes warns against the Platonist inclination to reify the abstracted geometrical (or arithmetic) entities. Like Spinoza, Descartes regards the latter as nothing more than modes of thinking, as we have seen. This brief, Aristotelian sketch of Descartes' views of the ontological status of figures is meant to provide a framework for understanding how figures can be conceived both as nothing more than beings of reason (or modes of thinking) *and* as real properties of bodies. The solution is to distinguish between a notion of figure abstracted from body—what I called above figure per se—on the one hand, and a notion of figure *in body*, on the other. I have tried to show that this solution is exemplified in Descartes' handling of the matter as a basis for proposing something similar for how we understand Spinoza.

I should say that my sketch of Descartes' views is not meant to provide an interpretation of Descartes' ultimate position on the matter. Although I think it is a good approximation, to make this case I would have to address the Platonist tendencies of passages I have not considered, especially from Meditation Five.[27] I pass over these complications, since my aim is to illuminate Spinoza's views, not Descartes'.

Using Descartes to illuminate Spinoza presents problems, however, since even when Spinoza imports Cartesian concepts, he often transforms them in quite radical ways. In the present context, it is noteworthy that Spinoza is quite critical of Descartes' notion of extension. Since Descartes' understanding of extension in spatial terms is an important aspect of my case for realism about figures, Spinoza's criticisms of extension cannot be ignored. I will address these criticisms in Chap. 5, after having discussed Spinozan science. As I will show there, I do not think the criticisms touch the basic notion that extension implies spatial dimensions. For the time being, let us take this for granted.

A further difference is the fact that, for Descartes, finite bodies are substances, which is obviously inconsistent with Spinoza's monism. Bodies are modes (of substance), in Spinoza, not substances. But unless this is

---

[26] I am indebted here to Nolan's discussion of Cartesian abstraction in terms of selective attention (1998, 167, 174).

[27] Nolan (1997) provides an anti-Platonist, conceptualist reading of Meditation Five's immutable essences with which I am generally sympathetic. For a Platonist reading, see Kenny 1970. Schmaltz (1991) outlines a "middle way between Platonic realism and conceptualism" (170) according to which immutable essences exist in God.

taken to mean that finite bodies do not really exist (the acosmist thesis), then the difference here does not affect the question of the *reality* of figure. Although finite bodies are modes, they are nevertheless individuals with their own natures and properties, including figural properties. This, at least, is my claim. To support this claim, it is necessary to turn to Spinoza's theory of individual bodies. I will argue that while Spinoza defines physical individuals in terms of motion and rest, not figure, figural properties are implicated nevertheless, as other texts bear out. I will also provide an explanation for why Spinoza avoids defining physical individuals in terms of figure.

3.3.2 *Spinoza's Theory of Corporeal Individuals and Figure*

In the concise digression on bodies following E2p13 (which I will henceforth call, following David Lachterman, the "Physical Digression"), Spinoza defines an individual body as follows:

> When a number of bodies, whether of the same or of different size, are so constrained by other bodies that they lie upon one another, or if they so move, whether with the same degree or different degrees of speed, that they communicate their motions to each other in a certain fixed manner, we shall say that those bodies are so united with one another and that they all together compose one body or individual, which is distinguished from the others by this union of bodies. (E2p13d/G 2: 99–100)

The key to individuation is the "certain fixed manner" in which the constituent parts of an individual communicate their motions to one another, thus establishing a "union of bodies." Elsewhere Spinoza speaks of this more concisely as a fixed "ratio of motion and rest" (E2p13lem5/G 2:101). The union can be maintained even if the parts of the individual are replaced with others (of the same nature) (E2p13lem4) and even if the parts composing the individual "become greater or less" (E2p13lem5), so long as the same ratio of motion and rest is preserved. These parameters accommodate the growth and change of an individual over time.

Spinoza's conception and definition of the individuality of bodies gives rise to significant interpretive perplexity.[28] In the first place, it is not clear

---

[28] For discussion of Spinoza's physical theory and the interpretive questions to which it gives rise, see Manning 2016 and Jaquet 2005.

what to make of the fixed ratio of motion and rest that determines the individuality of bodies, for Spinoza.[29] Inasmuch, moreover, as Spinoza uses the notion of bodies in defining an individual body, the definition leaves questions concerning the principles of bodily individuation on the table.[30] Despite these difficulties, a detailed analysis of which is beyond the scope of this study, we can still use Spinoza's theory of individuation to say something about the determinations that define bodies and distinguish one from another. As we have seen, the determinations that allow us to distinguish the simplest bodies and define composite bodies are determinations of motion and rest. It must be admitted that in his discussion of bodies and their individuation in the Physical Digression, Spinoza seems studiously to avoid any talk of shape or figure and to stick as much as possible to motion and rest. Despite such apparent efforts, however, there is abundant textual evidence in the Physical Digression and elsewhere that Spinoza regards figure among the determinations that characterize individual finite bodies.

Even in the Physical Digression itself, Spinoza has recourse at several points to the notion of surface, which implies figure. In his discussion of

[29] An analogy from chemistry may be of some use. Chemical compounds, such as sodium chloride, are analogous to individuals, because in sodium chloride, the constituents, sodium and chlorine, bind together in a fixed, determinate relation. Mixtures, such as saltwater, by contrast, provide an analogue for what fails to constitute an individual because while salt and water may be physically intermingled, they do not form any chemical bond and, as a result, are much easier to separate than the constituents of a compound. While this distinction between chemical compound and mere mixture may illustrate the sort of thing that Spinoza may have been trying to define (despite its anachronism), it does little to clarify the terms of the definition itself. In particular, scholars have debated whether the *ratio* of motion and rest should be understood in numerical terms or not. For a numerical reading, see Lachterman 1978, 85–6. For a criticism of the numerical reading, see Lin 2005, 248–54. I do not take a position on this matter here. A numerical reading would, of course, have to be squared with what I said about numbers as beings of reason above.

[30] If Spinoza's definition of an individual in E2p13d is a definition of a *composite* body (as it seems to be), then what individuates the bodies that make up the composite body? One place to look is Spinoza's definition of body ("*corpus*") in E2d1 as "a mode that in a certain and determinate way expresses God's essence insofar as he is an extended thing" (G 2:84), but this is very general and raises precisely the questions about what makes something a "determinate" expression of God's essence *qua* extended that one might have hoped Spinoza's Physical Digression would clarify. Another place to look is immediately prior to the definition of individual bodies in the Physical Digression, where Spinoza describes the "simplest bodies" as "distinguished from one another only by motion and rest, speed and slowness" (E2p13a2″/G 2:99). It is far from clear, however, how motion and rest, speed and slowness, could distinguish bodies unless they were already individuated.

the simplest bodies, for instance, he presents a law of reflection according to which when a body strikes another body that does not give way, the first body will be reflected off of the unmoved body, "and the angle of the line of the reflected motion with the surface [*plano*] of the body at rest which it struck against will be equal to the angle which the line of the incident motion makes with the same surface [*plano*]" (E2p13a2″/G 2:99). Discussing composite bodies, Spinoza attributes the hardness and softness of bodies to the size of the surface over which their parts lie: "the bodies whose parts lie upon one another over a large surface [*superficies*], I shall call *hard*; those whose parts lie upon one another over a small surface, I shall call *soft*" (E2p13a3″/G 2:100).

Spinoza's engagement with Boyle's experimental case for corpuscularism in Letter 6 provides a valuable complement to the Physical Digression in the *Ethics*. In addition to shedding light on Spinoza's attitude toward the use (and abuse) of experimental evidence—a topic I will take up in the next chapter—Letter 6 also illuminates Spinoza's thinking regarding the true, as opposed to merely apparent, properties of bodies. Articulating something similar (in outline if not detail) to Locke's later, more famous distinction between the primary and secondary qualities of bodies, Spinoza writes,

> I would think that notions derived from ordinary usage, or which explain Nature, not as it is in itself, but as it is related to human sense perception, ought neither to be counted among the chief kinds, nor to be mixed (not to say confused) with pure notions, which explain Nature as it is in itself. Of the latter kind are motion, rest, and their laws; of the former are visible, invisible, hot, cold, and as I will say at once, also fluid and solid, etc. (G 4:28)

The "notions" that Spinoza is talking about in this passage are notions regarding the properties of physical, or material, nature. As in the *Ethics*' Physical Digression, Spinoza avoids mention of figure, but conceives the true nature of physical things in terms of motion and rest (adding "and their laws"). On the other hand, Spinoza had a perfect opportunity to list figure among the notions that explain nature only as it is related to human sense perception, and not as it is in itself, had he wanted to make it clear that figure belongs no more in a proper ontology of physical things than heat. So Spinoza's statement in Letter 6 about the true properties of physical things is no more helpful in deciding the question whether figure counts as a true property than Spinoza's definition of physical individuality in the *Ethics*. However, just as other remarks from the Physical Digression speak in favor of figure as a true property, so also do other remarks in Letter 6. Perhaps most decisive is Spinoza's response to Boyle's attempt "to show," as Spinoza puts it, "that all the tangible qualities depend only on motion, shape, and the remaining mechanical affections" (G 4:25). Far from taking issue with Boyle's claim, Spinoza objects instead to the fact that Boyle attempts to prove the claim experimentally, "since," Spinoza explains, "it has already been more than adequately demonstrated by Bacon and later by Descartes" (G 4:25).

The *Ethics*' Physical Digression and Letter 6 represent Spinoza's most extended discussions of the nature and properties of physical bodies. While Spinoza provides clear and consistent statements of the basic properties of bodies in terms of motion and rest, omitting mention of figure, surrounding textual evidence suggests that figure is, in fact, a genuine property of bodies. But even if the overall impression imparted by these, and other,[31] texts favors a place for figure in the ontology of bodies, the result would be more satisfying if we had an explanation for why Spinoza omits figure in his statements on the basic properties of bodies, when, as I am claiming, figures are among the genuine properties of bodies. Fortunately, there is an explanation.

At the culmination of the Physical Digression, Spinoza explains how his theory of physical individuality can be extended to accommodate ever-higher orders of physical individuality. That is, at the lowest order, an individual "is composed only of bodies which are distinguished from one another only by motion and rest, speed and slowness, i.e., which is composed of the simplest bodies" (G 2:101). But this individual, Spinoza goes on to explain, can join with other individuals to form a higher-order individual. So long as the individuals maintain some stable set of relations of motion and rest vis-à-vis one another, they satisfy Spinoza's definition of physical individuality. Spinoza continues:

---

[31] In Letters 39 and 40, Spinoza argues for the superiority of circular (or spherical) lenses. (I discuss these letters in Chap. 5.) In Letter 32, Spinoza speaks of "size and shape" (*magnitudinis, et figurae*) (G 4:171a), along with motion and rest, in explaining the nature and composition of bodies. Finally, in E1p15s, Spinoza provides a kind of unofficial definition of body as follows: "by body we understand any quantity, with length, breadth, and depth, limited by some certain figure" (G 2:57). I call this a kind of unofficial definition because, as we saw above, Spinoza defines body officially in E2d1 as "a mode that in a certain and determinate way expresses God's essence insofar as he is considered as an extended thing" (G 2:84).

> But if we should further conceive a third kind of Individual, composed of many individuals of this second kind, we shall find that it can be affected in many other ways, without any change of its form. And if we proceed to infinity, we shall easily conceive that the whole of nature is one Individual, whose parts, i.e., all bodies, vary in infinite ways, without any change of the whole Individual. (G 2:102)

So, Spinoza thinks a physical individual can be infinite, constituting the whole of physical nature.[32] There are two things to note about this infinite physical individual that help to make sense of the fact that Spinoza defines physical individuality in terms of motion and rest, while omitting figure as part of the definition. First, an infinite physical individual is characterized by relations of motion and rest. Second, an infinite thing cannot have a figure. Let me demonstrate these points in turn.

The fact that an infinite physical individual is characterized by relations of motion and rest, and thus, relations of motion and rest are viable properties of an infinite individual (and not just a finite one) is perhaps already evident from what we have seen from the Physical Digression thus far. But further confirmation is provided by the examples that Spinoza gives in Letter 64 of the infinite modes of which he speaks in *Ethics* Part 1. Spinoza distinguishes between two kinds of infinite modes in *Ethics* Part 1: a kind that follows immediately from one of God's attributes and a kind that follows via the mediation of the first infinite mode, and thus only indirectly from the attribute (E1p21–2; G 2:65–6). Per common scholarly practice, I will refer to the former as the *immediate* infinite mode and the latter as the *mediate* infinite mode. In the case of the attribute of extension, Spinoza explains that the immediate infinite mode is motion and rest, whereas the mediate infinite mode is "the face of the whole Universe, which, however much it may vary in infinite ways, nevertheless always remains the same" (Ep. 64/G 4:278). At this point Spinoza references the scholium to Lemma 7 from which I just quoted, suggesting that the infinite individual spoken of there is "the face of the whole Universe," or the mediate infinite mode spoken of in Letter 64. Since this infinite mode or infinite individual follows from motion and rest, motion and rest are clearly fundamental to its nature and constitution.

---

[32] There is a debate about the extension of Spinoza's notion of individuality, centering, in particular, around the question of whether a political state can be an individual. But even skeptics of the state qua individual, such as Steven Barbone, accept the whole of physical nature as an infinite individual. On this, see Barbone 2002.

Turning now to the second point, Spinoza says in Letter 50 (discussed above), "it's manifest that matter as a whole, considered without limitation, can have no shape, and that shape pertains only to finite and determinate bodies" (Ep. 50/G 4:240b).[33] Putting these two points together, then, an infinite physical individual *can* be characterized by motion and rest (and, indeed, must be), but *cannot* be characterized by figure. Since Spinoza thinks there is an infinite physical individual—that, in particular, of which all finite individuals form part—then it makes sense that he would want his definition of physical individuality to cover the infinite physical individual as well as finite physical individuals. To accommodate the infinite physical individual, however, Spinoza needed to omit any mention of figure, since "matter as a whole…can have no shape." This explanation of Spinoza's definition of physical individuality in terms of motion and rest makes sense of both the omission of figure from the definition and why surrounding textual evidence speaks in favor of figure as a genuine property of physical individuals. Whereas the definition seeks to accommodate both finite and infinite physical individuals, and thus cannot be couched in terms of figure, the focus of the discussions in both the Physical Digression and in Letter 6 is generally on finite physical individuals, which *are* characterized by figure, and the discussions reflect as much accordingly.

After having discussed Spinozan science, I will address a further objection to my realist interpretation of figure, and advance an additional argument in support of my interpretation. In what remains of this chapter, however, I want to address some more specific questions concerning the ontology of figural properties (and then say something about numbers).

3.3.3   *What Are Figures in Spinoza?*

I hope to have established by this point that there is good reason to think that figures feature in Spinoza's ontology of extended nature, despite the fact that ideas of figures per se (or figures *considered* per se) count as beings of reason (lacking extra-mental existence). I have suggested that figures exist as determinations, or properties, of finite bodies. One might wish to

---

[33] As John Grey pointed out to me, we might also derive this point from E1d2: "That thing is said to be finite in its own kind that can be limited by another of the same nature" (G 2:45). If we interpret this to mean that something can be limited by another of the same nature, if *and only if* it is finite, then it follows that if something is not finite, then it is not limited by something of the same nature. Thus, it cannot have any shape.

know more about what these properties are, and the manner in which they exist in bodies. When we predicate sphericity, say, of multiple individuals, what is going on? Are figures universal properties multiply instantiated across particular instances, or are figural properties themselves particular?[34]

Spinoza's statements about universals are ambivalent. Given the discussion in the first section of this chapter, it will come as little surprise that he is often critical of the notion of universals. In the CM, Spinoza says that God knows only singular things, not universals (except insofar as he knows human minds), reinforcing the idea of universals as a figment of the human imagination (CM 2.7/G 1:263). Elsewhere, he criticizes the notion of mental faculties, such as intellect and will, by comparing them to "stoneness," and dismissing them as "either complete fictions or nothing but Metaphysical beings, or universals" (E2p48s/G 2:129).

On the other hand, perhaps more surprisingly, Spinoza also seems to have his own positive conception of universals. He considers the second kind of knowledge, reason, as a means of forming "universal notions" (E2p40s2/G 2:122), and since reason is an adequate form of knowledge, this implies the possibility of adequate universal notions. Indeed, Spinoza seems to regard the common notions, which provide the foundations of reason, as themselves universals of sorts, suggesting that reason begins and ends in adequate knowledge of universal notions. It seems that Spinoza is critical about universals when they are products of the imagination, but not when they are products of reason.[35] I do not wish to develop this line of thought further here, however. Greater clarity about Spinoza's

---

[34] In contemporary terminology, the question is whether Spinoza is a moderate nominalist or a realist. Extreme nominalism (the third major category) was ruled out earlier in the chapter. For an overview of the contemporary debates concerning universals, see Moreland 2001.

[35] Cf. Newlands 2017. Newlands highlights the ambivalence in Spinoza's treatment of universals, as I have done, but interprets it as an inconsistency. By contrast, I have suggested that the ambivalence can be resolved if we distinguish between universals formed through the imagination, on the one hand, and universals (or quasi-universals) formed through reason, on the other. Spinoza rejects the former but embraces the latter. Newlands (2017, 84–5) acknowledges this interpretive move, but questions whether Spinoza is entitled to the distinction. I think Spinoza does have a fairly compelling argument for distinguishing his common notions (at least) from imaginative universals. I do not interpret common notions to be abstractions as Newlands does. I discuss the origins and adequacy of common notions in the next chapter. For a more sympathetic handling of Spinoza's ambivalence about universals (i.e., which does not see it rooted in inconsistency), see Hübner 2015, 66–8. I discuss Hübner's interpretation in Chap. 6.

conception of reason and the sort of universals that he might embrace therein will have to wait until our discussion of Spinozan science in the next chapter.

No less ambivalent are Spinoza's remarks on another matter germane to the interpretation of figural properties, namely, natures, such as human or equine nature. This is a topic I will take up in more detail in subsequent chapters, but it is worth making some general points here. At times Spinoza speaks as if human nature (for instance) is something that can be shared by multiple individuals (for instance, in E1p17s2). At other times, he speaks of essences as individuating (in particular, in E2d2). ("Nature" and "essence" can be treated interchangeably for present purposes.) If Spinoza were unequivocal on the matter of whether essences can be shared or not, this might give us a basis for surmising his position on the analogous question of whether figural properties can be shared or not. But he is not unequivocal on the question of shared essences. Just as it is prima facie unclear, then, whether, for Spinoza, Plato and Socrates should be regarded as sharing the same human nature or exemplifying numerically different, albeit resembling, natures, that is, human nature$_1$ and human nature$_2$, so it is prima facie unclear whether two soap bubbles share the same property of sphericity or exemplify numerically different, but resembling, properties, that is, sphericity$_1$ and sphericity$_2$.[36]

The principle of the identity of indiscernibles is potentially relevant here. Melamed invokes this principle in discussing the question of the reality of geometrical figures.[37] It holds that two things must be distinguished from each other by a difference in their respective properties. Two things, in other words, cannot have all of the same properties. Spinoza voices something along these lines in E1p4: "Two or more distinct things are distinguished from one another, either by a difference in the attributes of the substances or by a difference in their affections." Melamed argues that this rules out the possibility that geometrical figures are real, since the parts of geometrical figures are indistinguishable. His example is that

---

[36] See Carriero 1995 for a useful discussion of this issue in relation to the Aristotelian notions of substance and accident. What I am speaking of as numerically different, but resembling, properties, Carriero (1995, 256–59) speaks of as particular or individual accidents. Like Carriero (and *contra* Bennett, whose position on the matter, along with Curley's, Carriero criticizes) I see nothing about the notion of property itself that would determine one way or the other whether properties are particular or universal (or both). Cf. Bennett 1984, 94.

[37] Melamed 2000, 15–16.

nothing distinguishes the vertices of a cube.[38] This is certainly the case if we are talking about cubes per se. I agree that figures per se are beings of reason sans extra-mental existence. It is much less clear to me, however, that indiscernibility is a problem if the cube exists not per se, but as the property of a finite body. In that case, there are two potential bases for discernibility. Either the vertices in the cubic body are distinguished from each other by other features of the body (such as the motions of the parts composing the respective vertices) or the vertices are slightly different from one another, but approximate a cube nevertheless. Even if the latter possibility means that no body could be precisely cubic, it does not mean that bodies cannot be more or less cubic.

This raises an important epistemological point. It may well be the case that no real thing is so simple as to be (perfectly) cubic. The shapes of real bodies may be far too complex. This complexity puts limits on our knowledge of the shapes of bodies, but not on the existence of the latter. Even Descartes, the arch geometrical realist, admits that perfectly simple geometrical entities like triangles may not exist in nature, writing to Gassendi:

> Geometrical figures are composed for the most part of straight lines; yet no part of a line that was really straight could ever affect our senses, since when we examine through a magnifying glass those lines which appear most straight we find they are quite irregular and always form wavy curves.[39]

This admission does not compromise Descartes' commitment to the relevance of geometry to physics, however.[40] Nor should it. Even if no perfect triangles exist in nature, still, bodies are more or less triangular. Some bodies will exhibit properties very similar to the perfect geometrical triangle. In this case, our geometrical knowledge of triangles will enable us to understand something about the properties of the imperfect triangular body (such as why it serves poorly as a wagon wheel).

---

[38] Melamed 2000, 16.
[39] CSM 2:262/AT VII:382.
[40] Palmerino finesses a similar distinction between the ontology of mathematical entities and epistemological constraints on our knowledge of them with respect to Galileo. Referencing a passage from the *Assayer* in which Galileo acknowledges the indefinability of infinitely complex irregular lines, Palmerino writes, "In Galileo's eyes the problem is hence not that irregular lines (and physical accidents) are not mathematical, but rather that their mathematical structure is beyond the reach of our intellectual skills" (2016, 39).

To this end, it is important that our abstract geometrical conceptions of triangles are true in form and genetically conceived. Even feigning a cause at will through which to think the figure, we are able to adequately deduce its properties. This enables us to make predictions about what to expect for triangular things (or entities of other shapes). In this way, our geometrical conceptions can function as heuristics. Even if they do not correspond precisely to natural bodies, the latter must approximate more or less closely to our conceptions. I will develop this line of thought in more detail in the next two chapters.

I have not provided any definitive answers to the questions concerning the precise nature of figures qua properties raised in this subsection. I am not certain whether the figural properties of finite bodies should be considered as multiply exemplifiable universals or as non-multiply exemplifiable particulars. Considerations of the infinite complexity of finite things and the principle of the identity of indiscernibles may well point us in the latter direction.[41] This subtle metaphysical point comes out in the epistemological wash, however, since regardless what the truth of the matter is about the metaphysics of figural properties, the following crucial points hold: (1) bodies have figural properties; (2) our finite minds, incapable of handling infinitely complex objects, must have recourse to geometrical abstractions in studying finite bodies; and (3) these abstractions, even if not precisely corresponding to the actual properties of finite bodies, necessarily approximate them to a greater or lesser extent, thereby grounding their usefulness in the science of bodies. When I discuss Spinoza's science of bodies in the next two chapters, these points will receive further confirmation and elaboration.

3.4 True Ideas of Number?

Before bringing this chapter to a close, I want to return briefly to the status of numbers and raise a question prompted by what we have seen to be the case with figures. That is, figures are beings of reason, and yet, it is

---

[41] For an additional consideration in favor of interpreting modes as non-multiply exemplifiable particulars, see Melamed 2013, 58. Melamed presents the counterfactual possibility that there are two substances, A and B, sharing mode *m*. He argues that, if we assume a change in *m*, the change must come from either A or B. But if A, say, caused the change in *m*, then A would have caused a change in B (since *m* is also a mode of B). But this would violate Spinoza's prohibition against causal interaction between substances. From this, Melamed concludes that modes are unrepeatable properties.

possible to have true ideas of figures—even if only true *in form*. Can the same be said for numbers? Can we have true-in-form ideas of numbers? Would such ideas exemplify the nature of truth to the same extent as true ideas of figures?

What more obvious exemplification of a truth than 2 + 3 = 5? one leaps to point out. The objection might be raised, however, that the distinguishing mark of the exemplary ideas of figures in the TIE was that they were genetically conceived, or conceived through causes. Can the same be said for arithmetical truths? Perhaps, in adding 2 + 3, one *generates* 5. Perhaps similar points could be made with respect to other arithmetic functions besides addition.[42] This is speculative, since Spinoza provides no analysis of arithmetic truths per se.

Spinoza does, on occasion, use arithmetic formulations for illustrative purposes, however. The most notable example is the fourth proportional problem, which he uses to illustrate differences between the kinds of knowledge. Since the example ostensibly works to illustrate aspects of adequate, as well as inadequate, kinds of knowledge, the fourth proportional problem is something that it should be possible to apprehend adequately, implying that purely arithmetic truths can serve to exemplify truth, though only the *form* of truth, for the same reasons that apply to geometrical truths.[43]

But even if arithmetical examples are able to exhibit the form of truth as well as geometrical ones, this does not mean that the two are

---

[42] In discussing Spinoza's fourth proportional example, Matheron claims that proportions and ratios can be genetically conceived. It is unclear whether he thinks this applies to arithmetic operations in general. See Matheron 1986, 127–28.

[43] In the TIE, Spinoza says, somewhat surprisingly, that through the fourth mode of knowing, "we know that two and three are five, and that if two lines are parallel to a third line, they are also parallel to each other, etc." (TIE 22/G 2:11). This is surprising since the TIE's fourth mode of knowing is the most perfect form of knowledge, but the simple mathematical truths cited in this comment are beings of reason, and beings of reason do not supply the content of the most perfect form of knowledge, as Spinoza indicates on numerous occasions (TIE 75/G 2:28–9; TIE 95/G 2:35; TIE 99/G 2:36). Furthermore, the fourth mode of knowing "comprehends the adequate essence of the thing" (TIE 29/G 2:13), but a number of passages suggest that number can have nothing to do with the essence of anything (E1p8s2/G 2:50–1; Ep. 50/G 4:239b). As a result, I think the mathematical examples cited here should be dealt with in the same way as the fourth proportional example. They may represent the form of true ideas (grasped through the fourth mode of knowing, in this case), but do not provide the proper content of true ideas (or the proper content of intuitive knowledge, *pace* Sandler 2005, 84). It must be admitted that the comment is bedeviling, nevertheless.

interchangeable, have the same capacities, or serve the same functions. I argued that despite the fact that figures per se are beings of reason, figural properties nevertheless have a place in Spinoza's ontology among the determinations that define finite bodies. I am much less confident that anything analogous can be said for numbers. Numbers do not appear to be among the determinations that define finite bodies. While bodies are spherical, cuboid, and pyramidal, they are not defined by numerical properties. This does not mean that they are not defined by ratios. (We know, after all, that Spinoza defines bodies in terms of a ratio of motion and rest.) For instance, there is some ratio between circumference and diameter that defines a circle, but the number, π, by which we define the proportion, is a being of reason and does not itself exist in the circle itself (for reasons given above).

So, there is an asymmetry between figure and number, and thus between geometry and arithmetic. According to Descartes, both geometry and arithmetic can be used to train the mind to recognize truth. (These are the sciences that Descartes picks out in the *Rules for the Direction of the Mind* as being the only ones capable of training the mind properly in the recognition of certainty.[44]) However, when Descartes says that his entire physics is nothing but geometry, there is good reason why he does not include arithmetic. Galileo, too, thought the characters of nature's language were geometrical figures, not numbers. In my reading of Spinoza, the same asymmetry applies to him as well.

References

Aristotle. 1984. The Complete Works of Aristotle. 2 vols., edited by Jonathan Barnes. Princeton, NJ: Princeton University Press.

Barbone, Steven. 2002. "What Counts as an Individual for Spinoza?" In Spinoza: Metaphysical Themes, edited by Olli Koistinen and John Biro, 89–112. New York: Oxford University Press.

Bennett, Jonathan. 1984. *A Study of Spinoza's* Ethics. Indianapolis, IN: Hackett.

Carriero, John Peter. 1995. "On the Relationship between Mode and Substance in Spinoza's Metaphysics." *Journal of the History of Philosophy* 33(2): 245–73.

Della Rocca, Michael. 1996. *Representation and the Mind-Body Problem in Spinoza.* New York, NY: Oxford University Press.

Frege, Gottlob. 1980. The Foundations of Arithmetic. Translated by J. L. Austin. Evanston, IL: Northwestern University Press.

---

[44] CSM 1:10–13.

Gueroult, Martial. 1968. *Spinoza I: Dieu (Éthique, I)*. Paris: Aubier-Montaigne.

Hegel, Georg Wilhelm Friedrich. 1995. Lectures on the History of Philosophy, Vol. 3. Translated by E.S. Haldane and Frances H. Simson. Lincoln, NE: University of Nebraska Press.

Hobbes, Thomas. 2005. *The English Works of Thomas Hobbes of Malmesbury*. Vol. 1. Translated by William Molesworth. London: John Bonn, 1839. Replica edition, Elbiron Classics.

Homan, Matthew. 2014. "Spinoza and the Problem of Mental Representation." *International Philosophical Quarterly* 54: 75–87.

Hübner, Karolina. 2015. "Spinoza on Negation, Mind-Dependence, and the Reality of the Finite." In *The Young Spinoza: A Metaphysician in the Making*, edited by Yitzhak Y. Melamed, 221–237. Oxford, UK: Oxford University Press.

Jaquet, Chantal. 2005. "Le problème de la différence entre les corps" in *Les expressions de la puissance d'agir chez Spinoza*. doi :https://doi.org/10.4000/books.psorbonne.151. Publications de la Sorbonne.

Kenny, Anthony. 1970. "The Cartesian Circle and the Eternal Truths." *Journal of Philosophy* 67: 685–700.

Lachterman, David R. 1978. "The Physics of Spinoza's Ethics." In Spinoza: New Perspectives, edited by Robert W. Shahan and J. I. Biro, 71–112. Norman: University of Oklahoma Press.

Lear, Jonathan. 1982. "Aristotle's Philosophy of Mathematics." *The Philosophical Review* 91(2): 161–192.

Lin, Martin. 2005. "Memory and Personal Identity in Spinoza." *Canadian Journal of Philosophy*. 35(2): 243–268.

———. 2019. *Being and Reason: An Essay on Spinoza's Metaphysics*. New York, NY: Oxford University Press.

Manning, Richard. 2016. "Spinoza's Physical Theory," *The Stanford Encyclopedia of Philosophy*. Edward N. Zalta (ed.), URL = https://plato.stanford.edu/archives/win2016/entries/spinoza-physics/.

Marshall, Eugene. 2008. "Adequacy and Innateness in Spinoza." *Oxford Studies in Early Modern Philosophy* 4: 51–88.

Matheron, Alexandre. 1986. "Spinoza and Euclidean Arithmetic: The Example of the Fourth Proportional." In Spinoza and the Sciences, edited by Marjorie Grene and Debra Nails, 125–150. Boston: D. Reidel.

Melamed, Yitzhak Y. 2000. "On the Exact Science of Nonbeings: Spinoza's View of Mathematics." *Iyyun, The Jerusalem Philosophical Quarterly* 49: 3–22.

———. 2010. "Acosmism or Weak Individuals?: Hegel, Spinoza, and the Reality of the Finite." *Journal of the History of Philosophy* 48: 77–92.

———. 2013. *Spinoza's Metaphysics: Substance and Thought*. Oxford, UK: Oxford University Press.

Moreland, J. P. 2001. *Universals*. Montreal, CA: McGill-Queen's University Press.

Morrison, John. 2015. "Restricting Spinoza's Causal Axiom." *Philosophical Quarterly* 65(258): 40–63.
Mueller, Ian. 1970. "Aristotle on Geometrical Objects." *Archiv für Geschichte der Philosophie* 52(2): 156–171.
Newlands, Samuel. 2017. "Spinoza on Universals." In *The Problem of Universals in Early Modern Philosophy*, edited by Stefano Di Bella and Tad M. Schmaltz. DOI: https://doi.org/10.1093/acprof:oso/9780190608040.001.0001.
Nolan, Lawrence. 1997. "The Ontological Status of Cartesian Natures." *Pacific Philosophical Quarterly* 78: 169–194.
———. 1998. "Descartes' Theory of Universals." *Philosophical Studies* 89: 161–180.
Palmerino, Carla Rita. 2016. "Reading the Book of Nature: The Ontological and Epistemological Underpinnings of Galileo's Mathematical Realism." In The Language of Nature: Reassessing the Mathematization of Natural Philosophy in the Seventeenth Century, edited by Geoffrey Gorham et al., 29–50. Minneapolis, MN: University of Minnesota Press.
Peterman, Alison. 2015. "Spinoza on Extension." *Philosopher's Imprint* 15: 1–23.
Sandler, Ronald. 2005. "*Intuitus* and *Ratio* in Spinoza's Ethical Thought." *British Journal for the History of Philosophy* 13(1): 73–90.
Schliesser, Eric. 2014. "Spinoza and the Philosophy of Science: Mathematics, Motion, and Being." In *The Oxford Handbook of Spinoza*, edited by Michael Della Rocca. DOI: https://doi.org/10.1093/oxfordhb/9780195335828.013.020.
Schmaltz, Tad M. 1991. "Platonism and Descartes' View of Immutable Essences." *Archiv für Geschichte der Philosophie* 73: 129–170.
Suárez, Francisco. 1995. *On Beings of Reason: Metaphysical Disputation LIV*. Translated by John P. Doyle. Milwaukee, WI: Marquette University Press.
Wilson, Margaret D. 1991. "Spinoza's Causal Axiom (Ethics I, Axiom 4)." In God and Nature: Spinoza's Metaphysics, edited by Yirmiyahu Yovel, 133–60. Leiden: E.J. Brill.

CHAPTER 4

Reason and Imagination in Spinozan Science

Geometrical figures exist in Spinozan nature as the properties of finite bodies. So, I argued, in the last chapter, if this is right, we should expect geometry, as the science of figure, to contribute to the knowledge of finite bodies. To follow up this prediction, we turn to the question of the sort of adequate knowledge of finite bodies available to us. Although the third kind of knowledge promises adequate, *intuitive* knowledge of finite bodies, I reserve discussion of it for a separate chapter, given the special interpretive complexities to which it gives rise. My focus here will be the relatively more pedestrian, tentative, methodical engagement with natural bodies that we have come to associate with scientific inquiry and the role of imagination and reason (the first and second kinds of knowledge) therein.

Our broadly contemporary notion of science was in its germinal stages yet when Spinoza was writing, and he does not have a term that is equivalent to "science" as we understand it today.[1] Nevertheless, Spinoza speaks of the method of interpreting nature and examining the natural world,

[1] In the TTP, Spinoza uses the term *scientia* to connote natural (as opposed to supernatural) knowledge, meaning the kind of knowledge of things that can be attained through employment of the mind's natural faculties. While this usage often encompasses what we would today understand by scientific knowledge, it clearly has a much wider scope. (See Curley 2:638 for references.) It is also noteworthy that in the part of the TTP where Spinoza discusses scientific methodology, and comes closest to modern notions of science, he does not employ "*scientia*," but instead most often speaks of the interpretation of nature (*inter-*

© The Author(s), under exclusive license to Springer Nature Switzerland AG 2021
M. Homan, *Spinoza's Epistemology through a Geometrical Lens*,
https://doi.org/10.1007/978-3-030-76739-6_4

and in doing so clearly has in mind a scientific approach to acquiring knowledge of nature. Thus, it is not anachronistic to speak of Spinoza's philosophy of science or his scientific method. If it turns out that geometry has a role to play in Spinoza's scientific method, this will serve to confirm that geometrical figures feature in Spinozan nature. At the same time, considering geometry's role in Spinoza's scientific method can help to clarify the workings of the latter. I take up the question of geometry in Spinozan science in the next chapter. It is first necessary to elucidate how Spinoza's scientific method is supposed to work in general. This is the task of the present chapter.

To piece together an interpretation of Spinozan science we need to juxtapose Spinoza's comments on method from the *Theological-Political Treatise* and his comments on reason from the *Ethics*. While both texts are quite schematic on their own, they provide mutual illumination when considered together (and other texts will be enlisted for supplement). The connecting thread is the common notions, which provide the basis of reason and play a pivotal, foundational role in the scientific method. A primary focus of the first part of this chapter, then, will be to get clear on the nature of the common notions, their adequacy, and their connection to laws of nature (whose relevance to an understanding of Spinozan science is evident). Despite the overlap, however, it is impossible to equate reason and Spinozan science. In the first place, there is the question of intuitive knowledge (which, as already noted, I will address later). What is more important for present purposes, however, is the imagination. Indeed, it would be fair to say that Spinozan science just is the orderly, methodical interplay of the first and second kinds of knowledge (and, perhaps, the third as well). But the imagination's integral role raises difficulties for the adequacy of the results of Spinozan science. These difficulties will be the subject of the second half of the chapter.

I will ultimately defend a hypothetico-deductive interpretation of Spinoza's scientific method. My interpretation will be distinctive (and, I believe, compelling) insofar as the notion of an idea true in form that I expounded in the last two chapters is perfectly suited, I will argue, for making sense of the role and epistemic status of hypotheses in Spinozan science.

---

pretatio naturae) (TTP 7.26/G 3:102). For discussion of the connotation of "*scientia*" in Spinoza's day, see Gabbey 1996, 143–48.

4.1 Reason and Spinozan Science

In the TTP, Spinoza says that the method of interpreting Scripture is analogous to that of interpreting nature (TTP 7.6/G 3:98). While his remarks about nature in this context are very schematic, and intended to illustrate the interpretation of Scripture, it is possible to tease out the broad contours of a theory of scientific method nevertheless, by tracing the logic of Spinoza's analogy.[2] In the case of interpreting both Scripture and Nature, it is helpful to see the method as having three parts. I will describe the three parts of the method first using Spinoza's scriptural examples (which are relatively fleshed out), and then show how this translates to the study of nature.

The method begins with data collection and organization, or with the compilation of what Spinoza calls, in Baconian terms, a "history" (*historia*).[3] In the case of scriptural interpretation, this includes information about the language in which the books of Scripture are written; the organization of the various utterances of the various books according to subject matter; and the cataloging of ambiguities, inconsistencies, and obscurities, as well as information about the books' authors, audiences, and reception histories. Once this history has been put together, the next step is the identification of common points of agreement across the data. This means paying attention to the teachings common to all of the scriptural prophets. As examples of such universal teachings, Spinoza cites the existence of one, omnipotent deity, who loves all, is alone to be worshipped, and so on (TTP 7.27/G 3:102). These *universalia* provide the

---

[2] This strategy for interpreting Spinoza's views on scientific method has been recognized by some commentators. See Schliesser 2014, 4–8. Gabbey (1996, 170), Klever (1986, 185–86), and Savan (1986, 98–99) touch on TTP 7 briefly in discussing Spinoza's scientific methodology. I am not aware of anyone who has pursued the strategy in depth.

[3] Spinoza explicitly approves this aspect of Bacon's method in Ep. 37 (G 4:189a). Gabbey (1996, 170–80) provides a discussion of Bacon's influence on Spinoza's methodological thought in the context of surveying Spinoza's scientific method more generally. While acknowledging the importance of a Baconian *historia* for the purpose of gathering data, Gabbey (1996, 176–77) argues that whereas Bacon's inductive method could use the *historia* for deriving the causes of things, this is not the case for Spinoza, since the *historia* is derived from the imagination, whereas the causes of things must be ascertained through the intellect. This is true, but Spinoza's method *integrates* experiential data with intellectual conceptions, as I argue in this chapter. In this respect, what A. I. Sabra (1967, 36–7) says about Descartes could be said equally about Spinoza: in his hands the *historia naturalis* is made to serve an essentially deductive method.

basis for the third part of the method, which consists in the derivation of less universal and particular things therefrom. Examples of such less universal things include "all the particular external actions of true virtue" (TTP 7.29/G 3:103).[4] To illustrate this third part of the method, Spinoza cites Christ's dictum that mourners are blessed. This may well have been cataloged as a point of ambiguity in the initial history, since it is unclear what sorts of things it is appropriate to mourn. Are those who mourn the loss of fortune, for instance, blessed? This sort of ambiguity can be cleared up in light of the universal teachings identified in the second part of the method. The universal of relevance here appears to be the primacy and uniqueness of God as the supreme good for human beings. In this light, Spinoza explains that by mourners, Christ must mean those who mourn the justice human beings have neglected, since this is the only appropriate object of mourning for true subjects of the kingdom of God (TTP 7.30/G 3:103).

By analogy with the foregoing sketch of the method of scriptural interpretation, then, the interpretation of nature (i.e., scientific method) begins with a *historia naturae*, a collection of observations of natural phenomena. Universal features are then identified that all members of the *historia* have in common. Finally, the properties of less universal and particular things are derived from (or reconciled with) the universal features. I have presented the method as having three components for the sake of clarity and convenience. Alternatively, the method might be viewed as having two components—an a posteriori component, reasoning from effects to first causes, and an a priori component, reasoning from first causes to effects. (This would be similar to what Hobbes describes in *De Corpore* with his distinction between analysis and synthesis.[5]) The first, a posteriori component would correspond to the transition between what I above

---

[4] Spinoza speaks of the derivation of "less universal things" at key points in articulating his conception of method without explicitly mentioning particulars. (See TTP 7.27–29/G 3:102–3.) While this phrasing in itself leaves it unclear whether the derivation is supposed to descend all the way to particulars, I take the passage just quoted regarding the "particular external actions of true virtue" to make it clear that Spinoza means for particulars to fall within the umbrella of "less universal things."

[5] Hobbes 2005, 65–6. Descartes, of course, also introduced a well-known distinction between analysis and synthesis (CSM 2: 110–11), and this is explicitly invoked in Meyer's preface to Spinoza's DPP (G 1:129). Nevertheless, like other scholars, I see Spinoza's methodology as closer to Hobbes' understanding of the distinction than to Descartes'. On this, see A. Garrett 2003, 103–122.

called the first and second parts of the method, while, the second, a priori component would correspond to the transition between the second and third parts. Whichever way we consider the structure of the method (I do not think it matters much one way or the other), the fulcrum on which the whole thing turns are the universals or common points of agreement among all the data comprising the history.

In the TTP, Spinoza identifies "the things most universal and common to the whole of nature" as "motion and rest, and their laws and rules, which nature always observes and through which it continuously acts" (TTP 7.27/G 3:102). Although he does not say so explicitly, there can be little doubt that these universal and common features of natural things correspond with the "common notions" of *Ethics* Part 2, and, more specifically, the objects thereof. Upon introducing the latter ("What is common to all things") in E2p37, Spinoza refers the reader to a lemma from the Physical Digression, the demonstration of which specifies that all bodies agree "in that they involve the concept of one and the same attribute (by D1), and in that they can move now more slowly, now more quickly, and absolutely, that now they move, now they are at rest" (E2p13lem2dem/G 2:98). In short, all bodies agree in being extended and having capacities for motion and rest. Ideas of extension, then, and of motion and rest, count as common notions. (While Spinoza mentions only motion and rest in the TTP passage, extension is surely implied, since motion and rest are inconceivable without extension.) Spinoza calls common notions the "foundations of our reasoning" (E2p40s1/G 2:120) and says that our ability to derive knowledge of other things from common notions (and from "adequate ideas of the properties of things" about which I will say something below) constitutes the second kind of knowledge or reason (E2p40s2/G 2:122). Thus, I take reason, the second kind of knowledge, to have a prominent place in Spinoza's conception of how scientific reasoning works. (Imagination, the first kind of knowledge, also has an important role, as we will discuss below.)

4.1.1 *Common Notions as Foundations of Reason and Laws of Nature*

A notable feature of common notions (or their objects) is that they "can only be conceived adequately" (E2p38/G 2:118). This promises to help explain why they are able to function as foundations of reasoning (and of science). Spinoza's demonstration of this claim of inherent adequacy appeals to the fact that God's idea of common features of bodies will be adequate insofar as he constitutes the essence of the human mind, and, as E2p11c teaches, anything that is adequate in God's mind insofar as he constitutes the human mind is adequate in the human mind. The demonstration would be more helpful if it addressed *why* God's idea of common features of bodies is adequate insofar as he constitutes the essence of the human mind, but I think what Spinoza is getting at here is that we do not need any ideas beyond those that we have of the affections of our bodies in order to have adequate ideas of what is equally in the part and in the whole. This is because an idea of the part (such as we get when we perceive the affections of our bodies) is just as good in this case as an idea of the whole (such as God has when he perceives the affections of our bodies *and* their external causes).[6]

To see why this might be the case, consider a rod sticking two feet out of the ground. In observing the visible two feet of the rod, we have only a partial idea of the whole rod, but we have a perfectly adequate idea of the rod's extendedness, a common notion. That is to say, the extendedness of the rod would not be further confirmed or clarified by pulling it out of the ground and determining that it is in fact four feet long. Similarly, when we have an image of an external body, we only perceive the way in which the body affects us, not the way the body exists in itself, as we saw in the last chapter. So, when we perceive the external object, we are actually having an idea of our own bodies qua affected by the external object, and our idea of the object is partial (an idea of effects absent causes) and inadequate. But our idea of the extendedness of the object is perfectly adequate. The affection of our own bodies itself represents extendedness just as well as the part of the rod sticking out of the ground. We would not understand extendedness any better if we were able to observe external objects directly

[6] Cf. Bennett 1984, 183–4. Calling E2p38d "enormously obscure," Bennett offers, by way of explanation, that whereas ideas of the imagination are inadequate because the causal flow from the environment to the human body involves a "bump" (i.e., "a qualitative discontinuity of which the metal counterpart is mutilation"), there is no such "bump" when the causal flow involves only features which the body shares with the environment. I agree that there is no mutilation in the case of common notions, but Bennett's "flow" and "bump" metaphors here are potentially misleading, since I do not see that there is any need for information from the outside to "flow" into the human mind (with or without a bump) for the formation of common notions. The requisite information is already contained in the human mind's idea of its own body. (I take up the related question of the innateness of common notions below.) For interpretations of Spinoza's reasoning in E2p38d that are more congenial with my own, see Wilson 1996, 111–12, and Marshall 2008, 65.

(*per impossibile*), and not just insofar as they affect our own bodies. The same points could be made regarding the motion of external bodies.

Recall Spinoza's claim (from the TIE and discussed in Chap. 2) that the idea of God cannot be abstract because it is not possible for this particular idea to extend more widely than its uniquely infinite object. As a result, it must necessarily be a true idea. There is a similar sort of logic in the case of the adequacy of the common notions, except instead of it being impossible for common notions to extend more widely than their objects, it is the reverse—they cannot, as it were, extend less widely than their objects; they cannot be partial. As a result, they must necessarily be adequate ideas. I think this tends to confirm that Spinoza's strategy for grounding his system via the idea of God in the TIE was not an anomaly. In the cases of both the idea of God in the TIE and the common notions in the *Ethics*, Spinoza appears to argue for an inherent "fit" between object and idea by appeal to the inherent "extension" of each. I said in Chap. 2 that in the case of God the strategy seems question-begging without a reason to believe that an infinite object exists (though I also suggested that the ontological argument provides this reason). A similar complaint can be raised against the strategy in the case of common notions. The argument only works if there *is* a property that is equally in the part and in the whole. Unlike the idea of God, however, the common notions are not meant to ground Spinoza's system.[7] They are affirmed only once much ground has been laid out, including the nature and existence of the attributes and infinite modes. Within this context, Spinoza's presupposition of a property equally in the part and in the whole strikes me as reasonable, and, thus, Spinoza's interesting strategy for establishing the inherent adequacy of common notions via a priori considerations of "fit" between idea and object is pro tanto on solid ground.

The inherent adequacy of common notions goes some way toward explaining how they are able to function as foundations of reasoning. This is especially the case when we consider Spinoza's further claim that any ideas derived from common notions are also adequate (E2p40/G 2:120). (I take this to be a straightforward matter of the truth preservation of valid deductive inferences.) However, it is not entirely clear how much of anything *could* be derived from ideas of extension, or motion and rest alone.

---

[7] In Chap. 7, I will argue that the idea of God can be regarded as itself a common notion. This does not prevent God from being uniquely foundational, however, vis-à-vis the objects of other common notions.

As Schliesser has argued, these notions seem too general and qualitative to serve as useful foundations for science.[8]

Recall that Spinoza identifies the "things most universal and common to the whole of nature" in the TTP with "motion and rest, and their laws and rules, which nature always observes and through which it continuously acts." Shifting from ideas of motion to ideas of *laws* of motion points to a more promising basis for scientific reasoning. This depends, however, on how we interpret Spinoza's talk of laws here. According to Schliesser, when Spinoza speaks of laws, he does not mean laws of nature as we are accustomed to thinking of them in a scientific context. Instead, he is referring only to a more general, metaphysical notion of lawful*ness*.[9] Admittedly, Spinoza never specifies a definitive set of laws of nature as, for instance, Descartes does in the *Principles of Philosophy*. As noted previously (and as I will discuss in more depth later), Spinoza never managed to work out the details of a physical theory. Nevertheless, I read Spinoza's talk of "laws and rules" to signify more than rejection of caprice.[10]

Earlier in the TTP, Spinoza gives an example of "a universal law of all bodies, which follows from a necessity of nature," namely, "that a body which strikes against another lesser body loses as much of its motion as it communicates to the other body" (TTP 4.2/G 3:58). This is a kind of principle of conservation of motion. In the *Ethics*' Physical Digression, moreover, we find a version of the law of inertia: "From this it follows that a body in motion moves until it is determined by another body to rest; and that a body at rest also remains at rest until it is determined to motion by another" (E2p13lem3c/G 2:98). Spinoza also presents a law of reflection in the same context:

> When a body in motion strikes against another which is at rest and cannot give way, then it is reflected, so that it continues to move, and the angle of

---

[8] Schliesser 2014, 25–28.
[9] Schliesser 2014, 6.
[10] That Spinoza's talk of laws refers, at least sometimes, to specific laws of nature, such as those regarding conservation and inertia, is widely accepted by commentators. See, for instance, Curley 1969, 47–9; Lachterman 1978, 88–90; Yovel 1991; Miller 2003; and LeBuffe 2018, 91. Schliesser cites Gabbey's (1996) point that Spinoza eschews Descartes' language of "laws of nature" in the DPP. But even Gabbey, who generally downplays Spinoza's credentials as a scientific thinker, says that Spinoza largely accepted Descartes' laws of motion and that the latter heralded the natural philosophy in which the *Ethics* is grounded (1996, 155, n. 55).

the line of the reflected motion with the surface of the body at rest which it struck against will be equal to the angle which the line of the incident motion makes with the same surface. (E2p13a2″/G 2:99)

These statements of natural laws remain both general and qualitative, to be sure.[11] But they are markedly less general than ideas of extension, motion and rest per se, and the conservation principle and law of reflection appear, at least, to offer the possibility of quantification, inasmuch as motion and angles of motion are measurable.[12] In any case, Spinoza clearly intends such laws to provide foundations for scientific reasoning. In reference to the "things most universal and common to the whole of nature" (i.e., "motion and rest, and their laws and rules"), he says, "From these we proceed gradually to other, less universal things" (TTP 7.27/G 3:102). Analogous statements of the fertility of such universals can be found elsewhere.[13]

If I am right in construing Spinoza's talk of laws of nature in terms of scientific foundations, what is the relation between these laws of nature and the ideas of extension, motion, and rest that Spinoza calls common notions? Should laws of nature such as the principle of inertia or the law of reflection quoted above be construed as common notions as well?[14] To answer these questions, we need to examine a bit more closely Spinoza's conception of laws of nature.

---

[11] See Garber 2016, 134–159, for an insightful discussion of the relationship between laws of nature and mathematics in the seventeenth century. Garber argues that the two are more independent of one another than we might expect from the vantage point of subsequent scientific development.

[12] Some commentators (Miller 2004, 572–73; LeBuffe 2018, 88–89) have viewed mathematical and geometrical laws (in addition to natural laws) as themselves examples of common notions. There are two issues with this suggestion. First, if by mathematical and geometrical laws are meant laws involving numbers and figures (respectively) per se, then, as we have seen, ideas of these entities are beings of reason, which may exhibit the form of truth, but cannot be (in themselves) robustly true. Second, I argued that although figures (not numbers) exist as the determinations of finite bodies in the last chapter, they are properties only of finite bodies, not the whole of extended nature (which is infinite). This means that geometrical properties (if such are understood to involve figure) cannot be properties equally of the part and of the whole of nature. I will discuss in the next chapter how geometry may contribute to a science of finite bodies nevertheless.

[13] TIE 101–3/G 2:36–7.

[14] For an interpretation which identifies common notions with laws of nature, see Miller 2004, 572–3.

In the TTP, Spinoza distinguishes between laws that follow "from a necessity of nature," on the one hand, and laws that depend on human decision, on the other. I am concerned here with the former, about which Spinoza writes: "A law which depends on a necessity of nature is one which follows necessarily from the nature or definition of a thing" (TTP 4.1/G 3:57). This suggests that to understand laws of nature, the emphasis needs to be on the term *nature*. Anything that has a nature (or can be defined or has an essence) has properties which follow by necessity from that nature.[15] To cite an example frequently used by Spinoza, it follows necessarily from the nature of a triangle for its three angles to equal two right angles (E1pp16–17/G 2:60–1). As I understand the passage just quoted from TTP 4, anything that has a nature also has laws that follow by necessity from that nature. Thus, having angles equal to two right angles might just as well be considered a *law* of triangles as a *property* of them.[16]

If this is right, universal laws of extension (or motion and rest) are just properties that pertain to the whole of extension qua attribute (or motion and rest qua infinite mode).[17] I think we should also understand these laws

[15] Viljanen (2011, 41–5) makes a strong case for reading the relation between natures (or essences) and the properties that follow therefrom as a relation of formal causation.

[16] Melamed (2013, 51) draws a tripartite distinction between the properties constitutive of the essence of a thing, properties that follow from (but do not constitute) the essence of the thing (i.e., *propria*), and properties that are at least partially caused by external causes (i.e., accidents, or extraneous properties). According to this distinction, it is important to note that the properties I am talking about here are not accidents or extraneous properties, but properties that follow from the nature of the thing itself. I am less certain about Melamed's distinction between properties constitutive of the essence of the thing, which are included in the definition of the thing, and *propria*, which, Melamed argues, must not be included in the definition. This is because I do not see that Spinoza provides any clear way of distinguishing properties that are constitutive of the essence of some thing from "*propria*." Consider that Spinoza compares the way infinite things (including modes) follow from God's nature with the way that it follows from the nature of a triangle for its three angles to equal two right angles (E1p17s/G 2:62). Since modes, according to Melamed, are *propria* (with the attributes being what constitute God's nature), the property of its angles equaling two right angles is, thus, a *proprium* of triangles. However, elsewhere (E2p49dem), Spinoza claims that having angles equaling two right angles pertains to the essence of a triangle, implying that it is a property constitutive of the essence, not a *proprium*. I return to the question of the relation between definition and essence in Chap. 6.

[17] Yovel (1991) argues that laws of nature are all infinite modes. It may be true that the infinite mode (i.e., motion and rest under the attribute of extension) is the first "level" (if we begin with the attributes) at which laws of nature are found that are determinate enough to be applicable in scientific inquiry. But I am using the notion of "law of nature" in a broader

as *constraining* anything that follows from the attribute (and immediate infinite mode), which is to say, all finite extended modes. While particular finite bodies have their own natures and laws that follow therefrom qua particulars, they will also be constrained (or "governed") by the laws of the attribute as a whole insofar as they are modes of the latter.[18] In this way, I suggest, the laws of the attribute and infinite mode can be understood to be equally in the whole and in the part. As such, ideas of universal laws of nature, which follow from the nature of the attribute and infinite mode, should count as common notions no less than ideas of extension and motion and rest themselves.[19]

This is a welcome result since common notions are foundations of reasoning, and it is much easier to make sense of laws of nature as such foundations than of ideas of extension and motion and rest alone. Spinoza also speaks of laws of nature as scientific foundations in TTP 7, as we have seen, and elsewhere.[20]

In order to see how universal laws of nature might function as foundations for the derivation of knowledge about less universal things, consider Edwin Curley's explanation of how optical laws can be derived from general laws of motion in Descartes:

> on the Cartesian account of vision, to know how vision works requires knowing the laws of motion. It is an essential part of the Cartesian hypothesis about the nature of vision that light be thought of as an action or tendency toward movement which 'follows the same laws as does movement.' E.g. by construing the situation in which a ray of light strikes a smooth, flat

---

sense than Yovel, a sense which is, in my view, more in keeping with the notion that Spinoza articulates in the TTP. See Miller (2003) for further argument that Spinoza's notion of laws of nature is expansive enough to encompass laws pertaining to attribute and finite modes, in addition to infinite modes.

[18] In addition to laws relative to particulars and laws governing all modes in an attribute, there are also local laws, governing groups of particulars. I discuss these in the section at the end of this chapter on the peculiar common notions of E2p39. Miller (2003, 258–59) lays out a useful taxonomy of the levels at which the notion of natural law can apply in Spinoza (and in the seventeenth century more generally).

[19] Cf. Miller 2004, 573. I agree with Miller that laws of nature are common notions, but not with his claim that "all common notions are laws of nature."

[20] Another example is the following statement from the preface of *Ethics* Part 3: "the laws and rules of nature, according to which all things happen, and change from one form to another, are always and everywhere the same. So the way of understanding the nature of anything, of whatever kind, must also be the same, viz. through the universal laws and rules of nature."

surface as analogous to that in which a body traveling at a constant velocity strikes a flat and perfectly hard surface, Descartes purports to explain the law of reflection. We know how a moving body would behave under these admittedly ideal conditions. Knowing this, and assuming light to be a tendency toward movement, we come to understand a law of optics.[21]

Curley takes this to be the kind of way in which common notions (qua laws of nature) could serve as foundations of reasoning for Spinoza. We have already seen that Spinoza embraces a version of the law of reflection for the motion of bodies. Later, I will discuss Spinoza's optical writings, which make it clear that he accepts the assumption that light is a kind of motion (or at least can be treated as such). We can imagine that information about the behavior of light would form part of a history of natural things. We can also imagine questions regarding the nature and behavior of light left open by that history. For instance, is light a body? Does light obey the law of reflection? The history itself might not answer these questions definitively any more than a history of biblical passages would answer the question regarding the appropriate parameters of mourning. However, they are answerable in light of general laws and principles. For instance, if light is motion, it must follow the laws of bodily motion. Among these is the law of reflection. Therefore, light obeys the law of reflection.

4.2 Imagination in Spinozan Science and Issues of Adequacy

Up to this point, our discussion of Spinoza's scientific method has focused on the common notions that function as scientific foundations. I argued that laws of nature count as common notions, and just gave an example of how they allow for the derivation of knowledge of less universal things. This is the province of reason, the second kind of knowledge, which Spinoza defines as the perception of things and formation of universal notions "from the fact that we have common notions and adequate ideas of the properties of things (see E2p38c, 39, 39c, and 40)" (E2p40s2/G 2:122). Spinoza's parenthetical citation here might indicate that by "adequate ideas of the properties of things," he has in the mind the "peculiar

---

[21] Curley 1973, 51. For Descartes' confirmation (in face of critical scrutiny) that light must follow the same laws of motion as bodies (even though light is the propagation of motion through a medium, and not a moving body itself), see CSMK, 73–4.

common notions" that he discusses in E2p38–39.[22] I will have more to say about these, as well as the adequacy of the knowledge yielded by Spinoza's scientific method later in this chapter. It is necessary first to address the other kind of knowledge indispensable to the method: imagination. As we know from the last chapter, *imaginatio* is Spinoza's term roughly for what we now more naturally understand as sensory experience (and which I will speak of as experience *tout court* for brevity's sake). Depending upon how we divvy up the parts of Spinoza's scientific method, experience features in all or, at least, in the first and third parts, of the method.[23]

Experience is obviously responsible for the *historia naturae* with which the method begins. Somewhat less obviously experience is also instrumental in the descent from universal to less universal things, that is, in the transition from the second to the third part of the method. Particular (or even "less universal") things cannot be deduced a priori from universal things. The latter are simply too general to admit of deductions on their own, at least for a finite mind. Spinoza explains in the TIE that the deduction of knowledge of particular, finite things from universals must be guided by experimental and empirical data, because "to conceive them all at once [i.e., all the singular things that can be deduced from the first principles] is a task far beyond the powers of the human intellect" (TIE 102/G 2:37).[24] For instance, it would not be possible (for us) to deduce anything about the properties of light from the most general laws of bodily motion (which make no mention of light) a priori. Instead, this deduction is guided by experience of light and its behavioral properties. This is why I spoke of clarifying questions or ambiguities left open by the "history" (in this case, observations about light). The universal laws are able to clarify the nature of light's behavior, by determining, for instance, that if light is

---

[22] I say it *might* indicate this, but it is ambiguous, since rather than referring to a different kind of common notion (i.e., peculiar common notions), the phrase "adequate ideas of the properties of things" could instead be simply a gloss on "common notions." The parenthetical citation is consistent with both possibilities.

[23] Excellent discussions of the role of experience in Spinoza's scientific thought and epistemology more generally include Curley 1973, Klever 1990, and Gilead 2000, 209–22.

[24] Spinoza's point here is very similar to one that Descartes makes in Part 3 of his *Principles of Philosophy*: "The principles which we have so far discovered are so vast and so fertile, that their consequences are far more numerous than the entire observed contents of the visible world; indeed, they are so numerous that we could never in a lifetime make a complete survey of them even in our thought" (CSM 1:249). Spinoza includes this concession to a need for experience in the third part of the DPP, indicating that he may have been influenced in this regard by his study of Descartes' *Principles*.

in fact a body (as experience might appear to suggest), it must obey the law of reflection. (Similar points could be made about the scriptural example of deriving knowledge of mourning from universal biblical teachings.)

While experience is an indispensable component of Spinoza's scientific method, it also introduces difficulties from an epistemological point of view. As we know, the deliverances of the imagination are inadequate ideas. How can a process of reasoning claim adequacy for its results if it depends upon inadequate raw materials? There is a finer-grained way of putting this question to distinct parts of Spinoza's method. First, there is the transition from the first to the second part of the method, from the *historia naturae* to the common notions. While Spinoza is vague about the details of this transition, what he does say suggests that knowledge of common notions is inferred from the history (TTP 7.7/G 3:98). How can we be assured of the adequacy of the common notions if this is the case? Second, there is the transition from the common notions to the knowledge of less universal things. Spinoza says that whatever is derived from common notions is necessarily adequate. If, in practice, the derivation depends upon experience, however, as we have seen it must, how can this be the case? Addressing these questions is an important task for an interpreter of Spinoza's epistemology. I will address each in turn, beginning with the shift from experiential ideas to common notions.

4.2.1 From the Historia Naturae to Common Notions

Just as human beings form universal notions of dogs via the imagination according to the salient traits that happen most to affect any given individual, so we also form imaginative universal notions about bodies in general and about motion in general in the same way. It was long thought that whereas celestial beings have perpetual motions, sublunary bodies tend toward rest, since this is how we experience the latter. We also tend to believe that the world is full of empty space, since there is much that does not affect the senses at all. Descartes regarded these kinds of beliefs as "preconceived opinions" that we acquire as children when we form beliefs on the basis of the senses rather than reason.[25] He, of course, dismissed them as errors in need of purgative doubt and reevaluation from a rational standpoint.

---

[25] CSM 1:193, 218–9.

For Spinoza, the shift from imaginative to rational notions does not run through a process of hyperbolic doubt as it does for Descartes. Indeed, Spinoza seems to have thought this was neither possible nor necessary.[26] There is, nevertheless, an analogous transition in Spinoza from the preconceptions of the imagination to rational notions. He articulates its contours in the following passage from *Ethics* Part 2:

> I say expressly that the Mind has, not an adequate, but only a confused and mutilated knowledge, of itself, of its own Body, and of external bodies, so long as it perceives things from the common order of nature, i.e., so long as it is determined externally, from fortuitous encounters with things, to regard this or that, and not so long as it is determined internally, from the fact that it regards a number of things at once, to understand their agreements, differences, and oppositions. For so often as it is disposed internally, in this or another way, then it regards things clearly and distinctly. (E2p29s/G 2:114)

Spinoza distinguishes here between two sharply contrasting cognitive comportments. On the one hand, ideas and perceptions are determined by fortuitous encounters with things. This way of conceiving things clearly corresponds to the imagination. On the other hand, ideas and perceptions can be determined internally, on the basis of considering many different kinds of things at once, and the agreements and differences between them. This comportment recalls the second stage of the method of interpreting nature as described in TTP 7 when the history of natural phenomena is scrutinized for agreements (and differences), and thus corresponds to reason (or at least the foundation of reason[27]).

---

[26] Cartesian hyperbolic doubt depends on the independence of will from intellect. Spinoza rejects Descartes' distinction between will and intellect, and thus the possibility of hyperbolic doubt as conceived by Descartes. As discussed in Chap. 2, the process of grounding the system of knowledge against skepticism begins with reflection on the nature of a true idea (however it was acquired). This leads to the idea of God, which fully grounds the system.

[27] Since Spinoza officially defines reason in E2p40s2 in terms of what can be derived from our grasp of common notions (and adequate ideas of the properties of things), it is an open question whether the knowledge of the common notions themselves should count as reason. A similar interpretive ambiguity attaches to the third kind of knowledge. Spinoza defines the latter in terms of the derivation of adequate ideas of the essences of singular things from adequate knowledge of the attributes. In this case, does the knowledge of the attributes themselves count as knowledge of the third kind? Is a single kind of knowledge responsible for the grasp of the starting points of both reason and intuitive knowledge? Relatedly, it has also been wondered what kind (or kinds) of knowledge is responsible for the various propositions of the *Ethics* itself. Scholars have interpreted these questions in a range of different ways

How does this transition come about? How is the mind activated, as it were, so that it follows the laws of its own nature, rather than being determined by external causes "like waves of the sea tossed by contrary winds" (E3p59s/G 2:189)? Spinoza does not himself address this matter in any detail, but here is what I take to be a plausible account. If one happens to live in a region with only short-tailed sheep—to use one of Spinoza's own examples from the *Short Treatise* (KV 2.3/G 1:56)—and is determined externally to perceive only short-tailed sheep as a result, one will come to think of sheep as short-tailed and will be astonished upon encountering a long-tailed specimen. The astonishment issues from the realization that one's imaginative generalization that all sheep are short-tailed is false. We can imagine that this realization prompts a reevaluation of what it means to be a sheep and the question of the true definition of sheep. At this point the mind is active, internally determined. It considers the differences between the short-tailed and long-tailed sheep and searches for what they have in common. It questions whether there are other kinds of sheep still, what the differences and similarities there are between these others and the ones presently known, and so on. This seems to describe just the consideration of agreements and differences between many kinds of things that Spinoza attributes to the internal determination of reason.

Spinoza's discussion in the *Short Treatise* of the astonishment at seeing long-tailed sheep is supposed to illustrate the passion of wonder. Far from facilitating active inquiry, however, Spinoza thinks that wonder in and of itself arrests the mind in the contemplation of an object. So wonder is not the beginning of philosophy for Spinoza as it was for Plato and Aristotle— "there is no wonder in him who draws true conclusions," he says (KV

---

according to their interpretations of the second and third kinds of knowledge and the differences between them. (See, for instance, Parkinson 1973 and Fløistad 1973.) I defend a method interpretation of the difference between reason and intuitive knowledge in Chap. 7, according to which the kinds of knowledge are only differentiated in their process of derivation. This leaves it unclear how to categorize the knowledge of the starting points themselves. (I argue that the attributes are common notions, so the starting points of the kinds of knowledge overlap no less than the terminations.) However, on my particular version of the method interpretation, intuitive knowledge is just the perfection of reason. This means that intuitive knowledge could in fact be regarded as a species of reason. Thus, in the end, there is only a single candidate for grasping the axioms, attributes, or starting points. Whether we call this adequate knowledge, reason, or intuitive knowledge is a matter of little consequence, since each of these categories overlaps in this case. I expand on these matters in detail in Chap. 7.

2.3.3/G 1:57).[28] The account I have just sketched of the transition to active inquiry needs to be modified, then. Wonder or astonishment cannot in and of itself be credited with facilitating the transition to active inquiry. I suspect that the affect of joy must be part of the story, as several commentators have argued.[29] It seems especially relevant that Spinoza allows for passive joy, that is, an increase in one's power of acting (as is constitutive of joy) that is caused by external forces (and, hence, is passive). This is because passive joy does not presuppose the possession of adequate ideas (as active joy does), and yet serves to increase power of action.[30] Whereas, then, one might get stuck in wondering at the long-tailed sheep's long tail, nevertheless, insofar as the sheep has many things in *common* with its short-tailed counterparts, this is no cause for wonder, but, we might imagine, elicits the joy of recognizing similarities between disparate things. Although this joy comes initially from the outside, it plausibly has the capacity to stimulate the mind into an activity characterized by adequate ideas and active joy. So long as one is led to a consideration of *both* similarities and differences, then, as Spinoza says happens in the internal determination of reason, and slack-jawed astonishment does not freeze the gears of thought, wonder could be one part, along with joy, of a more complicated cognitive transition to activity in which the mind passes fluidly from the consideration of differences to similarities, and vice versa.[31]

---

[28] See also Spinoza's discussion of *admiratio* (wonder) in E3defaff4/G 2:191–2. Compared to Plato, Aristotle, and Descartes, who all see in wonder an epistemic virtue (although Descartes also recognizes that wonder can be excessive), Spinoza's relative disdain is quite striking. For Descartes' discussion of wonder, see CSM 1:353–56.

[29] For accounts of the transition from imagination to reason that stress the role of joy, see Deleuze 1990, 280–88, and Charles 2002. James (2011), by contrast, stresses the social context favorable to the transition, specifically the acceptance of certain elements of the "true religion" that Spinoza outlines in the TTP. I think James is right that social factors can inhibit the transition from imagination to reason, and that the right social context can help to facilitate the transition. Even so, an affective-cognitive account at the level of the individual is still necessary to explain how the transition is possible within a favorable social context. For a helpful general discussion of the role of the affects (both passive and active) in the acquisition of human freedom and knowledge, see Goldenbaum 2004.

[30] The question of how passive joy could increase power of action (given that its epistemic correlate is inadequate cognition) poses an interpretive difficulty. For discussion, see LeBuffe 2009, 211–18.

[31] E5p9dem: "An affect is only evil, or harmful, insofar as it prevents the mind from being able to think (by 4p26 and p27). And so that affect which determines the mind to consider many objects together is less harmful than another, equally great affect which engages the mind solely in considering one, or a few objects, so that it cannot think of others" (G 2:286).

Encountering a contradiction or conflict in one's system of beliefs strikes me as a plausible explanation (or at least a component in a plausible explanation) for what stimulates the transition from the passive comportment of the imagination to the active comportment of reason, but I do not wish to put too much stress on this particular account of the affective-cognitive mechanism that brings it about. *However* the mind is able to transition from being externally determined to being internally determined, the main point for my purposes is *that* the transition happens, and when it does the mind shifts from conceiving things passively and inadequately to conceiving things actively and adequately.

I want to consider a similar account of the transition from the inadequate conceptions of motion and extension discussed above to adequate conceptions of these objects. The purpose will not be to argue further for an account of the mechanism of the transition, but to discuss a separate difficulty that arises from Spinoza's claim that common notions can only be conceived adequately. Let us say, then, that one's imaginative belief in empty space is disturbed by new microscopic evidence of invisible particulate matter. One is then led from passive acceptance of empty space to a rational inquiry into the logic of that belief, which terminates ultimately in the rejection of vacua. The details of the transition, as I say, are not important.[32] Whatever they may be, the transition raises an epistemological difficulty. On the one hand, the foregoing account takes as its starting point ostensibly inadequate conceptions of extension and motion. On the other hand, we have seen that Spinoza insists that common notions—of which ideas of extension and motion are the prime examples—can only be conceived adequately. There is an apparent conflict here that needs to be addressed.[33]

---

[32] I certainly do not suggest that microscopic evidence of invisible particulate matter provides any kind of argument against a vacuum. The atomists postulated invisible atoms, after all. The arguments that Descartes and Spinoza advanced against the void, moreover, were of a rationalist, not empirical, nature. (For Descartes' arguments *contra* void, see CSM 1:229–30; for Spinoza's, see E1p15s and DPP2p3.) But rationalist arguments are not to the purpose in the present context, since to present rationalist arguments is already to be in an active cognitive state, whereas the question is how the transition from mental passivity to activity comes about. Given that Descartes diagnoses the error (from his perspective) of believing in a vacuum to stem from the childhood belief that all that exists is sensible (CSM 1:219), microscopic evidence of invisible particulate matter seems like the type of thing that could cast doubt on, and thus rethinking of, one's childhood preconception.

[33] Curley writes, "It is supposed to be impossible to perceive them [i.e., common notions] inadequately precisely because they are ideas of properties common to all objects we experi-

I think this problem could be resolved if, when Spinoza claims that the common notions of extension and motion can only be conceived adequately, he is speaking about extension per se (or qua extension) and motion per se (or qua motion). I attempted to explain the logic of Spinoza's claim above with the example of the rod sticking out of the ground. If my reasoning was on track, then it explains only the inherent adequacy of the idea of extension per se. It does not imply that all claims involving extension or about extension are adequate. If this is right, then an inadequate imaginative belief in the tendency to rest of terrestrial bodies or in the existence of a vacuum is consistent with Spinoza's claim that common notions of extension and motion can only be conceived adequately, since these imaginative beliefs are not ideas of extension and motion per se. It is only in the transition to active, rational inquiry regarding the objects of these beliefs—however that transition might be accomplished—that one comes to isolate extension and motion per se as objects of thought, and thus comes to enjoy an adequate idea. In this light, we can understand those commentators who have seen the emendation of the intellect as a process of cleansing inherently adequate ideas of impurity.[34]

ence [....] How Spinoza might have reconciled this view with the fact that people did, for many centuries, have inadequate ideas about motion, I do not know" (1973, 54).

[34] I have in mind, in particular, Aaron Garrett's emphasis on the notion of emendation in understanding the transition from inadequate to adequate ideas (2003, 86–93). (See also Savan 1986, 108.) For an argument that common notions, and all other adequate ideas, should be considered innate, see Marshall 2008, 81–7. I am sympathetic to seeing common notions as innate on the following grounds. The human mind has adequate ideas of the common properties of extended things just by virtue of having ideas of its own body (for reasons already laid out). But the nature of the mind is to be the idea of the human body (per E2p13/G 2:96). Thus, common notions follow from the nature of the mind itself as the idea of the human body. This plausibly makes common notions innate to the mind. I am less confident that the adequate ideas that can be derived from the common notions are also plausibly considered to be innate. This is due to the fact that they depend for their formation on input from the imagination, as I will argue in the next section. Admittedly, the data of the imagination are fitted into an adequate explanatory framework, and, thus, subsumed by the intellect (insofar as the resultant idea is adequate), but the result is still dependent upon input from external causes, and is true only in form, not robustly. Whether such derivative adequate ideas should also be considered innate depends, it seems to me, on one's notion of innateness. While it would be in keeping with Descartes' expansive notion of innateness, which encompasses any idea that we have "within ourselves the faculty of summoning up" (CSM 2:132), it would not, by contrast, be in keeping with other contemporary interpretations, such as that of Descartes' one-time friend and pupil, Regius (CSM 1:295). Given the wide range of interpretations of innateness in the seventeenth century, coupled with the fact that "innate idea" is not a notion that Spinoza himself explicitly uses, I think it is inadvisable

That is to say, the ideas of extension and motion per se are present implicitly (in all ideas of finite bodies), but in order to be appreciated explicitly, they need to be isolated from the imaginative illusions that have accumulated around them through naïve experience.[35]

4.2.2 Descending to Particulars

Spinozan science relies upon and incorporates experiential data of imagination both at the beginning of the method in the compilation of the history and in the descent from more universal to less universal things and ultimately to particulars. Since the products of the imagination are inadequate conceptions, the place of experience in Spinozan science raises a difficulty for the adequacy of the knowledge that Spinozan science yields. In the previous section I addressed the transition from the initial imaginative conceptions to adequate understanding of common notions and associated general laws and rules. What about the descent to particulars? How can it yield adequate knowledge about less universal things if experience must serve as guide?

---

to assimilate Spinoza's position on the matter to Descartes' (or Leibniz's). Spinoza does talk of "native power" (*vis nativa*) of the intellect (TIE 31/G 2:14) to refer to what is not caused in us by external causes, though, as A. Garrett notes (2003, 82), this inborn power applies as much to bodies as minds. In the end, despite my openness to seeing common notions as innate, I prefer to avoid talking of "innate ideas" in the case of Spinoza (and to stick to the intellect/imagination and adequate/inadequate dichotomies), given the ambiguity of the notion itself (especially in the case of adequate ideas derived from common notions on the basis of experiential input), and Spinoza's silence on the matter.

[35] It must be admitted that certain texts resist this attempt to reconcile Spinoza's claim that common notions can only be conceived adequately by all with its prima facie implausibility, but I do not see any other way of resolving the issue, and this solution at least seems plausible. The recalcitrant text I have in mind is the following passage from E2p40s1: "But some axioms, or notions, result from other causes which it would be helpful to explain by this method of ours. For from these explanations it would be established which notions are more useful than the others, and which are hardly of any use; *and then, which are common, which are clear and distinct only to those who have no prejudices*, and finally, which are ill-founded [....] But since I have set these aside for another treatise, and do not wish to give rise to disgust by too long a discussion, I have decided to pass over them here" (italics added). It is Spinoza's distinction in this passage between those notions which are common and those which are clear and distinct only to those who have no prejudices that raises the issue, since my interpretation of common notions suggested that they might need to be cleansed of prejudices in order to be grasped adequately (by all). The fact that Spinoza tables the issue for another treatise, however, suggests that he may not have fully worked out all of the details of his account. I think this leaves room for the sort of interpretation I have given.

I think there are two points that serve to mitigate this difficulty. The first involves the distinction between primary and secondary qualities. While no such distinction will show up in the initial *historia naturae*, by the time knowledge of less universal and particular things is drawn from the common notions, secondary qualities, I suggest, will have dropped out of the picture. The rejection of resemblance relations between sensory ideas and the external causes of sensation is one of the revolutionary consequences of the new mathematized view of nature associated with Descartes and Galileo. Spinoza explicitly credits Descartes (along with Bacon) with demonstrating the primary-secondary quality distinction, moreover, in Letter 6, and embraced a version of the distinction between primary and secondary qualities (albeit in the guise of other terminology). The distinction represents a significant refinement of how experiential data are treated and understood. Since, as Descartes says, primary qualities are those properties "comprised within the subject-matter of pure mathematics,"[36] a focus on primary rather than secondary qualities means a focus on those properties of external objects that are geometrically tractable. We will be discussing the role of geometry in Spinozan science in the next chapter. Now there is still another point to be made regarding the question of the adequacy of the results of Spinozan science.

As Descartes recognized, even if we can clearly and distinctly understand that bodies must have one size and shape or another, our sensory perceptions of any given body's particular size and shape involve a "high degree of doubt and uncertainty."[37] To put this in the language of Spinoza's epistemology, while extension and motion generally are equally in the part and in the whole, particular sizes, shapes, and motions are not, and so our perceptions of them are not inherently adequate like the common notions. While some body may well be spherical, my perception that that particular body over there is spherical reflects the way the object affects my body rather than its own nature.

I think this is where hypotheses must become part of the story of Spinoza's scientific method. (This is the second mitigating point mentioned above.) If, in hypothesizing that an entity is spherical, we are able successfully to derive some of its other properties, we have some reason to believe that our conception is getting something right about the object.

---

[36] CSM 2:55.
[37] CSM 2:55.

Of course, if it turns out that further evidence contradicts our hypothesis, then the hypothesis can be revised.[38]

There is evidence that Spinoza embraced this kind of hypothetico-deductive use of intellectual conceptions in conjunction with experience.[39]

---

[38] Cf. Klever 1990. Klever characterizes Spinoza as an "anti-falsificationist," so inasmuch as my talk of evidence contradicting hypotheses sounds like falsificationism, it appears that my proposal is in conflict with Klever's. But this is not the case on closer inspection. Klever's claim is that empirical evidence cannot falsify what can be known independently by the intellect. For example, Klever highlights Spinoza's discussion of Zeno's paradoxes of motion in the DPP (G 1:192–96) and Spinoza's criticism of Diogenes' attempt to refute them through experience. Instead, the paradoxes can be shown to be flawed on purely rational grounds. I agree with Klever that when it comes to what is knowable on the basis of the intellect alone, empirical evidence is useless for either verification or falsification. (Klever's analysis of Spinoza's epistolary engagement with Boyle's experimental philosophy is useful in this regard (1990, 130–33).) This would include what can be known about the basic principles of physical nature (though see the caveats in the previous section about the role of experience in arriving at the common notions). However, what I am talking about in the present context are non-universal natural phenomena that are *not* knowable by the finite intellect alone. In this domain, Klever's following qualification is germane: "Of course, observed facts can falsify and refute other…opinions, conjectures, hypothetical semi-rational constructions. Spinoza does not deny this sort of 'elimination'" (1990, 129). I would only object that there is no reason to regard hypothetical constructions as "semi-rational." Inasmuch as hypothetical constructions can exhibit the *form* of true ideas, they are fully rational, in my view.

[39] Cf. Bennett 1984, 20–23. Bennett also highlights evidence from the DPP (and elsewhere) of Spinoza's friendliness to hypothetico-deductive methodology. His main point, however, is to argue that the *Ethics* itself be viewed as a hypothetico-deductive system. Klever (1986) endorses and further develops this reading of Spinoza's more general philosophical methodology. As I understand the notion, a hypothesis is something whose truth is not self-evident, but needs to be tested or confirmed in some way. In this case, I disagree that the definitions (at least the *real*, if not the nominal ones) and axioms of the *Ethics* serve as hypotheses as Bennett and Klever argue, since, in my view, Spinoza thinks that they are self-evident (as I argue in Chap. 2 regarding the idea of God qua foundation of Spinoza's system), and do not need to be confirmed by what follows from them. (Bennett, at times, seems only to suggest that by reading the *Ethics* as a whole, one may come to better grasp the truth of the definitions and axioms. This may be true from a subjective, pedagogical standpoint, but does not signify that the definitions and axioms are in fact in *need* of any such confirmation.) This is why I prefer to restrict the attribution of hypothetico-deductive methodology to Spinoza's philosophy of science. On the latter, cf. Schliesser 2014, 9–10. Schliesser quotes Spinoza as saying, "it is sufficient for me here to have shown one [cause] through which I can explain it [i.e., the mechanics of image formation] as if I had shown it through its true cause" (E2p17s), then infers: "in this *limited* respect Spinoza shows himself a true Cartesian for whom causal explanations of natures are always merely hypothetical." Savan (1986, 113–18) also attributes to Spinoza a "principle of hypothetical explanation" and provides an excellent discussion of Spinoza's scientific method with which the one presented in this

He makes the following statement regarding the use of hypotheses in natural science in the DPP:

> since the best way to understand the nature of Plants and of Man is to consider how they gradually come to be and are generated from seeds, we shall have to devise such principles as are very simple and very easy to know, from which we may demonstrate how the stars, earth and finally all those things that we find in this visible world, could have arisen, as if from certain seeds—even though we may know very well that they never did arise that way. For by doing so we shall exhibit their nature far better than if we only described what they are now. (DPP 3 preface/G 1:226)

The concessive clause which follows the dash reminds us of what Spinoza says about the genetic conception of the sphere in the TIE, that is, that it is a true conception even though we know that no sphere in nature was ever generated in that way. Here we find Spinoza applying the same notion of hypothetical genetic conception to the natures of plants and human beings. He goes on a few paragraphs later to reprise mathematical examples in illustrating the use of hypotheses. He says that if one wishes to explain a parabola drawn on paper, it does not matter whether one explains it as having been first cut out of a cone and then pressed on the paper, or as having been described by the motion of two straight lines, or in some other way,

> provided that he demonstrates all the properties of the Parabola from what he supposes. Indeed, even though he may know it to have come to be from the pressing of a Conic section on the paper, he will nevertheless be able to feign any other cause he pleases, which seems to him most convenient to explain all the properties of the Parabola. Similarly we are permitted to assume any hypothesis we please to explain the features of nature, provided that we deduce all the Phenomena of nature from it by Mathematical consequences. (DPP 3 preface/G 1:227–28)

---

chapter is in many ways congruent. However, Savan suggests that insofar as a hypothesis is not adequate and true, it must be inadequate (1986, 114–15). This strikes me as a mistake, since it implies that the hypothesis is imaginative, whereas it is certainly possible, and indeed necessary, for hypotheses to be intellectual. My notion of an idea that is true *in form* better captures the status of hypotheses formed by the intellect and serves to bridge the gap between ideas which are completely (or robustly) adequate and true and those which are inadequate.

Spinoza's point about the parabola is very similar to one he makes about equivalent ways of explaining an ellipse in TIE 108.[40]

While any evidence drawn from the DPP for interpreting Spinoza's own views is problematic, since the DPP presents Descartes' philosophy rather than Spinoza's own, the coincidence with TIE 108 suggests that Spinoza agrees with the points regarding hypotheses that he is voicing on behalf of Descartes.[41] The evidence from the DPP also jibes with a remark Spinoza makes in the TTP concerning our knowledge of particular things. Although, Spinoza explains, human actions, for instance, depend on universal laws of nature, this consideration does not in itself afford us any particular knowledge of human actions, since "we are completely ignorant of the order and connection of things itself, i.e., of how things are really ordered and connected" (TTP 4.4/G 3:58). In other words, the particular way in which human actions are determined by universal laws is beyond

---

[40] "The mind can determine in many ways the ideas of things that the intellect forms from others—as, for example, to determine the plane of an ellipse, it feigns that a pen attached to a cord is moved around two centers, or conceives infinitely many points always having the same definite relation to some given straight line, or a cone cut by some oblique plane, so that the angle of inclination is greater than the angle of the cone's vertex, or in infinite other ways" (TIE 108/G 2:39).

[41] Spinoza also mentions hypotheses in a footnote to a passage in the TIE in which he is discussing a kind of thought experiment, in particular, the idea of a candle burning on its own, surrounded by nothing (in which case, it is inferred, there is no cause for the flame's destruction). About the thought experiment, Spinoza says, "there is no fiction, but true and sheer assertions" (*verae ac merae assertiones*) (TIE 57/G 2:22). (I take Spinoza to use "true" (*verae*) here in the sense of "genuine" or "veritable," not in the epistemic sense of agreeing with an object. Curley concurs. See Curley 1:26, n. 44.) The footnote in question is attached to this comment, and reads:

> The same must also be understood concerning the hypotheses [*de hypothesibus*] that are made to explain certain motions, which agree with the phenomena of the heavens; except that when people apply them to the celestial motions, they infer the nature of the heavens from them. But that nature can be different, especially since many other causes can be conceived to explain such motions. (TIE 57n)

In saying that "[t]he same must be understood," Spinoza means that astronomical hypotheses are, like the thought experiment with the candle, not fictions, but "true and sheer assertions." Unfortunately, I do not think it is very clear what Spinoza means by "assertions" in this context. Spinoza condemns inferring the nature of things from hypotheses, on the grounds that the nature can always be different than the hypothesis suggests, but this simply follows from the nature of hypotheses. Overall, I do not think the footnote reveals much about whether Spinoza endorses the use of hypotheses or not.

the capacity of a finite mind for reasons already adduced. Thus, Spinoza infers, "for practical purposes it is better, indeed, necessary to consider things as possible [*possibiles*]" (TTP 4.4/G 3:58). When Spinoza says that we must consider things as possible, here, I take him to mean that we must make use of hypotheses in investigating the natures of particular things.[42] A hypothetical explanation, after all, is one that is possibly true.

4.3 Peculiar Common Notions

Earlier in this chapter I said, on the basis of remarks in TTP 4, that a law of nature should be understood in terms of what follows from the nature or definition of a thing. Since my goal, then, was to explain universal laws of nature, my focus was on what follows from the whole of extension qua attribute and from its immediate infinite mode. But Spinoza's conception of natural law also admits of local and even individual incarnations. TTP 4 opens with the following statement: "The word *law* [*legis nomen*], taken without qualification, means that according to which each individual, or all or some members of the same species, act in one and the same fixed and determined way" (TTP 4.1/G 3:57). Just as universal laws govern the behavior of all bodies, so there are less universal laws governing the behavior of certain kinds of bodies, such as human bodies, and particular laws governing the behavior of individual bodies. There is, then, a spectrum of laws from universal to particular governing a correlative spectrum of natures.[43] The notion of shared natures in Spinoza is problematic and will be taken up in Chap. 6. For the present, I will bracket such issues, since my interest now is in the notion of non-universal or local laws. Given what

---

[42] Cf. Spinoza's definition of *possibile* in E4d4: "I call...singular things possible, insofar as, while we attend to the causes from which they must be produced, we do not know whether those causes are determined to produce them" (G 2:209). On the one hand, this definition of "possible" suggests something slightly different than my gloss of TTP 4 in terms of "hypothesis" might suggest, since Spinoza says here that to conceive something as possible is to conceive the causes from which it *must* be produced, whereas a hypothetical conception posits the manner in which something *might* be caused. On the other hand, both conceptions of "possible" represent *causal* conceptions of an object. If, then, the causes of a thing are themselves what is in question, as is the case in TTP, it seems in keeping with the spirit of Spinoza's E4d4 definition of "possible," to regard a hypothetical conception of the causes of a thing in terms of possibility. Savan (1986, 112–17) also connects Spinoza's notion of "possible" with the notion of the hypothetical.

[43] See Miller (2003, 258–59) for further discussion of the spectrum (or different levels) of laws of nature in Spinoza.

I just argued in the previous section, our knowledge of local laws, such as those governing human action, must be hypothetical. I think this is right, but it is in some tension with comments Spinoza makes in the *Ethics* about a certain kind of common notion that I have not discussed yet. Before concluding this chapter, I want to look at these other common notions.

E2p39 reads: "If something is common to, and peculiar to, [*commune est et proprium*] the human body and certain external bodies by which the human body is usually affected, and is equally in the part and in the whole of each of them, its idea will also be adequate in the Mind" (G 2:118). Spinoza's restriction of these notions to what the human body and *certain* external bodies have in common sets them in contrast with the universal common notions (or UCNs) discussed above, which are ideas of what is common to *all* bodies. To mark this contrast, I will adopt Curley's translation of *proprium* and refer to the common notions of E2p39 as *peculiar* common notions (or PCNs). Spinoza's demonstration of the adequacy of PCNs consists in stipulating that such notions exist, and proceeding to argue that in this case the idea of such peculiar common features will be adequate in God insofar as God constitutes the nature of the human mind alone, thereby invoking the E2p11c doctrine of adequate ideas. This is similar to Spinoza's demonstration of the adequacy of UCNs, and similarly unhelpful in explaining why we should believe that such things *are* identical to (whole) ideas in God's mind. To understand what PCNs might be and why they should be adequate, the definition stated above is the best guide.

It helps to break the definition into three components as follows:

(i) The objects of PCNs are *common and peculiar* to the human body and *certain* external bodies
(ii) The "certain external bodies" are ones by which the human body is *usually affected*; and
(iii) The objects of PCNs are equally in the part and in the whole *of each of them* (i.e., the human body and the certain external bodies)

The first component distinguishes the PCNs from the UCNs by restricting these notions to what is common to the human body and only *certain* external bodies. These notions are not only common to a certain subset of bodies, however, but *peculiar* to them. In other words, the objects of PCNs do not exist external to the relevant subset of bodies. This suggests that we are talking about either the *nature* that is common and peculiar to a certain subset of bodies (which includes the human body) or a *property* (or properties) of that nature (or both nature and properties). The most obvious (but by no means the only) candidate for a nature that is common and peculiar to the human body and certain external bodies is, of course, human nature.[44]

The third component of the definition of PCNs helps to reinforce and sharpen this suggestion. Echoing the primary criterion of UCNs, the third component specifies that PCNs must be equally in the part and in the whole of each individual member of the relevant subset of bodies. This serves to rule out the possession of noses, for instance, as a candidate object of PCNs. While noses may be a feature shared in common by a given subset of bodies, noses are not equally in the part and in the whole of any individual member of the relevant subset. What is equally in the part and in the whole of the members of an exclusive subset of bodies? Again, the most obvious candidate is a shared nature or essence, such as human nature. Since Spinoza defines bodies in terms of a ratio of motion and rest, it is plausible to think that it is this ratio, in particular, that is equally in the part and in the whole. Thus, in some sense, my white blood cells, for instance, must involve and express the ratio of motion and rest essential to me just as I, as a whole, must.[45] Of course, my white blood

---

[44] Spinoza affirms that we have a shared (rational) nature in common with other human beings in *Ethics* Part 4 (see E4p35). The logic of Spinoza's definition of the PCNs suggests that we might have common and peculiar natures in common with all members of the class of animals insofar as we are members of this class. Thus, we would have PCNs of animal nature. However, Spinoza never talks explicitly of shared animal nature (as far as I am aware), while he frequently talks of shared human nature. Hence, I say, the latter is the most obvious (but not the only) candidate for PCNs.

[45] I am not suggesting that the mind has an adequate idea of white blood cells. This suggestion would contradict E2p24: "The human mind does not involve adequate knowledge of the parts composing the human body." I am suggesting instead that the mind has an adequate idea of *human nature* (and, perhaps, the ratio of motion and rest that defines human nature), and that the reason for this is that human nature is equally in the part (e.g., in white blood cells) as in the whole. It might be further objected, however, that I do not have an explicit idea of human nature as involved in or expressed by my white blood cells. To respond to this potential objection, if the fact that I do not have an explicit idea of the human nature involved or expressed in my white blood cells is taken to be a problem for the adequacy of my idea of human nature, then, by parallel logic, the fact that I do not have an explicit idea of the *extension* of my white blood cells should pose a problem for the adequacy of my idea of extension. Since the latter does not in fact appear to be a problem for the adequacy of the UCN of extension, the former should not be a problem for the adequacy of the PCN of human nature.

cells must have their own distinct ratio of motion and rest that defines them as individuals. Nevertheless, insofar as they make up constituent parts of my nature, and are in turn constrained by the laws of my nature, I propose, they *also* involve and express *my* ratio.[46] Since the precise meaning of this ratio is unclear, however, I will speak less technically and more colloquially simply in terms of human nature (or equine nature, or what have you) for the purposes of this discussion.[47]

The third component is the only one that could explain the adequacy of PCNs. Since being equally in the part and in the whole is a criterion common to PCNs and UCNs, it will be well to recall what I argued above about the significance of this criterion for the adequacy of UCNs. The key point was that since the objects of UCNs, such as extendedness or motion, are equally in the part and in the whole of *everything*, in having an idea of *anything*, I must be having a perfectly complete and adequate idea of a universally common feature. It is impossible, in other words, to have a partial idea of such a feature, and, since only partial ideas are inadequate, it is impossible to have an inadequate idea of such a feature. The same line of reasoning should apply for PCNs, except in this case the common features are restricted to those peculiar to a given subset of bodies. Since, then, the objects of PCNs, such as human nature, are equally in the part and in the whole of a given subset of bodies—in this case, human bodies—in having the idea of any human body, I must be having a perfectly complete and adequate idea of human nature.[48]

---

[46] I am grateful to Christopher Martin and John Grey for prompting me to clarify this point.

[47] Parkinson associates PCNs with the propositions of sciences such as physiology, explaining, "Such a science is not true of the whole of Nature, as physics is, but only of 'individuals'...of a certain degree of complexity" (1954, 165). In order for this reading to be acceptable, the objects of the physiological propositions in question (or propositions of other special sciences) would have to be equally in the part and in the whole. It is not clear to me exactly what sort of propositions Parkinson had in mind, but it seems unlikely that their objects would satisfy this criterion. My interpretation has more in common with that of Gueroult, who interprets the PCNs as correlated with commonalities among types or species of individual of a certain complexity. (For Gueroult's excellent analysis of PCNs, see 1974, 335–52.) As Gueroult points out, this suggests a hierarchy of PCNs. Thus, there could be PCNs for organic entities qua organic, for animals qua animal, for humans qua human, and so on. I do not follow Gueroult, however, when he states that insofar as we are composed of less complex individuals, such as blood, lymph, chyle, iron, and water, we must share peculiar common properties with such things (1974, 342), since these less complex individuals are not equally in the part and in the whole of my body.

[48] While Gueroult agrees that an example of a PCN would be human nature (or human essence) itself, he astutely raises the difficulty that this appears to conflict with Spinoza's

In discussing UCNs, above, we ran into the following difficulty: Spinoza's claim that we can have only adequate ideas of UCNs is contradicted by the prevalence of inadequate ideas about motion, extension, and so on. (Recall the discussion of belief in empty space and a natural tendency to rest.) In response, I argued that Spinoza must mean that we can have only adequate ideas of extension qua extension (or motion qua motion). In other words, in the event that we properly isolate the relevant object in our minds, *then* we can be sure of its adequacy. I think something similar must apply here in the case of PCNs. Naturally, Spinoza must recognize the possibility of inadequate ideas of human nature. He argues explicitly against conceptions of human beings as substances. To reconcile this patent fact with E2p39, we can say that an adequate conception of human nature is available to us, and its adequacy is assured, *if* we can properly isolate it from related imagination-based confusions.

What about the second component in the definition of PCNs? It specifies that the human body is "usually affected" by the certain external bodies with which it shares a common and peculiar feature. This component plays no manifest role in Spinoza's demonstration of E2p39 and might seem unhelpfully vague. Nevertheless, I think it suggests an important point. I might think that even if I were never affected by another human body, I have ideas of my own human body, and since my human nature is equally in the part and in the whole of my own body, I have no need to be affected by another human body in order to have an adequate idea of human nature. This would be a mistake, however. Perception happens only in the interaction with external bodies. Thus, Spinoza's "usually affected" clause may imply the very interesting claim that unless I were affected by other human bodies, I would never have the idea of my own human body or any ideas of human nature. The same could also be said of the UCNs: if I were never affected by any external bodies I would have no ideas of extension or motion. The only difference is that UCNs are generated by all my interactions, whereas PCNs are generated only by certain

claim (in E2p37) that common notions do not constitute the essence of any individual. Gueroult's proposal for resolving this difficulty is to distinguish between the way reason grasps human essence, that is, from the outside, and as a property, on the one hand, and the way intuitive knowledge grasps human essence, that is from the inside, and as essence proper, on the other hand (1974, 342–43). I do not believe there is any such distinction to be drawn between reason and intuitive knowledge, as I will explain in Chap. 7. I think the way to solve the problem is instead to recognize that the idea of human essence at the species level is a being of reason, not a true essence. I defend this view in Chap. 6.

interactions with things that share some common and peculiar features with me.[49]

So much for what can be gleaned from Spinoza's definition of PCNs. It is now time to address the issue that initially prompted this foray into Spinoza's (somewhat peculiar) doctrine of peculiar common notions. The previous discussion of Spinozan science and laws of nature implied that any knowledge of local laws, such as those governing human action, must be hypothetical. E2p39, by contrast, affirms the inherent adequacy of our ideas of certain non-universal objects, such as human nature. If we can have inherently adequate ideas of human nature, however, we need not rely on hypotheses. The question, then, is whether Spinoza is entitled to the more bullish epistemic outlook that might be suggested by E2p39?

I do not think so. I argued above that the adequacy of PCNs would need to be established in a way analogous to the adequacy of UCNs. In both cases, the argument is that, being equally in the part and in the whole of their respective domains, both PCNs and UCNs cannot be conceived only partially, since a partial conception is equal to a complete conception. This only works, however, if the metaphysical reality of the domain in question is itself assured. Extension, as an attribute of God, exists through itself. As such, its metaphysical reality can be known with certainty a priori. The case of motion and rest is less straightforward, since it is a mode, even if an infinite one. Nevertheless, Spinoza takes motion and rest qua infinite mode to follow immediately from the attribute of extension. Moreover, he takes this to be knowable a priori. By contrast, while an infinite intellect might be able to deduce the existence of human nature from God's nature a priori, this is not the case for finite intellects.[50] This means that the metaphysical reality of human nature cannot be rationally grounded a priori, at least by us. To be sure, anything that exists must have some nature. So, *I* must have some nature. *You* must have some nature. But there is no a priori basis for assuming that my nature is shared with you or anything else[51] nor (as far as I can see) for assuming the existence of discrete species essences.[52]

---

[49] The fact that UCNs and PCNs are generated only through the interaction with external bodies does not in and of itself mean that they are passive. On this, see the discussion of the activation of common notions in Sect. 4.2.1 of this chapter on the transition from the *historia naturae* to common notions.

[50] I discuss the implications of this discrepancy further in the final section of Chap. 6.

[51] I think the same can be said for shared (peculiar) properties, if we are talking about properties rather than natures. While all members of a given attribute share properties universal to that attribute, I see no a priori reason for thinking that there are properties that are shared only locally (i.e., only by subsets of the members of a given attribute).

[52] Perhaps, for instance, species essences are required by some principle of plenitude, but if so, I am not sure how or why.

Does Spinoza assume the existence of discrete species essences, such as human nature and equine nature? Sometimes it appears as if he does. Throughout Parts 3 and 4 of the *Ethics*, which are devoted to advancing a science of human affects, he frequently treats human beings as possessing a shared nature. If humans did not have a shared nature, then a science of human affects would not be possible. While Spinoza attributes affects to non-human animals, he insists that they "are different in nature from human affects" (E4p37s1/G 2:237), and he distinguishes, for example, between equine lust and human lust (E3p57s/G 2:187). Sometimes he speaks as if agreement of natures is an all-or-nothing affair: the nature of one human agrees with that of another human, but not with that of a non-human. It is on this basis that Spinoza condones using non-human animals "at our pleasure" (E4p37s/G 2:237). But this cannot be right. After all, Spinoza concedes equine lust and equine gladness to horses, and analogous affects to fish and insects. There must be *something* in common between equine joy and human joy, and thus, by extension, between equine nature and human nature.[53] By the same token, Spinoza acknowledges that the affects of the inebriate differ from those of the philosopher, implying a difference in nature as well. So, while Spinoza sometimes talks as though there are discrete species essences, it is difficult to find a sound basis for this view in his philosophy, and he often seems to acknowledge as much.

There is one approach to establishing the adequacy of peculiar common notions that I have not considered yet. This approach argues that adequacy comes in degrees.[54] The more we have in common with something, the

---

[53] Cf. Wilson (1999, 347): "Why *should not* my belief (after Spinoza) that a squirrel in my yard, or an osprey over the water—or for that matter a centipede in the bathtub—experiences joy in the life that it has, inhibit my eliminating that life, even *if* I think that its joy is 'different in nature' from mine, and that accordingly I cannot be 'friends' with it?" Wilson is making a normative point here about the ethical implications (or lack thereof) of differing natures, whereas I am questioning the extent of difference in nature in the first place. But Wilson's point that other animals experience their own kinds of joys is still congenial with my own. Wilson's paper (1999) provides a good overview of some of the aporias involved in Spinoza's doctrine of human and animal natures. See also Grey (2013).

[54] Della Rocca defends the idea that adequacy comes in degrees (2008, 114–16). Della Rocca's notion of degrees of adequacy appears to be motivated, at least in part, by his view that human beings are not capable of completely adequate ideas. The latter view is based on the following line of reasoning. In order for an idea to be adequate, it must not be caused by anything external, since ideas that are externally caused (even only partially so) are inadequate. But all human ideas are externally caused, at least in part, thus no human ideas are completely adequate. I disagree that all human ideas are externally caused in the relevant sense. The genetic geometrical conceptions from the TIE provide abstract examples of ideas that are fully caused by the human mind itself. The common notions provide non-abstract examples of such ideas, as argued above. In this regard, I agree, in general, with Eugene

greater the degree of adequacy of our ideas about what we have in common. This line of thought is congenial with what I just said about natures. Although there may be no discrete human nature, we have more in common with certain other individuals than others. It might also be thought to be congenial with the corollary to E2p39, which states: "the mind is the more capable (*aptior*) of perceiving many things adequately as its body has many things in common with other bodies" (G 2:119–20). This passage is, I think, ambiguous, and can be made to fit with a conception of adequacy as an all-or-nothing affair or as admitting of degrees.[55] Nonetheless, the notion that adequacy admits of degrees is an attractive interpretive option. For one, it offers a solution to the interpretive questions raised by the peculiar common notions. It could be conceded that peculiar common notions are not knowable a priori, and thus are not perfectly adequate like our ideas of things knowable a priori. At the same time, we would be able to make sense of Spinoza's claim that our peculiar common notions are adequate as a statement admitting of degrees. The *more* we have in common with something else, the more adequate our ideas of this thing can be. This interpretation also offers an appealing way to handle the interplay of intellect and imagination I said is a necessary feature of our scientific investigation of finite things. Insofar as our ideas have imaginative input, they are inadequate; insofar as they have intellectual input they are adequate. The combination of the two results in a partially adequate and partially inadequate idea. The degree of adequacy depends on the relative contributions of the intellect and the imagination in the idea.

This way of conceiving adequacy is very different from the one I have articulated in this study. In my view, even if agreement of natures comes in degrees, adequacy does not. An adequate idea, recall, is one that is internally complete. I argued in the previous chapter that internal completeness

---

Marshall's (2008) arguments in favor of the possibility of ideas that are totally caused by the human mind. Given this possibility, a motivation for the notion of partial adequacy is removed.

[55] That is, the passage could be interpreted to say (in line with a degree of adequacy view): as our bodies have more in common with other bodies, our ideas increase (by degree) in their adequacy. Or, the passage could be interpreted to say (in line with an all-or-nothing view of adequacy): as our bodies have more in common with other bodies, we are more capable of *having* adequate ideas. In my view, the capability language (*aptior*) fits better with the latter all-or-nothing reading. The degree of adequacy view suggests that the mind should *automatically* (or *ipso facto*) enjoy an increase in the (degree of) adequacy of its ideas by having more in common with other bodies, not just gain greater *capability* for adequate ideas.

is guaranteed when an object is thought through its cause, such that all of the object's properties can be deduced therefrom. But it is important that this guarantee is a guarantee *for* the mind conceiving the idea in question. This transparency of adequacy is, I take it, the significance of Spinoza's definition of adequacy in terms of *intrinsic* denominations. When we have an adequate idea, it is as if a light goes off in our minds by which we *see* the completeness of our idea. This is, of course, a metaphor, though it is one that Spinoza himself uses (E2p43s/G 2:124). Its significance is in tying the notion of adequacy to psychological certainty. To have a partially adequate idea would be to enjoy partial certainty. Upon inspection, however, the notion of partial certainty is incoherent, at least within a Spinozan framework as I understand it. Supposing an idea is made up of intellectual (adequate) elements and imaginative (inadequate) elements, does partial certainty consist in being certain of the intellectual elements and uncertain of the imaginative elements? If so, this situation is better analyzed in terms of two ideas—one wholly adequate and the other wholly inadequate. If, on the other hand, partial certainty does not consist in certainty about which parts of the idea are intellectual (or adequate) and which are imaginative (or inadequate), then I think the idea must be seen as confused, or wholly inadequate. Whichever way we attempt to understand partial certainty, then (I cannot think of any other construal), it breaks down under analysis. If, as I am suggesting, partial adequacy would imply partial certainty, we need to reject the one along with the other.

Fortunately, the notion of partial adequacy is not needed to make sense of the adequacy of PCNs. We can, alternatively, view them as true *in form* and treat them as equivalent to adequate hypotheses. It is reasonable to suppose (on the basis of experience) that there are subsets of bodies with which the human body shares common and peculiar features. When we interact with such bodies, moreover, and conceive their properties in terms of shared features of our own bodies, we have partial ideas that are, in this case, equivalent to ideas of the whole. But this must be regarded as a reasonable supposition (not an apodictic verity), albeit one that can receive ongoing confirmation or disconfirmation through experience.[56] As we have seen, discrete species essences cannot be deduced a priori from

---

[56] Although the "problem of other minds" is not an issue that Spinoza takes up, I imagine that the same points that I have just made regarding ideas of other bodies pertain mutatis mutandis to ideas of other minds.

universal principles. Thus, when Spinoza announces his intention to "consider human actions and appetites just as if it were a Question of lines, planes, or bodies" (G 2:138) in the Preface to *Ethics* Part 3, we should take this to mean, among other things, that the analysis of human actions and appetites is no less adequate than geometrical analyses, but equally no less constructed.[57]

Admittedly, Spinoza does not build in any such qualifications when arguing for the adequacy of PCNs in E2p39. But we have already seen that elsewhere, too, he elides the distinction I have drawn between *true-in-form* ideas and *robustly true* ideas. Nevertheless, I hope to have shown already that the distinction has a clear basis in the difference between Spinoza's analysis of constructed geometrical truths, on the one hand, and the self-grounding idea of substance, on the other. Interpreting non-universal adequate ideas as true-in-form hypotheses also strikes the best compromise between the deductive, a priori orientation of Spinoza's scientific methodology and the need to rely on sensory experience for knowledge of anything particular, as I hope to have demonstrated in this chapter. I will have more to say about the role of hypotheses in Spinoza's approach to scientific knowledge in the next chapter, which will focus explicitly on geometry's place in Spinozan science.

---

[57] I acknowledge that in the same passage Spinoza also compares the way in which he will treat the affects with the way he treated God and the mind in the first two parts of the *Ethics*. According to what I just said about his analysis of the affects, it should follow that Spinoza's analysis of God is also constructed (i.e., true in form only). Bennett (1984, 20–3), notably, interpreted all of the *Ethics* as hypothetico-deductive. But this reading does not comport with the distinction I made between the robust truth of our idea of God and our true-in-form ideas of finite things. To reconcile my interpretation of Spinoza's "lines, planes, or bodies" comment with my interpretation of Spinoza's views on the truth of God as robust (not hypothetical), it must be the case that the "lines, planes, or bodies" comment has another connotation in relation to God than I have suggested it has in relation to the affects. The obvious candidate for an alternative connotation is Spinoza's geometrical method of beginning with definitions and axioms and deriving propositions therefrom. This certainly applies to Spinoza's treatment of God, while being neutral on the question of whether the axioms and definitions are stipulations or claim genuine correspondence with real objects. This qualification weakens my interpretation of the "lines, planes, or bodies" comment in relation to the affects, but I do not think it undermines it completely, since there is an independent basis for treating our knowledge of God as distinct from our knowledge of finite affairs.

References

Bennett, Jonathan. 1984. *A Study of Spinoza's* Ethics. Indianapolis, IN: Hackett.
Charles, Syliane. 2002. "Le salut par les affects: le rôle de la joie comme moteur du progrès éthique ches Spinoza." *Philosophiques* 29(1): 73–87.
Curley, Edwin. 1969. *Spinoza's Metaphysics: An Essay in Interpretation*. Cambridge, MA: Harvard University Press.
———. 1973. "Experience in Spinoza's Theory of Knowledge." In Spinoza: A Collection of Critical Essays, edited by Marjorie Grene, 25–59. Notre Dame, IN: University of Notre Dame Press.
Deleuze, Gilles. 1990. *Expressionism in Philosophy: Spinoza*. Trans. by Martin Joughin. New York: Zone Books.
Della Rocca, Michael. 2008. *Spinoza*. New York, NY: Routledge.
Fløistad, Guttorm. 1973. "Spinoza's Theory of Knowledge in the Ethics." In Spinoza: A Collection of Critical Essays, edited by Marjorie Grene, 101–127. Notre Dame, IN: University of Notre Dame Press.
Gabbey, Alan. 1996. "Spinoza's natural science and methodology." In The Cambridge Companion to Spinoza, edited by Don Garrett, 142–191. Cambridge, UK: Cambridge University Press.
Garber, Daniel. 2016. "Law of Nature and the Mathematics of Motion." In The Language of Nature: Reassessing the Mathematization of Nature in the Seventeenth Century, edited by Geoffrey Gorham et al., 134–59. Minneapolis, MN: University of Minnesota Press.
Garrett, Aaron V. 2003. *Meaning in Spinoza's Method*. Cambridge, UK: Cambridge University Press.
Gilead, Amihud. 2000. "The Indispensability of the First Kind of Knowledge." In Spinoza on Knowledge and the Human Mind, edited by Yirmiyahu Yovel and Gideon Segal, 209–222. Leiden: Brill.
Goldenbaum, Ursula. 2004. "The Affects as a Condition of Human Freedom in Spinoza's Ethics." In Spinoza on Reason and the 'Free Man,' edited by Yirmiyahu Yovel and Gideon Segal, 149–161. New York: Little Room Press.
Grey, John. 2013. "'Use Them at Our Pleasure': Spinoza on Animal Ethics." *History of Philosophy Quarterly* 30: 367–388.
Gueroult, Martial. 1974. *Spinoza II: L'Âme (Éthique, II)*. Paris: Aubier-Montaigne.
Hobbes, Thomas. 2005. *The English Works of Thomas Hobbes of Malmesbury*. Vol. 1. Translated by William Molesworth. London: John Bonn, 1839. Replica edition, Elbiron Classics.
James, Susan. 2011. "Creating Rational Understanding: Spinoza as a Social Epistemologist." *Proceedings of the Aristotelian Society Supplementary Volume* 85(1): 181–199.
Klever, W.N.A. 1986. "Axioms in Spinoza's Science and Philosophy of Science." *Studia Spinozana* 2: 171–95.

———. 1990. "Anti-Falsificationism: Spinoza's Theory of Experience and Experiments." In Spinoza: Issues and Directions. The Proceedings of the Chicago Spinoza Conference, edited by E. M. Curley and Pierre-François Moreua, 124–135. Leiden: E. J. Brill.
Lachterman, David R. 1978. "The Physics of Spinoza's Ethics." In Spinoza: New Perspectives, edited by Robert W. Shahan and J. I. Biro, 71–112. Norman: University of Oklahoma Press.
LeBuffe, Michael. 2009. "The Anatomy of the Passions." In A Cambridge Companion to Spinoza's Ethics, edited by Olli Koistinen, 188–222. New York, NY: Cambridge University Press.
———. 2018. *Spinoza on Reason*. New York, NY: Oxford University Press.
Marshall, Eugene. 2008. "Adequacy and Innateness in Spinoza." *Oxford Studies in Early Modern Philosophy* 4: 51–88.
Melamed, Yitzhak Y. 2013. *Spinoza's Metaphysics: Substance and Thought*. Oxford, UK: Oxford University Press.
Miller, Jon. 2003. "Spinoza and the Concept of a Law of Nature." History of Philosophy Quarterly 20: 257–76.
———. 2004. "Spinoza and the *a priori*." *Canadian Journal of Philosophy* 34(4): 555–590.
Parkinson, G.H.R. 1954. *Spinoza's Theory of Knowledge*. London: Oxford University Press.
———. 1973. "Language and Knowledge in Spinoza." In Spinoza: A Collection of Critical Essays, edited by Marjorie Grene, 73–100. Notre Dame, IN: University of Notre Dame Press.
Sabra, A. I. 1967. *Theories of Light: From Descartes to Newton*. New York, NY: American Elsevier Publishing Company, Inc.
Savan, David. 1986. "Spinoza: Scientist and Theorist." In Spinoza and the Sciences, edited by Marjorie Grene and Debra Nails, 95–123. Dordrecht: D. Reidel.
Schliesser, Eric. 2014. "Spinoza and the Philosophy of Science: Mathematics, Motion, and Being." In The Oxford Handbook of Spinoza, edited by Michael Della Rocca. DOI: https://doi.org/10.1093/oxfordhb/9780195335828.013.020.
Viljanen, Valtteri. 2011. *Spinoza's Geometry of Power*. Cambridge, UK: Cambridge University Press.
Wilson, Margaret D. 1996. "Spinoza's theory of knowledge." In *The Cambridge Companion to Spinoza*, edited by Don Garrett, 89–141. Cambridge, UK: Cambridge University Press.
———. 1999. "'For They Do Not Agree in Nature with Us': Spinoza on the Lower Animals." In *New Essays on the Rationalists*, edited by Rocco Gennaro and C. Huenemann, 336–52. Oxford, UK: Oxford University Press.
Yovel, Yirmiyahu. 1991. "The Infinite Mode and Natural Laws in Spinoza." In God and Nature: Spinoza's Metaphysics, edited by Yirmiyahu Yovel, 79–96. Leiden: E.J. Brill.

CHAPTER 5

Geometry and Spinozan Science

The prevailing arc of Spinozan science runs from common notions and general principles and laws applying to the whole of nature to less universal things and ultimately down to particulars. That imagination-based, a posteriori reasoning has a role to play both in providing a basis for knowledge of common notions and in directing the downward deduction of particulars does not spoil the overall a priori character of Spinozan science. This is important because, as I have said before, knowledge, in Spinoza, mirrors reality. Per Spinoza's doctrine of parallelism, the order of knowing is the same as the order of being. So, if, in the order of being, finite modes follow from infinite modes and attributes, our knowledge of finite modes should follow likewise from our knowledge of infinite modes and attributes.

We can see that this is borne out by the general structure of Spinozan science. The common notions are ideas of extension, motion and rest. Ideas of extension, of course, correspond to the attribute itself. Motion and rest is that in terms of which Spinoza defines the immediate infinite mode of extension. Thus, in having common notions, ideas of extension, motion and rest (and their laws), we have adequate ideas (since common notions can only be conceived adequately) of the attribute and the immediate infinite mode. The mediate infinite mode, which follows via the mediation of the immediate infinite mode, and thus only indirectly from

© The Author(s), under exclusive license to Springer Nature Switzerland AG 2021
M. Homan, *Spinoza's Epistemology through a Geometrical Lens*, https://doi.org/10.1007/978-3-030-76739-6_5

its attribute, encompasses all of the finite modes.[1] (Recall that Spinoza calls the mediate infinite mode of extension "the face of the whole universe.") Thus, in moving from common notions and general principles to less universal, and, ultimately, to particular things, we move from the attribute and the immediate infinite mode to the mediate infinite mode. In this way, Spinozan science reproduces the general structure of Spinozan reality.

Where do figures fit into this harmonious picture? If figures have a place in Spinozan reality, which, I argued in Chap. 3, they do, and if Spinozan science must mirror the contours of Spinozan reality, then geometry (understood as the science of lines, planes, and solids[2]) should feature in Spinozan science. It is the task of this chapter to follow up on this proposition. Now that we have sketched out the framework of Spinozan science, we are in a position to do so.

Figure, recall, is not a property of physical nature as a whole because an infinite thing can have no shape. This, I argued, makes sense of why Spinoza defines physical individuals in terms of motion and rest, which are properties of infinite extension, but not in terms of figure, which is a property only of finite physical individuals. Incidentally, this also makes sense of why figure is not listed by Spinoza as a common notion (at least, of the universal sort)—since figure is not a property of the whole, it cannot, of course, be equally in the part and in the whole, as common notions must be. This implies that geometry is not relevant to the elaboration of the most general principles and laws, governing the whole of physical nature.

---

[1] For further discussion in support of this reading of the infinite modes as encompassing the finite modes (such that the latter are the parts of the former), see Melamed 2013 130–32.

[2] Geometry was classically defined as the science of (continuous) magnitudes, but I think it is clear that this is insofar as magnitudes can be determined in various ways (e.g., as points, lines). Cf. Hobbes' statement of the subject matter of geometry in *De Corpore* (with his particular emphasis on motion):

> first we are to observe what effect a body moved produceth, when we consider nothing in it besides its motion; and we see presently that this makes a line, or length; next, what the motion of a long body produces, which we find to be superficies; and so forwards, till we see what the effects of simple motion are; and then, in like manner, we are to observe what proceeds from the addition, multiplication, subtraction, and division, of these motions, and what effects, what figures, and what properties, they produce; from which kind of contemplation sprung that part of philosophy which is called *geometry*. (Hobbes 2005, 71)

On the other hand, since figure *is* a property of all finite physical individuals, geometry should be relevant to knowledge of the latter, and thus we should expect it to figure in the descent, as it were, from common notions and general principles to less universal, particular things.

It must be admitted that given the very schematic level at which Spinoza lays out his thoughts on science and the sort of knowledge of finite bodies that it is capable of producing, he says nothing explicit regarding the significance of mathematics for scientific knowledge of finite bodies. Fortunately, there are certain texts in which Spinoza himself engages in geometrico-scientific analyses of finite bodies. I have in mind, in particular, Spinoza's epistolary writings on optics. These offer valuable insight into the place of geometry in Spinozan science.

5.1 Spinoza on the Geometry of Optical Lenses

Spinoza was well respected by contemporaries for his practical skills in grinding optical lenses. While his skills as a theoretician of optics were perhaps more modest, he took up theoretical questions nevertheless, in part, at least, in the service of his lens-grinding practice.[3] In Letter 36, for instance, Spinoza argues that convex-plane lenses have the advantage of a shorter focal length than convex-concave lenses. In making his case, Spinoza relies on equations formulated by his correspondent, Johannes Hudde, in the latter's optical text, *Specilla circularia*. In addition to basing his calculations on Hudde's optical theory, Spinoza defers to Hudde in judging the merits of his use of the theory, writing at the end of the letter, "But I have no doubt that you have already considered these things before, and made more accurate calculations, and finally settled the matter. So I ask your judgment and advice about this matter" (Ep. 36/G 4:187). Letter 36 shows Spinoza engaging a question of theoretical optics, but not from the standpoint of his own theoretical understanding. It is in this respect that Letters 39 and 40 offer more insight into Spinoza's own thinking, since there Spinoza appears to present his own understanding of

---

[3] See Petry 1985, 97. Petry describes Huygens' admiration for Spinoza's practical skills in optics and doubts about Spinoza's capacity to contribute to optical theory. Cf. Von Duuglas-Ittu (2008c), who questions Petry's evidence on this score. See also Vermij (2013, 66), whose assessment is more in line with Petry's.

a question of optics, even though, as I will contend, his remarks need to be interpreted in light of Hudde's treatise.[4]

In both Letters 39 and 40 to Jarig Jelles, Spinoza presents an argument on behalf of circular (or spherical) lenses.[5] The subject is raised in response to Descartes' explanation of the size of images formed at the base of the eye (in, I assume, the Seventh Discourse of Descartes' *Optics*[6]). Spinoza claims that Descartes does not consider any cause for the size of images formed at the back of the eye beside the point at which the rays coming from different points of the object initially cross each other and how far that point is from the base of the eye. The factor that Spinoza alleges that Descartes neglects is "the size of the angle the rays make when they cross each other on the surface of the eye" (Ep. 39/G 4:194b). Spinoza proceeds to opine that the reason Descartes neglected this factor is that "he did not know any means of collecting those rays, which proceed from different points into so many other points." I think Spinoza must be referring here to a point Descartes makes in the Fifth Discourse of his *Optics* regarding the imperfections of vision. Descartes writes:

> Whatever shape the parts of the eye have, it is impossible for them to cause the rays coming from different points to converge in as many other different points [at the back of the eye]; and that the best they can do is to make all those that come from some particular point such as from X [at the center of the object of vision] assemble at some other point such as S, in the middle of the back of the eye; in which case, only some of those from point V [at the edge of the object of vision] can assemble exactly at point R [...] and the others have to scatter all around a little [....] And this is the reason that this picture is never distinct at its edges as it is in the middle, as has been sufficiently noted by those who have written of Optics; for it is because of this that they have said that vision takes place principally along the straight line which passes through the centers of the crystalline humor and of the pupil [...] which they call the axis of vision. (DM, 96; see Fig. 5.1)

---

[4] On Hudde's influence on Spinoza's optical thought and practice, see Vermij (2013, 79–81).

[5] Von Duuglas-Ittu (2008b) provides an insightful, in-depth reading of these letters with which the points I make below are largely sympathetic. Especially helpful is his speculative reconstruction of the questions from Jelles—in letters now lost—that prompted Spinoza's responses, as well as his discussion of the contemporaneous optical writings on which Jelles and Spinoza probably drew.

[6] See DM, 117–19.

5 GEOMETRY AND SPINOZAN SCIENCE   127

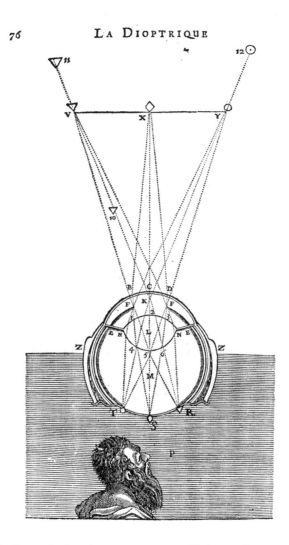

Fig. 5.1 The figure depicts the reconvergence of light rays from an object (V, X, Y) via refraction in the eye's cornea and lens (L), and the observation (by P) of the image thereby formed at the back of the eye (R, S, T) from within an enclosed chamber (Z). (*Discourse on Method for Rightly Directing One's Reason and Searching for Truth in the Sciences, Together with the Optics, Meteorology, and Geometry, Which Are Essays in This Method.* Leiden: Maire, 1637)

An ideal eye would refract light in such a way that rays coming from each point of the object converge again (after having spread out in traveling from the surface of the object to the surface of the eye) in a corresponding point at the back of the eye. In the passage just quoted, Descartes points out that regardless of the shape of the eye's lenses, it is impossible for the rays coming from different points on the object to be brought together in as many corresponding points at the back of the eye. This is because the more rays come from points farther from what Descartes calls the "axis of vision," the more they are scattered at the back of the eye around some point (as opposed to being focused in that point).[7]

Spinoza takes issue with Descartes' reasoning here. According to him, there is a shape uniquely suited to bring rays from different points of an object together in so many corresponding points at the back of the eye, namely, a circle. At whatever angle parallel rays hit a circular lens, they can be brought together at a single point on the other side of the circle. (See Fig. 5.2.) Spinoza's reasoning on behalf of this claim is characteristically pithy: "Because the circle is the same everywhere, it has the same properties everywhere" (Ep. 39/G 4:195b). (Spinoza thinks the assumption that the rays will be parallel from whichever angle they hit is justified in practice because "the opening of the Telescope is to be regarded as only like a point in relation to the distance" (Ep. 40/G 4:199b–200b).)

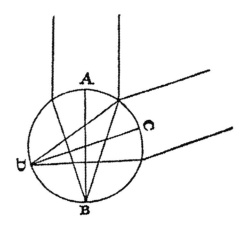

Fig. 5.2 The figure depicts Spinoza's contention that parallel rays entering a circular lens from any point are refracted so as to come together in a single point. (*Opera Posthuma.* J. Rieuwertsz, 1677, p. 532)

---

[7] For further analysis of Descartes' discussion of the imperfections of natural vision and means of enhancement in the *Optics*, see Ribe 1997.

Spinoza puts this point another way in Letter 40, explaining that in the case of a circular lens, "a line can be drawn from any point on the object which passes through the center of the circle" (Ep. 40/G 4:200b). He goes on to note: "What I say here about a Circle cannot be said about an Ellipse, or a Hyperbola, much less other more composite shapes, because one can only draw one line which passes through each focus from a single point on the object" (Ep. 40/G 4:200b–201b). Spinoza's remark here is once again directed against Descartes, who had argued for the superiority of hyperbolic and elliptical lens shapes in the Eighth Discourse of the *Optics*. The disagreement between Spinoza and Descartes on this score seems to come back to the question of whether there is, for most intents and purposes, a single "axis of vision" (per Descartes) or multiple axes of vision (per Spinoza). If there were only a single axis of vision, the fact that "one can only draw one line which passes through each focus from a single point on the object" in the case of a hyperbola and ellipse would not be a point against these shapes, and a point in favor of circles, as Spinoza takes it to be.

Alan Gabbey charges that Spinoza's reasoning on behalf of the circle in the letters to Jelles represents "an unaccountable blunder."[8] Gabbey's point seems to be that Spinoza fails to understand that the problem of spherical aberration undermines his claims on behalf of the circle. Spherical aberration is the phenomenon of increased refraction on the part of light rays that enter a spherical lens nearer to the edge of the lens (at a sharper angle). As a result of spherical aberration, it is not possible for all parallel rays entering a spherical lens to come together in a single focal point. It is for this reason that Descartes promoted hyperbolic and elliptical lens shapes in his *Optics* over spherical lens shapes.[9] According to Gabbey's critique, Spinoza is apparently oblivious to the problem of spherical aberration as well as the solutions to the problem that Descartes outlines prominently and at length in the *Optics* (and also in the second book of the *Geometry*). Spinoza clearly is well aware of Descartes' arguments for the ellipse and the hyperbola, however, since he references those shapes explicitly in both Letters 39 and 40. Obliviousness is off the table, then. This leaves the question of why Spinoza opts for the circle over the ellipse and hyperbola if he was aware of Descartes' arguments and the problem of spherical aberration. Did Spinoza simply fail to understand the nature of

---

[8] Gabbey 1996, 153.
[9] DM, 160–1.

the problem? Even if he was known more for his practical than for his theoretical optical skills, it would be surprising if this were the case. Fortunately, a more sympathetic interpretation of Spinoza's arguments on behalf of circular lenses is also more plausible.[10]

A clue to Spinoza's understanding of the issue is his parenthetical insertion in the following remark from Letter 40:

> since a limited segment of a circle can have the effect that (*mechanically speaking*) it brings together all the rays proceeding from one point into another point on its diameter, it will also bring together all the others which come from the other points on the object into as many other points. (Ep. 40/G 4:200b, emphasis added)

When Spinoza says that the circle has the effect of bringing together the rays from different points of an object into as many corresponding points *mechanically speaking*, he means that it does so *grosso modo*. This signification would be in line with the following terminological clarification that Descartes makes in the Second Book of his *Geometry*: "we understand by 'geometry' that which is precise and exact, and by 'mechanics' that which is not" (DM, 191). When Spinoza qualifies his claim about the circle with the phrase "mechanically speaking," he means to convey his recognition that his claim does not meet the standards of mathematical precision. Further evidence that this was Spinoza's intention comes from the optical treatise by Hudde that Spinoza references in Letter 36.

Hudde's *Specilla circularia* was published in 1656, subsequently lost, and rediscovered only relatively recently. Rienk Vermij and Eisso Atzema, who rediscovered it, translate the full title as follows: "Circular lenses, or how one can construct all kinds of optical instruments by circular figures only, both microscopes and telescopes, so that they produce the same effect as elliptical or hyperbolic figures, or at least come as close as possible."[11] In the *Specilla circularia*, Hudde takes up the problem of determining the lens shape best suited for bringing together parallel rays of light into a single point. He does not take issue with Descartes' arguments for the hyperbola and ellipse from a mathematical perspective, but explains that these shapes are too difficult to produce in practice, and

---

[10] Von Duuglas-Ittu (2008a) also rejects Gabbey's interpretation.
[11] Vermij and Atzema 1995, 106.

argues for the practical superiority of spherical lens shapes.[12] In laying out his case, Hudde says that the point into which parallel rays must be gathered can be considered either mathematically or mechanically. While admitting that a circle cannot bring together rays into a mathematical point, he argues that the circle can achieve a mechanical point, which he defines as one that is not mechanically divisible or one whose parts are not worth considering.[13]

Since we know from Letter 36 that Spinoza made a careful study of Hudde's text, there can be little doubt that Spinoza's arguments on behalf of the circle in Letters 39 and 40, which were composed just a few months after the letter to Hudde, should be interpreted in light of the *Specilla circularia*. Thus, when Spinoza argues for the circle in Letters 39 and 40, he does so from a "mechanical" perspective, fully aware both of Descartes' mathematical arguments and of the practical constraints confronting the working lens grinder. Spinoza indeed invokes the notion of a "mechanical point" himself in correspondence with Leibniz, defining it as a "small space" (Ep. 46A/G 4:232b).

Although my aim is not to vindicate Spinoza's arguments on behalf of circular lenses, but to advance an interpretation of Spinoza's epistemology, the foregoing analysis of Spinoza's optical writings affords valuable insights into his view of the relationship between geometry and science, and between geometrical figures and finite bodies—both of which are of central importance for understanding Spinoza's epistemology. In the first place, the epistolary optical writings confirm that geometry does indeed have a place in Spinozan scientific investigation of the nature and properties of natural bodies. Even if the focus is on the construction of artificial lenses, both Descartes' *Optics* and Spinoza's letters make clear that the study of optics is just as significant for understanding the nature and

---

[12] See Vermij and Atzema 1995, 113.

[13] See Vermij and Atzema 1995, 113–14. The relevant section of Hudde's text reads, "The crucial thing is that we cause the preponderance of parallel rays to be refracted by the glass through which they pass in such a way that they tend afterward to one and the same point. But this point can be considered either mathematically or mechanically [*aut mathematice aut mechanice*]. And although it is certain that circular figures have neither the power nor property (as do elliptical or hyperbolic figures and many others more composite) to refract parallel rays in such a way that afterward they tend to one mathematical point, nonetheless a preponderance of them can be turned toward the same place, such that that space in which they all converge can be considered a mechanical point. Now, I call a point mechanical either when it is not divisible in mechanical terms or when its parts are not worth consideration" (my translation).

properties of natural eyes as it is for the design and production of artificial lenses.[14] While it might seem obvious that geometry would have a place in Spinozan science, Spinoza never says as much explicitly to my knowledge in any of his philosophical works. Moreover, as we have seen, the remarks that he does make about mathematics and mathematical entities serve as much to cast doubt on the relevance of mathematics to natural knowledge as they do to support it. As a result, some have doubted that mathematics even applies to uncovering Spinozan reality.[15] In this light, then, Spinoza's optical letters provide welcome confirmation of geometry's application.

Perhaps more importantly, the letters shed light on *how* geometry can be used to illuminate the nature and properties of natural bodies. First, they reveal how geometry can be useful in examining natural bodies even though geometrical figures (conceived *per se*) have the status of beings of reason. As the distinction discussed above between mathematics and mechanics demonstrates, the fact that a natural body does not display the properties of ideal geometrical notions with mathematical exactness is no obstacle to understanding the body in terms of the geometrical notion nevertheless. Despite the fact that a mathematical point is a being of reason, Spinoza embraces the mechanical correlate of a mathematical point in describing the properties of circular lenses. Similarly, even if no object in nature is perfectly circular, and the notion of a perfect circle is a being of reason, he deploys the notion of circularity to explain and predict the properties of natural bodies, nevertheless.

As Spinoza notes in his letter to Leibniz, even if no lens of any shape is able to bring rays together into a mathematical point, the rays come together nevertheless "in a small space (which we usually call a mechanical point), which is larger or smaller" (Ep. 46A/G 4:232b). That is to say, the fact that mathematical points are beings of reason does not mean that natural bodies do not have, more or less, the nature of points. Similarly, even if no natural body is perfectly circular, every natural body is more or

---

[14] See also CSM 1: 288: "I do not recognize any difference between artefacts and natural bodies except that the operations of artefacts are for the most part performed by mechanisms which are large enough to be easily perceivable by the senses...so it is no less natural for a clock constructed with this or that set of wheels to tell the time than it is for a tree which grew from this or that seed to produce the appropriate fruit." I am grateful to John Grey for pointing me to this passage. It is well known that Spinoza goes even further than Descartes in subsuming everything under the same laws of nature, inasmuch as he includes therein the workings of the human mind (E3pref).

[15] See n. 32 in Chap. 1.

less circular, and the extent to which it is more or less circular has a bearing on its properties. In the case of the eye, for instance, Spinoza writes, "although the eye itself is not so precisely constructed that all the rays coming from the different points of the object meet in exactly as many other points in the back of the eye, nevertheless, it is certain that those shapes which can produce this result are to be preferred to all others" (Ep. 40/G 4:200b). The properties of the eye can be understood in light of the optical properties of circles, even if the eye is not itself perfectly circular. It is the extent to which it is *not* circular that explains why the lens fails to bring together rays from different points into as many other different points at the back of the eye.

Second, the optical letters provide a rare example of Spinozan science in action. In the last chapter, I provided an overview of Spinoza's philosophy of science, in particular, his views regarding scientific method. We can now glimpse how (and the extent to which) that method works in practice. For the sake of analysis, I will regard Spinoza's reasoning as having two parts, and consider each in turn: (1) the framing of the question and (2) the answer to the question.

The question that Spinoza is addressing in Letters 39 and 40, as we have seen, is the optimal lens shape for bringing together parallel light rays coming from different points of an object (at different angles) into as many other different points via its refractive properties. The framing of this question rests on a few notable assumptions. First and foremost, the motivation of the question stems from the assumption that vision depends upon the reconvergence of light rays from the different points of the object of vision in the eye. While there is no doubt that Spinoza accepted this premise (even if it is not explicitly stated in his exchange with Jelles), it is unclear on what basis he would have accepted it. The prospect that this could be known a priori seems doubtful (especially since, as Descartes argues, vision itself does not require any resemblance between what stimulates a perception and the object of the perception[16]). A more likely basis is the experimental evidence that Descartes lays out in the Fifth Discourse of his *Optics*, namely, the inverted images formed in pinhole cameras and similar phenomena that can be produced in the detached eye of a large mammal.[17] As a student of Descartes, it is likely that Spinoza accepted this evidence (or evidence like it) as the basis for his assumption regarding the

[16] DM, 87–91.
[17] See DM, 91.

nature of vision.[18] Even more basic assumptions guiding Spinoza's inquiry into optimal lens shape include the law of refraction and the most general laws of motion governing the movement of light (when it is treated like a body). These assumptions are themselves based partially on experiential evidence of the behavior of light.

So the initial framing of the question and the settling of guiding assumptions and principles depends on evidence from experience and experiment. But the experiential information is not passively gathered, and the inferences are not externally determined. The investigative and experimental enterprise is conducted in relation to the most general laws and principles, such as the laws governing bodily motion. It is not clear-cut whether the questions were prompted by certain experiences (such as the experience of contradictions in one's externally determined opinions, as discussed in the last chapter), or the experiences were induced experimentally for the sake of answering questions (thus generating a kind of chicken and egg problematic). Even if we distinguished between a first and second stage of the scientific method in the last chapter—the compilation of the history and the determination of general principles, respectively—in practice, the method is not beholden to strict rules of order. Hence, it is preferable to speak of an *interplay* between experiential evidence and the formulation of general principles, so long as it is understood that the interplay is not haphazard. In order to count as Spinozan *science*, the interplay between experiential evidence and general principles must be internally, not externally, determined. This means that it must be guided by an a prioristic conception of what counts as understanding, where *a priori* reasoning has its original meaning of proceeding from an understanding of causes to a derivation of effects, rather than vice versa.[19] In considering the framing of Spinoza's question concerning the optimal shape of lenses, then, we see the contours of the first two stages of Spinozan science outlined in the previous chapter, though it is their reason-guided interaction that stands out in practice.

Turning now to Spinoza's answer to the question concerning optimal lens shape, we know his view that a circle (or sphere) is best for reconverging parallel rays coming from different points of an object (at different

---

[18] For further discussion of Descartes' account of vision in the *Optics*, see Osler 2008, 134–36.

[19] For discussion of the history of the term "a priori" and Spinoza's usage of it therein, see Miller 2004, 556–66.

angles). We have also seen that his reasoning on behalf of the circle is consistent: it is because the circle is uniquely "the same everywhere" and thus has "the same properties everywhere" (specifically, all points can be regarded as lying on the optical axis). Of course, it seems likely that his focus on the circle was guided by his own experience with lenses of different shapes (not to mention practical considerations regarding the ease of grinding certain lens shapes compared with others). Descartes writes in the *Optics* of the "infinity of shapes" (DM, 117) that could be devised to solve a given optical problem, thus underscoring that some reliance on experience is unavoidable.

But even if that is the case, haphazard experiences with sundry lens shapes would not have satisfied Spinoza. As we saw in the last chapter, he regards the deliverances of sensory experience as inadequate. And even if some aspects of experience, in particular, extension and motion, are "equally in the part and in the whole," and thus can only be conceived adequately, this is certainly not the case for the shapes of finite bodies. Even if all finite bodies must have one shape or another, there is no particular shape that is equally in the part and in the whole of all finite bodies. For this reason, any perception we have of the particular shape of some external body reflects the nature of our own body as much as the nature of the external body and thus is inadequate.

Hence, any adequate account of optimal lens shape must be aprioristic, and Spinoza's a priori reasoning on behalf of the circle is precisely what we should expect. On the other hand, since Spinoza is making a claim about finite external bodies, and since the claim cannot be known by us with necessity a priori, it must be understood to be hypothetical. As a hypothesis, the claim that circular lenses are best suited to converge parallel rays is subject to empirical confirmation and falsification. Although Spinoza is not explicit on this point, we might regard his concession regarding the circular lens's inability to achieve reconvergence of points with mathematical precision as being based on experience. At any rate, Spinoza appears open to the possibility that lens shapes other than the circle could turn out to be superior in his epistolary exchange with Leibniz, even if he also harbors his doubts.[20]

In Spinoza's answer to the question of optimal lens shape, then, we see, again, an interplay between experiential evidence and

---

[20] I have in mind Spinoza's offer to "suspend judgment" until Leibniz has had a chance to explain further his own arguments in favor of a lens shape other than the circle (G 4:233b).

hypothetico-deductive reasoning that is guided, ultimately, by reason (and, thus, internally determined). This fits with what I said in the last chapter about the third stage of Spinoza's scientific method. While this stage is predominantly a priori, consisting in the downward deduction of less universal and particular things from general principles, the downward deduction must nevertheless be guided by reliance on experiential evidence (due to the plethora of things deducible *a priori* from general principles).

Overall, the optical letters provide a valuable example of Spinozan science in practice that both accords well with the account of Spinozan scientific methodology outlined in the last chapter and shows how geometry fits seamlessly into that method. To recap, since geometrical figures are genuine (i.e., mind-independent) properties of finite bodies, understanding such properties is an important component of the science of finite bodies. Unlike common notions, however, geometrical figures are not equally in the part and in the whole, so imaginative conceptions of bodily shapes derived from the senses will always remain inadequate. In face of this, I argued that Spinoza can make recourse to hypothetical intellectual conceptions. So, for instance, even if my sensory experience of the eye suggests that it is roughly spherical, I do not truly understand the eye's sphericity unless I have an intellectual conception of sphericity in terms of which I can understand the nature and properties of the eye. This intellectual conception is hypothetical, but as a hypothesis, it can receive confirmation or falsification in light of experience and remains revisable in light of further evidence. Because geometrical figures can be conceived clearly and distinctly, exhibiting what, in Chap. 2, I spoke of as the *form* of truth, they make ideal hypothetical categories for understanding the nature and properties of finite bodies.

5.2 Response to an(other) Objection from Letter 12

Perhaps the text most frequently cited by antirealist interpreters of mathematical entities in Spinoza is Letter 12 (and a nearly identical passage in E1p15s[21]), where Spinoza criticizes certain imaginative conceptions of quantity. I touched on some aspects of this critique back in Chap. 3, but I now want to examine a couple of key passages more closely. Here they are:

[21] G 2:59.

But if you ask why we are so inclined, by a natural impulse, to divide extended substance, I reply that we conceive quantity in two ways: either abstractly, or superficially, as we have it in the imagination with the aid of the senses; or as substance, which is done by the intellect alone. So if we attend to quantity as it is in the imagination, which is what we do most often and easily, we find it to be divisible, finite, composed of parts, and one of many. But if we attend to it as it is in the intellect, and perceive the thing as it is in itself, which is very difficult, then we find it to be infinite, indivisible and unique, as I have already demonstrated sufficiently to you before now. (Ep. 12/G 4:56)

And if the Modes of Substance themselves are confused with Beings of reason of this kind, or aids of the imagination, they too can never be rightly understood. For when we do this, we separate them from Substance, and from the way they flow from eternity, without which, however, they cannot be rightly understood. (Ep. 12/G 4:57–58)

When Spinoza speaks of "Beings of reason of this kind, or aids of the imagination" in the second passage, he seems clearly to be referring to the trio of particular ways of conceiving of quantity, namely, time, measure, and number, that he singles out in the lines (here omitted) between the two passages just quoted. It will be recalled that I discussed this trio in Chap. 3, casting doubt on the idea, maintained by some antirealists, that Spinoza's critique of measure encompasses geometrical figures. Nevertheless, in light of the first passage quoted above, it is possible to interpret Spinoza as mounting a more general campaign against imaginative conceptions of extension in Letter 12, which encompasses not only measures of quantity but also quantity measured, which is to say, quantity that is finite, determinate, and figural.[22] In this case, we do not separate modes from substance and the way they flow from eternity *only* in measuring quantity (in terms of units of measure); we do so as well insofar as we conceive them as finite and figural at all. The latter way of conceiving modes is abstract, superficial, and inadequate, and must not feature in an adequate conception of reality. Much of what I said in Chap. 3 in response to antirealist arguments about figure is relevant to this line of objection, but I want to revisit it now, having presented my interpretation of Spinozan science, and the place of figural conceptions of modes therein. In particular, I want to show that figural conceptions of bodies do not necessarily imply

[22] See Peterman 2015, 6–7.

the separation of modes from substance (and of the way they flow from eternity).

The first thing to note in responding to this line of criticism against the reality of figure is that it is not a criticism of conceptions of quantity as finite *simpliciter*. If it were, then this would make it impossible to adequately conceive finite modes of extended substance, or, in other words, finite bodies, in any way. But this is certainly not what Spinoza means (lest we embrace acosmism). A better appreciation for the context of Spinoza's criticism of imaginative conceptions of quantity in Letter 12 helps to bring his intentions into focus. The target in both texts is anyone who attempts to argue that extended substance cannot be infinite, because extended substance is composed of parts, and nothing composed of parts can be infinite.[23] In this vein, Spinoza remarks in Letter 12, "they talk utter nonsense, not to say madness, who hold that Extended Substance is put together of parts, or bodies, really distinct from one another" (Ep. 12/G 4:55). He then goes on to explain why this is such a common mistake to make, and that is when he introduces the distinction between intellectual and imaginative conceptions of quantity. So, the butt of his criticism there is not conceptions of quantity as finite, but rather conceptions of quantity as consisting of real parts. To conceive quantity as having real parts is to conceive it—whether temporal quantity or spatial quantity—as composed of indivisible, or atomistic, parts.[24]

For Spinoza, to conceive quantity as consisting of such real parts is to mistake modes of substance for substance itself. As he says in E1p15s, "parts are distinguished in it [i.e., matter] only insofar as we conceive matter to be affected in different ways, so that its parts are distinguished only modally, but not really" (G 2:59). As he explains in the last paragraph of the extended passage from Letter 12 quoted above, moreover, we make

---

[23] On the question of the identity of Spinoza's targets in these texts, Wolfson writes, "It is safe to say that whomsoever in particular and directly Spinoza may have had in mind when assailing his opponents for denying the infinity of corporeal substance, it is ultimately the views and arguments advanced by Aristotle that he is contending with" (1934, 265).

[24] Cf. Spinoza's critique of Zeno in the DPP:

> He supposes, first, that bodies can be conceived to move so quickly that they cannot move more quickly, and second, that time is composed of moments, *just as others have conceived that quantity is composed of indivisible points.*
>
> Both assumptions are false. (DPP2p8s, emphasis added)

the mistake of affirming real (i.e., substantial) distinctions among the parts of substance when we confuse modes of substance with beings of reason and when "we separate them [i.e., the modes of substance] from Substance, and from the way they flow from eternity." These texts suggest that modes of substance, including finite modes of substance, are not a problem per se, so long as we avoid confusing them with beings of reason (such as the units of measure considered before), and separating them from substance and from the way they flow from eternity.

There are a few ways in which we can provide satisfaction that in conceiving extended modes as finite and figural we do not run afoul of these provisos. First, we can simply offer assurance that in conceiving something, say, a soap bubble, as finite (and figural), we are not conceiving it as a substance, but as a *mode* of substance. But how do we make good on this assurance? What is the difference between conceiving a soap bubble as a substance in its own right, on the one hand, and conceiving it as a mode of substance, on the other? For one thing, we can insist that we will not draw the inferences from our conception of the soap bubble to which Spinoza demurs. That is, we will not cite the existence of the soap bubble, or any of its material constituents, as evidence that extended substance cannot be infinite.

Another point is suggested by Spinoza's example of two ways of conceiving of water in E1p15s:

> we conceive that water is divided and its parts separated from one another—insofar as it is water, but not insofar as it is corporeal substance. For insofar as it is substance, it is neither separated nor divided. Again, water, insofar as it is water, is generated and corrupted, but insofar as it is substance, it is neither generated nor corrupted. (G 2:60)

This passage can be read to suggest an inherent ephemerality in finite modes, which must always undergo generation and corruption. Spinoza's example of water is particularly well suited to illustrate this point. We might think of modes on the model of eddies, currents, or waves, which have a fleeting reality as particular aspects of the water qua water, changing as the water qua water, like substance, remains the same. (Alternatively, we can think of Bennett's thaw moving across a countryside.[25]) I think the

---

[25] Bennett 1984, 89. See also, more generally, the "field metaphysic" interpretation that Bennett gives of substance and its modes (1984, 88–106). Bennett's field metaphysic inter-

same point can be extended to the figural properties of finite bodies. No object is permanently one shape or another. No object is perfectly one shape or another. As argued earlier in this chapter, figures are best viewed as ideal states with respect to which a given body more or less closely approximates. Bodies are more or less spherical, for instance, without being perfectly spherical. Hence, figures conceived as geometrical ideals can be used as hypotheses, but remain hypothetical. This use of figures respects the modal status of finite bodies and the distinction between beings of reason and modes of substance. So, by treating figures as ideals with respect to which finite bodies can approximate more or less, and as hypothetical categories, we avoid confusing modes of substance with beings of reason.

I have discussed how to avoid confusing finite modes with beings of reason, but what about ensuring that we do not "separate them from Substance, and from the way they flow from eternity, without which, however, they cannot be rightly understood"? What does it mean to understand finite modes in relation to (not separation from) substance and the

---

pretation of extension has proven controversial insofar as it attributes (divisible) spatial extent or dimensionality to God qua extended substance. One problematic implication of this view is that by analogy with God's having spatial extent (qua extended), he also has temporal extent (Bennett 1984, 206). Schmaltz criticizes Bennett on this score, drawing a contrapositive lesson from the space-time analogy: since God does *not* have temporal extent (but is eternal), God also does not have spatial extent (Schmaltz 1999, 199). I agree with Schmaltz that God is eternal, but I do not follow him in concluding that God is extended only in an eminent (not formal) sense (Schmaltz 1999, 188). Schmaltz's main motivation for considering God to be extended only eminently appears to be his concern that viewing God as actually (or formally) extended (i.e., as having "spatial extent") would make God divisible, but God qua substance is not divisible. Schmaltz's arguments raise metaphysical issues that it is not possible to delve into here. (I touch on some of these issues in the next chapter, though only cursorily.) I will just say that what is most important in my view is Spinoza's distinction between intellectual and imaginative conceptions of substance qua extended. When we conceive extended substance using the imagination (i.e., *inadequately*), we conceive it as divisible, having parts, enduring, and so on. When we conceive it, by contrast, via the intellect (i.e., *adequately*), we conceive it as indivisible, eternal, and so on, *but also as extended*. In this light, I agree with Bennett's reading that God is spatially extended and with Schmaltz's point that God is eternal (not enduring). This suggests perhaps that the space-time analogy breaks down on an intellectual view. I will return to the eternity/duration distinction in the next chapter.

way they flow from eternity? Do finite bodies still have figural determinations conceived in that manner?[26]

The above analysis of geometry and Spinozan science provides an outline for answers to these questions. While Spinoza's talk in Letter 12 of the way modes of substance "flow from eternity" is rather Delphic, it is reminiscent of TIE 101 where he speaks of "fixed and eternal things, and at the same time the laws inscribed in these things, as in their true codes, according to which all singular things come to be, and are ordered" (TIE 101/G 2:37). Some commentators have connected the "fixed and eternal things" from this passage with the "common notions" of the *Ethics* and TTP.[27] The language of "laws" and the way singular things are "ordered" seems further to suggest a connection to scientific foundations and what follows therefrom. If this is right, and if invoking TIE 101 in this context is apt, then the interpretation developed above of Spinoza's scientific method may serve to illuminate Spinoza's talk in Letter 12 of the way modes of substance flow from eternity. I argued that Spinoza envisions the deduction of subordinate laws and singular things from the common notions. I used the deduction of optical laws from general laws of bodily motion as an example of this kind of procedure and cited some of Spinoza's letters on optics as evidence that Spinoza thought that the properties and nature of lenses of various shapes (including in the eye) could be ascertained in this way. If it is acceptable to associate the deduction from common notions of less general laws and particular things with Spinoza's obscure notion of relating the modes of substance to the way they flow from eternity in Letter 12, then his criticisms of imaginative conceptions of quantity in Letter 12 do not in fact raise problems for my interpretation that cannot be addressed by pointing to what I have already laid out.

It might be objected further, however, that this association is not acceptable on the grounds that in Letter 12 Spinoza is critical not of

---

[26] Cf. Melamed 2000, 15: "For when we prove a certain mathematical property of a body, we are completely uninterested in the way this body 'flows from eternity,' or even whether a body, which has such proportions, is instantiated in the extended world at all" (2000, 15). Here Melamed appears to invoke the Aristotelian notion that mathematicians study natural mathematical properties, but not *qua* naturally instantiated. In other words, mathematicians study objects abstracted from material instantiation (and the way bodies flow from eternity). Granting this to be the case, it still does not preclude the subsequent application of mathematical conclusions to the properties of natural bodies, at which stage instantiation would be of interest.

[27] Wilson 1996, 115.

separating finite modes from common notions, but of separating modes from substance. Insofar as the foregoing interpretation manages to relate knowledge of finite modes to common notions, but not to substance, it fails to meet the objection. To relate the knowledge of finite modes to common notions *is*, however, to relate finite modes to substance. After all, the common notions we have discussed are ideas of extension, motion and rest. Extension is, of course, an attribute of substance. Motion and rest are cited by Spinoza in Letter 64 as infinite modes which follow immediately from the absolute nature of the attribute of extension. Thus, in relating the knowledge of finite modes to the common notions, we are indeed relating finite modes to substance, as well as to the infinite modes which follow immediately from substance. Spinoza's worry in Letter 12 is about regarding extension as exclusively finite and divisible, while ignoring (or actively gainsaying) its infinity and the relation of the modes of extension to the infinite attribute. As should now be clear, the foregoing interpretation of Spinozan science does not consider extended substance only insofar as it is finite and divisible (i.e., in abstraction from substance). In deducing the natures of finite extended things from the common notions, Spinozan science as I have interpreted it consists precisely in relating the knowledge of finite things to the infinite attribute and the infinite modes from which they follow. Thus, my interpretation survives the doubts raised by Spinoza's criticisms of the imaginative conception of extension in Letter 12, and the reality of finite bodies with figural determinations survives along with it.[28]

5.2.1 *The Commensurability Response*

To this point I have responded to the criticism of a figural conception of finite bodies on the basis of Letter 12 by arguing that a fully contextualized interpretation of the criticism to which Spinoza is giving voice in these passages is actually consistent with a figural conception of finite bodies, so long as in conceiving finite bodies as figural (or otherwise), they are not confused with beings of reason or separated from substance. Before bringing this discussion of Spinoza's critique of imaginative conceptions of quantity in Letter 12 to a close, I want to add a distinct line of response. Let me begin with a counterfactual.

---

[28] For a discussion of how Spinozan mechanistic science can be reconciled with Letter 12 with which I am generally sympathetic, see Lecrivain 1986, 20–23.

Suppose that Spinoza's critique of imaginative conceptions of quantity does encompass figural conceptions of finite body. When we conceive finite bodies as figural, that is, we do precisely what Letter 12 prohibits, namely, we confuse them with beings of reason and separate them from substance. So, to conceive finite bodies properly we would have to conceive them in some way other than in terms of figural determinations. It is a mystery, however, what this would mean. I find it difficult to make any sense of the notion of finite body without figural determinations of one sort or another. But let us suppose that my problem stems from an overactive imagination (in Spinoza's sense of imagination—in the usual sense, my problem might be underactivity). It is only the imagination that conceives bodies as figural. By contrast, it is only by means of the intellect that finite bodies are viewed properly—*sans* figural determinations—in connection with substance and as they flow from eternity.

Even if it were possible to make sense of an intellectual conception of finite bodies that did not involve figural determinations, the result would be a sharp disconnect between intellectual and imaginative conceptions of finite bodies at odds with the interplay between reason and imagination that I have argued is at the core of Spinozan scientific method. In the previous chapter, the imagination was seen to play an indispensable role in Spinozan science. In particular, it is responsible for providing the raw data from which common notions and general laws are formulated, and it is also essential to guiding the downward process of deduction from common notions and general laws to particular things. For the interplay between imagination and reason (or the intellect) to be possible, imaginative conceptions must be translatable into intellectual conceptions and vice versa. Imaginative and intellectual conceptions must be, in other words, commensurable, at least to some extent. (This, in a nutshell, is what I am calling the "commensurability response" to the objection from Letter 12 against realism about figures.) Even if my imaginative conception of extension, for instance, is inadequate, it must share *something* in common with an adequate intellectual conception of extension qua common notion, otherwise it could not provide the basis for the apprehension of the adequate conception, as Spinoza seems in TTP 7 to suggest that it does. Likewise, if my imaginative conception of bodily shape is to play a role in testing the empirical applicability of my hypothetical, intellectual conception of shape, as, I argued, it needs to, then, once again, it must have *something* in common with the intellectual conception of shape.

Needless to say, my imaginative conception of bodies involves a number of sensible qualities that drop out in an intellectual conception, including color, texture, heat, and so on. But figure, surely, cannot be among these. For one thing, we already know that we can have intellectual conceptions of figures, since Spinoza uses geometrical figures as examples *par excellence* of adequate ideas in the TIE. So, figure, along with extension and motion, is among the properties that imaginative and intellectual conceptions of bodies have in common. If they did *not* have this in common, per the counterfactual raised above, Spinozan science would not be able to work in the way I have argued it does. Hence, the counterfactual scenario in which only improper, imaginative conceptions of body of the sort Spinoza is targeting in Letter 12 are figural, and proper, intellectual conceptions of body are somehow non-figural, must be rejected for being at odds with basic features of Spinozan scientific method (not to mention mystifying).[29]

5.3 Letters 80–83 and the Incompleteness of Spinozan Science

A second potential line of objection to the geometry-oriented interpretation of Spinozan science and knowledge I am advancing here is suggested by an epistolary exchange between Spinoza and Tschirnhaus that took place in the last year of Spinoza's life on the topic of the fundamental nature of the physical world and what can be deduced therefrom. One pillar of my argument for the reality of figure as a determination of finite bodies and the consequent relevance of geometry to Spinozan science has been an interpretation of the workings of Spinozan science, based, in part, on the evidence provided by examples of Spinozan science in action, in particular, optical examples. The portrait of Spinozan science that I have sketched as friendly to geometry is Cartesian in significant respects. Indeed, given Descartes' overt commitment to the mathematization thesis, stressing the Cartesian nature of Spinozan science has served to advance my interpretation of Spinoza as similarly committed to his own version of mathematized nature. Two things emerge in Spinoza's exchange

---

[29] My claim that intellectual conceptions of bodies are figural raises a question about the relation between conceiving the figural properties of a body and conceiving a body's essence. This is a difficult question that I take up at the end of the next chapter.

with Tschirnhaus in Letters 80–83 that call into question my rapprochement of Spinozan with Cartesian science.

First, Spinoza lambastes the principles of Descartes' natural philosophy as "useless, not to say absurd" (Ep. 81/G 4:332), suggesting that perhaps there is much less in common between Spinoza and Descartes on matters scientific than I have made out. This is potentially damaging to my argument, since if Spinozan science is unlike Cartesian science on fundamentals, then perhaps Spinoza and Descartes also diverge on the question of mathematization. Second, Spinoza makes it clear in Letter 83 that while he disagrees with Descartes on certain fundamental questions of natural philosophy, he has "not been able to set out anything concerning them in an orderly way" (Ep. 83/G 4:334). This creates a different problem for my interpretation. If Spinoza hasn't fully worked out his own views on fundamental aspects of natural philosophy, then how am I justified in using Spinozan science to support an interpretation of Spinoza's ontology and epistemology?

Let me start with the first issue—Spinoza's rejection of fundamental aspects of Descartes' natural philosophy. What precisely does Spinoza object to? In both Letters 81 and 83, Spinoza's target is Descartes' conception of matter in terms of extension. In Letter 83, he states, "Descartes defines matter badly by Extension" (Ep. 83/G 4:334), and in Letter 81, he makes clear what he understands by Descartes' definition of extension, namely, "a mass at rest" (*moles quiescens*) (Ep. 81/G 4:332). What is Spinoza's problem with Descartes' understanding of extension as a mass at rest? On the surface, his stated problem is that "it is not only difficult to demonstrate the existence of bodies, as you say, but completely impossible" (Ep. 81/G 4:332). Tschirnhaus had asked Spinoza in Letter 80 "how the existence of bodies, which have motion and shapes, is demonstrated *a priori*. For in Extension, considering the thing absolutely, no such thing occurs" (Ep. 80/G 4:331). Since Tschirnhaus seems to be asking about Spinoza's understanding of extension and how the existence of bodies might be derived therefrom, not Descartes', Spinoza's criticism of Descartes' notion of extension in response to Tschirnhaus' question reads like something of a non sequitur, if not an outright red herring. Presumably, Spinoza intends to make it clear that Tschirnhaus would be right to doubt that the existence of bodies could be demonstrated a priori from extension, *if* extension were understood as Descartes understands it. The implication, of course, is that Spinoza does not understand extension in the way Descartes does, but in such a way that the existence of bodies *can* be derived a priori. This implication remains tacit until it is made explicit by Spinoza in Letter 83.

This cannot be all there is to Spinoza's objection to Descartes' principles of natural philosophy, however, since Descartes is well aware that the existence of bodies cannot be derived a priori from extension on its own, but requires to be set in motion by God. It is unclear why Spinoza leaves out of his discussion of Descartes' theory of the derivation of diversity from extension the famous element of God's original jolt, and Tschirnhaus seems perplexed by this omission himself. Tschirnhaus politely corrects Spinoza on this point in his next letter, and attempts, once again, to elicit a response regarding Spinoza's own explanation (not Descartes') of how the existence of bodies can be derived a priori from extension. Whatever the explanation might be for Spinoza's curiously truncated depiction of Descartes' first physical principles, a more complete account of Spinoza's objection to Descartes' principles would seem to need to extend to the fact that, for Descartes, the diversity-inducing motion of matter requires an *external* cause and the fact that God is this external cause underscores the fact that Descartes' God is external to the physical world. By contrast, what is perhaps the most fundamental aspect of Spinoza's philosophy is the fact that God does not transcend the world of things, but relates to the latter rather as an *immanent* cause. Extension is not properly viewed, then, as something that God produced and then subsequently needed to set in motion, but rather, as Spinoza goes on to clarify in Letter 83, "an attribute which expresses eternal and infinite essence" (Ep. 83/G 4:334), that is, an attribute of God.[30]

---

[30] A number of commentators have interpreted Spinoza's criticism of Cartesian extension in Letters 81 and 83, as I have done, as a criticism of its intrinsic inertness, and the attendant need to invoke an external (transcendent) cause to bring about motion (and, thus, individuation). See, for instance, Lachterman 1978, 101–3; Klever 1988, 165–71; and Viljanen 2011, 76. Peterman (2012) argues that Spinoza's objection to Cartesian extension is more fundamental than the common reading would have it, applying even on the assumption that motion is imposed by God. Leibniz argues in *De Ispa Natura* (1989, 505) that (extrinsic) motion is unable to bring about the individuation of a uniform plenum (as he understands Cartesian extension to be), on the grounds that if there is no way to tell bodies apart prior to motion, there will be no way to tell them apart after the transposition of parts. (See Garber 1992, 179–81, for discussion of Leibniz's critique.) Spinoza may well have had something similar in mind, objecting, thus, to Descartes' physics not just because it requires God to transcend nature, but that it fails to account for individuation in any case. On either construal, Spinoza's objection is against the externality of motion to matter.

If the only distinction brought out by Letters 80–83 between Descartes and Spinoza regards the question whether matter's motion is caused externally or immanently, it is unclear how consequential this difference is for their respective views of science in general. Does the difference entail that Spinoza rejects other aspects of Cartesian physics, such as Descartes' laws of motion? Most relevant for present purposes is the question whether this difference entails that Spinoza rejects Descartes' commitment to mathematization. It is true that Spinoza's statement that the principles of Descartes' natural philosophy are "useless, not to say absurd" suggests a sweeping condemnation that may well extend to the specific laws of motion. If so, this would mean that Spinoza had come to adopt a much more critical view of Descartes' physics in 1676 than he expressed a decade or so earlier. Consider the following attempt on Spinoza's part to correct a mischaracterization of his views by Oldenburg in a letter from 1665: "As for what you write next—that I hinted that Descartes' Rules of motion are almost all false—if I remember rightly, I said that Mr. Huygens thinks this. I did not affirm that any of the Rules was false except the sixth" (Ep. 32/G 4:174a). While this may be nothing more than a simple fact check, it can also be read (without implausibility) to suggest that Spinoza accepted Descartes' rules of motion in general, objecting only to the sixth rule, in particular. It is certainly possible that over the course of the intervening decade, Spinoza had, like many of his contemporaries, come to notice problems with prominent aspects of Descartes' physics, such as the dubious conservation of quantity of motion.[31]

On the other hand, Spinoza's "useless, not to say absurd" comment might not have such expansive connotations. It might be narrowly limited to the point already examined that Descartes' conception of extension is useless in not being able to account (on its own) for the existence of bodies. But even if we take Spinoza's comment in the broader sense, would a more thoroughgoing critique of Descartes' physics actually jeopardize the mathematization thesis?[32] The thesis is not tied, after all, to any specific set

---

[31] See Iltis (1971) for discussion of the *vis viva* controversy sparked by Leibniz's criticisms of Descartes' principle of the conservation of the quantity of motion. On the other hand, Leibniz is reported to have said, after having met with Spinoza in November 1676 (and after Spinoza's letters to Tschirnhaus), that Spinoza did not see the problems with Descartes' laws of motion. (See Gabbey 1996, n. 55.) For further discussion of Spinoza's remarks about Descartes' laws in Ep. 32, see Gabbey 1996, 165–66.

[32] For an interpretation that answers this question affirmatively, see Peterman 2012. Peterman argues that Spinoza's critique of Descartes' physics encompasses the latter's con-

of physical laws. It may be inconsistent with *some* set of conceivable physical principles, but, as I have already argued, it is unclear what such principles would look like.

It is true that Spinoza reiterates the fact that he considers shapes as beings of reason, which, in the context of Letter 83, may gesture in some readers' minds toward a non-geometrical physics. However, a closer look at Spinoza's remark does not support any such reading. He is responding there to Tschirnhaus' suggestion that, contrary to what Spinoza claims in E1p16, it is possible to deduce from the definition of any given thing just one property. To make this point, Tschirnhaus used the example of the circle. In response, Spinoza concedes that while this may be true "for very simple things, or beings of reason (under which I include shapes also)," it is not true "for real beings," such as God (Ep. 83/G 4:335). This comment can be handled in the way I have handled all the other instances where Spinoza characterizes shapes as beings of reason—namely, by distinguishing between shapes or figures per se, on the one hand, and shapes or figures as the determinations of finite bodies, on the other. Indeed, Spinoza registered no objection to Tschirnhaus' characterization of bodies as having "motions and shapes" in Letter 80, which is just what we would expect, since in this context Tschirnhaus is talking about shapes as the determinations of finite bodies, not about shapes considered in themselves, or per se.

Given the unfinished state of Spinoza's thinking about natural philosophy, there is danger of *argumentum ad ignorantiam* both in favor of and against mathematization. Of course, uncertainty about the details of Spinoza's physics in itself suggests nothing one way or the other about mathematization. In any case, the evidence of Spinoza's late letters to Tschirnhaus, such as it is, must be considered alongside all the other evidence laid out in this and previous chapters regarding Spinoza's thinking about scientific knowledge of the physical world. The latter is consistent with Spinoza's admission in the letters to Tschirnhaus of having not been able to fully work out his physical theory. After all, we have seen that while Spinoza cites a couple of very simple and general physical laws, such as his

---

ception of extension itself in terms of spatial dimensionality; extension is spatial, for Spinoza, only as it is imagined, not as it is in itself. (This argument is developed in greater depth in Peterman 2015.) The "commensurability response" outlined above serves, in part, to respond to this mathematical antirealist line of argument. For another response to Peterman, see Schmaltz 2020, 232–37.

versions of the laws of inertia and reflection, it has been no secret all along that he is in possession only of a schematic idea of science, based on his theory of method, the common notions, and his theory of physical individuation.

Even so, the schematic vision is consistent on the following key points, which I have argued for in this and the previous chapter. The content of physical science is extension, motion, and the determinations of extended, mobile bodies that constitute and characterize individuals. The most general content of the physical world of which we possess common notions, that is, extension and motion, can only be conceived adequately. From this most general adequate knowledge we can deduce knowledge of less universal things and particular things. However, the derivation of less universal and particular things must be guided by the imagination. Although the imagination is an inadequate form of knowledge per se, certain features of our imaginative conception of things are commensurate with our intellectual or adequate conception (which certain other features are not); among these features are ideas of extension, motion, and figure. By turning our experiential data of these features into adequate hypothetical ideas, we can deploy a hypothetico-deductive methodology in the pursuit of ever-refined theories about the physical world. Since extension, motion, and figure provide the content of these theories, geometry, as the study of figure, has a supporting role to play. This central Spinozan vision of science supports the mathematization thesis, and nothing in Letters 81 or 83 directly or clearly challenges the central vision.

REFERENCES

Bennett, Jonathan. 1984. *A Study of Spinoza's* Ethics. Indianapolis, IN: Hackett.

Gabbey, Alan. 1996. "Spinoza's natural science and methodology," in *The Cambridge Companion to Spinoza*, edited by Don Garrett, 142–191. Cambridge, UK: Cambridge University Press.

Garber, Daniel. 1992. *Descartes' Metaphysical Physics.* Chicago, IL: University of Chicago Press.

Hobbes, Thomas. 2005. *The English Works of Thomas Hobbes of Malmesbury.* Vol. 1. Translated by William Molesworth. London: John Bonn, 1839. Replica edition, Elbiron Classics.

Iltis, Carolyn. 1971. "Leibniz and the Vis Viva Controversy." *Isis* 62: 21–35.

Klever, W.N.A. 1988. "Moles in Motu: Principles of Spinoza's Physics." *Studia Spinozana* 4: 165–95.

Lachterman, David R. 1978. "The Physics of Spinoza's *Ethics.*" In *Spinoza: New Perspectives*, edited by by Robert W. Shahan and J. I. Biro, 71–112. Norman: University of Oklahoma Press.

Lecrivain, André. 1986. "Spinoza and Cartesian Mechanics," in *Spinoza and the Sciences*, edited by Marjorie Grene and Debra Nails, 15–60. Dordrecht: D. Reidel.

Leibniz, Gottfried. 1989. *Philosophical Papers and Letters*. Edited and translated by Leroy E. Loemker. Dordrecht: Kluwer Academic Publishers.

Melamed, Yitzhak Y. 2000. "On the Exact Science of Nonbeings: Spinoza's View of Mathematics." *Iyyun, The Jerusalem Philosophical Quarterly* 49: 3–22.

———. 2013. *Spinoza's Metaphysics: Substance and Thought*. Oxford, UK: Oxford University Press.

Miller, Jon. 2004. "Spinoza and the *a priori*." *Canadian Journal of Philosophy* 34(4): 555–590.

Osler, Margaret J. 2008. "Descartes' Optics: Light, the Eye, and Visual Perception." In *A Companion to Descartes*, edited by Janet Broughton and John Carriero, 124–141. Malden, MA: Blackwell Publishing.

Peterman, Alison. 2012. "Spinoza on the 'Principles of Natural Things'." *The Leibniz Review* 22: 37–65.

———. 2015. "Spinoza on Extension." *Philosopher's Imprint* 15: 1–23.

Petry, M.J. (ed.) 1985. *Spinoza's Algebraic Calculation of the Rainbow and Calculation of Chances*. Dordrecht: Martinus Nijhoff Publishers.

Ribe, Neil M. 1997. "Cartesian Optics and the Mastery of Nature." *Isis* 88(1): 42–61.

Schmaltz, Tad M. 1999. "Spinoza on the Vacuum." *Archiv für Geschichte der Philosophie* 81(2): 174–205.

———. 2020. *The Metaphysics of the Material World: Suárez, Descartes, Spinoza*. New York, NY: Oxford University Press.

Vermij, Rienk, and Atzema, Eisso. 1995. "Specilla circularia: an Unknown Work by Johannes Hudde." *Studia Leibnitiana* 27: 104–121.

Vermij, Rienk. 2013. "Instruments and the Making of a Philosopher. Spinoza's Career in Optics." *Intellectual History Review* 23: 65–81.

Viljanen, Valtteri. 2011. *Spinoza's Geometry of Power*. Cambridge, UK: Cambridge University Press.

Von Duuglas-Ittu, Kevin. 2008a. "Spinoza's Blunder and the Spherical Lens." *Frames/sing* (blog). Posted June 21, 2008. Available at: https://kvond.wordpress.com/2008/06/21/spinozas-blunder-and-the-spherical-lens/

———. 2008b. "Deciphering Spinoza's Optical Letters." *Frames/sing* (blog). Posted August 17, 2008. Available at: https://kvond.wordpress.com/2008/08/17/deciphering-spinozas-optical-letters/

———. 2008c. "Spinoza: Not As Abused as Is Said." *Frames/sing* (blog). Posted September 14, 2008. Available at: https://kvond.wordpress.com/2008/09/14/spinoza-not-as-abused-as-is-said/

Wilson, Margaret D. 1996. "Spinoza's theory of knowledge." In *The Cambridge Companion to Spinoza*, edited by Don Garrett, 89–141. Cambridge, UK: Cambridge University Press.

Wolfson, Harry Austryn. 1934. *The Philosophy of Spinoza: Unfolding the Latent Process of His Reasoning*. Volume 1. Cambridge, MA: Harvard University Press.

CHAPTER 6

Spinoza's Notions of Essence

Having now treated the role of both imagination and reason in Spinozan science, and the place of geometry therein, we turn our sights to the pinnacle of Spinoza's epistemology, intuitive knowledge, which promises knowledge of the essences of singular things. Before embarking upon this final ascent, however, it will be necessary first to clarify Spinoza's notion of essence in general (although, as we will see, it is more accurate to speak of Spinoza's notions of essence in the plural). In line with the general strategy outlined in the introductory chapter of delving into Spinoza's metaphysics only when necessary for understanding his epistemology, I will restrict myself to discussing those aspects of essence relevant to the interpretation of intuitive knowledge and to the question of the nature of the essences of finite things raised in Chap. 2. This means that the present chapter by no means purports to offer a comprehensive interpretation of essence in Spinoza, and, in some cases, the significance of the points introduced here will become fully apparent only when deployed in the interpretation of intuitive knowledge in the next chapter. The aim is to handle a couple of salient issues in Spinoza's doctrine of essence and to sketch a framework for approaching intuitive knowledge.

Of particular relevance will be the question of what can be said to have essence, in Spinoza, that is to say, the extension of the concept. In this regard, I will argue that there are three "levels" of essences—that of attributes and infinite modes, that of finite individuals, and the species level, which is intermediate between the other two. Together these levels form a spectrum, although species essences are beings of reason. I will also attempt to clarify Spinoza's notions of formal essence (*essentia formalis*) and actual essence (*essentia actualis*), and the sense in which the essences of finite things enjoy non-durational existence in contrast with (and in addition to) durational existence. This will be relevant to interpreting intuitive knowledge, since Spinoza defines the latter in terms of formal essence. It will also afford me an opportunity to address Garrett's construal of the formal essences of singular things as infinite modes, which I discussed in Chap. 2 as an objection to my notion of ideas true only in form. In contrast to Garrett, I will defend a reading of the formal essences of singular things as finite.

6.1 Common Essence, Species Essence, and Individual Essence

Spinoza provides the following definition of essence at the beginning of *Ethics* Part 2:

> I say that to the essence of any thing belongs that which, being given, the thing is also necessarily posited and which, being taken away, the thing is necessarily also taken away; or that without which the thing can neither be nor be conceived, and which can neither be nor be conceived without the thing. (E2d2/G 2:84)

As he explains a little later in the same Part, he means for this definition to be understood in contrast with a conception of the nature or essence of a thing as that without which the thing can neither be nor be conceived. For instance, according to a standard Aristotelian conception, reason is the sine qua non of human nature. Whereas one can be human without being white or tall or male, one cannot be human without being rational, and, thus, reason is of the essence of human beings. Spinoza raises the following objection to this way of understanding essence: if that without which a thing can neither be nor be conceived pertains to the essence of a thing, then either the nature of God pertains to the essence of created things or the latter can be and be conceived without the former (E2p10s/G 2:93).[1]

---

[1] Curley (1:635) cites Descartes' conception of essence in terms of the "principal attribute" of a thing (CSM 1:210) as exemplifying the target of Spinoza's criticism in E2p10s. For instance, for Descartes, extension constitutes the essence of any corporeal substance, since it

Spinoza rejects both horns of this dilemma, and the understanding of essence from which it stems. Instead, in his own definition, he stipulates that the essence of a thing is that without which the thing can neither be nor be conceived *and* which can neither be nor be conceived without the thing. According to Spinoza's revisionist conception, the essence of a thing describes not only necessary conditions, but necessary and sufficient conditions, of the thing. Socrates cannot be defined, then, as a rational animal. Although "rational animal" may be given with "Socrates," the converse is not the case. It is not the case, that is, that when "rational animal" is given, "Socrates" is also given. The essence of Socrates, then, must define Socrates not qua human being, but qua individual (i.e., qua Socrates). Hence, according to E2d2, essences must be unique to each individual. I will call such essences *individual essences*.[2]

Other passages appear to contradict E2d2, however. Spinoza talks at a number of points as if individuals of the same kind share an essence. For instance:

> a man is the cause of the existence of another man, but not of his essence, for the latter is an eternal truth. Hence, they can agree entirely (*prorsus*) according to their essence. But in existing they must differ. And for that reason, if the existence of one perishes, the other's existence will not thereby perish. But if the essence of one could be destroyed, and become false, the other's essence would also be destroyed. (E1p17s/G 2:63)

This is not an anomaly. Spinoza speaks a number of times in the *Ethics* of the essence *of man* (*essentia hominis*), as well as of the essence of

---

is impossible to conceive the latter except as extended. This is actually similar to *one* of the notions of essence that I will attribute to Spinoza below (i.e., *common* essence), though there is no doubt that Spinoza does in fact criticize this conception in E2p10s. As we will see, Spinoza's usage of "essence" is not always consistent—hence, my distinction between different Spinozan conceptions.

[2] In this, I follow other commentators who similarly use qualifiers to distinguish Spinoza's E2d2 conception of essence from the conception of essences as shared or common to multiple individuals that Spinoza appears to espouse in other places. Hübner (2016), Soyarslan (2016), and Martin (2008), for instance, speak of "unique essences," on the one hand, and of "shared essences" (Soyarslan 2016) or "species essences" (Martin 2008; Hübner 2016), on the other. Below, I distinguish between essences common to *all* individuals of a given attribute (which I call "common essences") and essences common to only some individuals (which I call "species essences").

non-human animals.[3] Recall, moreover, Spinoza's distinction between human and equine affects (discussed in Chap. 4).

In some places, then, Spinozan essences are unique; in others, they are shared. Is Spinoza's doctrine of essences simply inconsistent? In a recent paper, Karolina Hübner has proposed a way of reconciling the apparent inconsistency that will be worth considering in outline.[4] According to Hübner, the only essences that exist independently of human minds are the individual essences unique to each concrete particular. Shared essences or "species essences," by contrast, exist only in human minds, as beings of reason. This might make it sound as if she takes a standard antirealist line against universals, but that is not the case. Hübner distinguishes between ideas of species essences formed through the imagination, on the one hand, (in the way Spinoza describes in E2p40s1), and ideas of species essences formed through reason, on the other. While she styles both kinds of ideas "constructions" (and her reading "constructivist"),[5] the latter, she argues, can be adequate or true ideas inasmuch as they are derived or generated on the basis of knowledge of properties that things do in fact share. Such properties, as we know, are the objects of what Spinoza calls common notions. I take Hübner's notion of constructions adequately derived from common notions to parallel the notion of true-in-form hypotheses I developed in previous chapters. The fact that they are true only *in form*, while not corresponding exactly (or necessarily) to an extra-mental concrete particular, is what (I take it) makes them count as constructions.[6]

Evidence that Spinoza countenanced a conception of universals or shared essences as adequate (or at least true in form) is provided by a passage from E2p49s:

> the will is something universal, which is predicated of all ideas, and which signifies only what is common to all ideas, viz. the affirmation, whose adequate essence, therefore, insofar as it is conceived abstractly, must be in each idea, and in this way only must be the same in all, but not insofar as it is considered to constitute the idea's essence; for in that regard the singular affirmations differ from one another as much as the ideas themselves do. For

---

[3] Examples include E2p10c/G 2:93 and E4d8/G 2:210.
[4] Hübner 2016.
[5] Hübner 2016, 59.
[6] One notable discrepancy between my reading and Hübner's is that whereas I have argued that notions adequately derived from common notions can only be true *in form*, for reasons laid out in past chapters, Hübner characterizes them as true *simpliciter* (Hübner 2016, 79).

example, the affirmation that the idea of a circle involves differs from that which the idea of a triangle involves as much as the idea of the circle differs from the idea of the triangle. (G 2:135)

This is a valuable passage, because Spinoza is dealing with the notions of shared essence and unique essence together. The shared essence in this case is the will or affirmation, which, according to Spinoza's doctrine of the identity of intellect and will, all ideas involve insofar as they are ideas. Individual essence, by contrast, is the essence of individual ideas insofar as they are individuated by distinct objects. Spinoza clearly gives priority to the notion of individual essence. Even if all ideas do involve will or affirmation, he denies that will or affirmation constitutes any idea's essence. Instead, their essence is individuating. This is what we should expect given Spinoza's definition of essence in E2d2. Nevertheless, it is also noteworthy that Spinoza does not dismiss the "universal" will or affirmation. On the contrary, he affirms that it is "common to all ideas" and, indeed, has an "adequate essence" that must be in each idea, insofar, at least, "as it is conceived abstractly." Thus, even if the "universal" will or affirmation does not characterize the essence of any idea qua individual, it might be said to characterize the essence of an idea *qua idea*, in other words, an idea qua general type.[7]

Spinoza's conciliating treatment of the universal notion of will in E2p49s needs to be juxtaposed and reconciled with a statement from the preceding proposition. Having refuted the notion of an absolute faculty of willing, he says:

In this same way it is also demonstrated that there is in the Mind no absolute faculty of understanding, desiring, loving, etc. From this it follows that these and similar faculties are either complete fictions or nothing but Metaphysical beings, or universals, which we are used to forming from particulars. So intellect and will are to this or that idea, or to this or that volition as 'stoneness' is to this or that stone, or man to Peter or Paul. (E2p48s/G 2:129)

---

[7] Cf. Hübner (2016, 76) for a different reading of this passage. Hübner emphasizes the qualification "insofar as it is conceived abstractly" in arguing that the conception of will that is perceived as common to all ideas is mind-dependent. As I explain below, if by "will" we mean an absolute faculty of willing, then this is certainly abstract. But if we mean the affirmation that all ideas must involve *qua* ideas, then I think this is a common property of ideas and exists *in* the idea just as extension exists *in* any body (and not just mind-dependently).

This passage might be read as denying what I just argued on the basis of E2p49s, namely that all ideas (qua ideas) share will or affirmation as a shared essence. Such universals here are dismissed, it seems, as complete fictions or nothing but Metaphysical beings. This is not quite right. Spinoza's target is not will or affirmation as a property common to all ideas. He is clear that they all involve will or affirmation *insofar as they are ideas* (E2p49/G 2:130). Instead, his target is the notion of an *absolute faculty* of willing. The significance of viewing the will as an absolute faculty for a philosopher, such as Descartes, is to distinguish it from other mental faculties, in particular, the intellect (with the result that the will and the intellect can operate independently). It is precisely this separation of the will from the intellect that Spinoza rejects as a fiction or Metaphysical being. This separation can be compared to the Platonist mathematician's mistake of separating the circle from the body, and then reifying the former, which we saw Descartes criticize in Chap. 3. (Spinoza, I guess, would charge Descartes with committing an error comparable to the one he himself warns against in separating the will from the intellect.)

At the end of the passage, Spinoza remarks that the relation of intellect and will to this or that idea or volition is like the relation of "stone-ness" to this or that stone or "man" to Peter or Paul. Since what is clear is that stone-ness and humanity (and intellect and will) can be no more than properties of individuals, how we interpret Spinoza's remark depends on how we interpret his understanding of properties. Are properties multiply exemplifiable, or can two things have, at most, resembling but numerically distinct properties? I discussed this question in Chap. 3 in connection with figural properties. I presented grounds for thinking that Spinozan properties are probably not multiply exemplifiable, but the argument was inconclusive, and I shifted to an epistemological point. I want to do the same thing here as well.

From an epistemological point of view (if not necessarily from a metaphysical or ontological one), there is an important difference between the will or affirmation common to all ideas, on the one hand, and the stone-ness common to this or that stone or the humanity common to Peter or Paul, on the other. The difference is this: we can be sure that there *are* ideas *and* that they all involve affirmation as an essential property. This is because ideation (which I understand in terms of mental representation) follows directly from the attribute of thought in the same way that motion and rest follow directly from the attribute of extension. I take this to be suggested by Spinoza's identification of "absolutely infinite intellect" as the infinite mode that follows immediately from thought (Ep. 64/G 4:278). This means that, like motion and rest in the attribute of extension, ideas are (or, if you prefer, ideation is) equally in the part and in the whole of thought. Since all ideas involve affirmation insofar as they are ideas, affirmation, too, is equally in the part and in the whole. Ideas of such pervasive properties are common notions. As we know from our earlier discussion, common notions can only be conceived adequately. This is why they can function as foundations of reasoning.

This is not the case for any ideas we might form of the shared essences of human beings or stones (just as it was not the case for ideas of the shapes of things). Neither human beings nor stones are equally in the part and in the whole. Although Spinoza describes a kind of common notion of a feature equally in the part and in the whole of a subset of bodies (i.e., *peculiar* common notions, or what I dubbed PCNs), and although shared natures provide the most plausible examples of such features, in Chap. 3 I presented reasons to believe that such notions cannot be adequate (contrary to what Spinoza himself says in E2p39), at least in the robust sense, given our need to rely on sensory experience to gain ideas of such features, and our lack of any a priori assurance of their true nature. This means that we cannot assume that any idea we have of human beings or stones does not reflect the affections of our own bodies more than the things themselves. (As Spinoza explains, this point applies to the human mind and body themselves, no less than to external bodies.[8]) The best we can do, then, vis-à-vis such natural phenomena as human beings and stones is apply the scientific method elaborated in the last two chapters. We certainly cannot rest content with our imaginative conceptions of human nature or stone nature, if we wish to have any chance of accurately conceiving such objects. We must instead construct (revisable) hypothetical conceptions in terms of primary qualities and consistent with higher-order laws of nature.

In this regard, ideas of species essences, even adequate ideas of species essences, are mind-dependent constructions, and I agree with the main outlines of Hübner's constructivist interpretation of such essences. But if ideas of what all stones or human beings have in common count as ideas of species essences, then ideas of what all bodies or all minds have in common should also count as shared essences. And, yet, as we have seen, such ideas are not mere constructions (insofar as "construction" implies

[8] See E2pp23–30.

mind-dependence). They are ideas of mind-independent, that is, real, pervasive properties. To mark this crucial distinction, I want to introduce a separate category for natures common to all things (of a given attribute), which I will call *common essences*. Thus, all bodies are essentially extended and mobile, just as all ideas are essentially volitional. It is true that Spinoza says that the objects of common notions cannot constitute the essence of any singular thing (E2p37/G 2:118). But in this case, he is talking about individual essences (per E2d2). We have seen that he also countenances a conception of shared essence (even in the context of talking about what *all* ideas involve *qua* ideas).

Another way to think about common essences is by recognizing that attributes (and infinite modes) are themselves individuals, concrete particulars (not abstractions). As such, they have their own unique, individuating essences. But they are strange kinds of individuals insofar as they (I am speaking of the attributes now) have (other) individuals as their modal properties. Thus, a stone (a modal individual) is a property of an attribute of substance. (This is what did not sit well with Curley and has exercised many interpreters of Spinoza's metaphysics.[9]) I enter this murky metaphysical terrain only to make the following point. The notion of common essence is really just the notion of the individual essence of attributes (or that of immediate infinite modes) *conceived not as individuating the attributes (or immediate infinite modes) but as pertaining to the modes that follow from the attributes (or immediate infinite modes)*. For example, the essence of extension pertains to a stone inasmuch as the stone *is* an

---

[9] Curley regarded modes as the "wrong logical type" to be properties of substance. See Curley 1969, 18 (and, more generally, 1–44). For more recent discussion of the mode-attribute-substance relation, and criticism of Curley's view, see Melamed 2013, 3–60. As suggested by my claim (above) that attributes have modes as their properties, I incline toward the view, defended by Melamed *contra* Curley, that modes do relate to attributes as predicate to subject in addition to relating to them as effects to causes. (Cf. Lin 2019, 102–36.) It is not clear to me that the dispute regarding the mode-substance relation has much consequence for interpreting Spinoza's epistemology. (Hence, I have not felt the need to treat this subject in any systematic manner in this study.) I think there is a reasonably good explanation for the lack of apparent significance: while the cause-effect relationship between attribute and mode is of paramount importance for Spinoza's epistemology (as should be very clear by now), it is not clear how much epistemological import the subject-predicate relationship has (assuming it obtains). Since the cause-effect relationship is agreed to by all parties, the implications of *that* relationship for the epistemology remain unaffected by any resolution of the dispute concerning the substance-mode relationship one way or the other.

extended mode (albeit one among infinitely many others). Extension, then, constitutes the stone's *common essence*. To summarize, in reference to the attribute itself, the essence of the attribute is individuating (i.e., an individual essence); in reference to the modes of the attribute, however, the same essence is shared by all modes (i.e., a common essence).

Let me make one further clarification about the notion of common essence and its relation to that of individual essence, as I understand it. Neither attributes nor immediate infinite modes have common essences. The distinction between common and individual essence pertains only to singular things which *share* with other singular things a common attribute (and immediate infinite mode) while also being differentiated from other singular things through their individual essence.

It might be wondered what the significance is of introducing this notion of common essence. The utility of the notion will (I hope) become more fully apparent in the next chapter when I turn to interpretation of Spinoza's third kind of knowledge (as will the utility of the other notions of essence I have introduced here, namely species essence and individual essence), but let me anticipate briefly what I will explain in more detail later. In certain texts where Spinoza says that we can have intuitive knowledge of the human mind, he seems to mean that we grasp (intuitively) the mind as a thinking thing (i.e., as a mode that follows from God's thinking essence). But this grasp of the mind individuates it not at all, while Spinoza says that intuitive knowledge is knowledge of the essences of things. The notion of common essence will help to make sense out of this, or so I shall argue. I ask, then, that the notion of common essence be accepted for the time being on a provisional basis, in addition to its individual and species essence counterparts.

The three kinds of essence form a spectrum. At one extreme is the essence of the attribute (and infinite mode), that is, the common essence. Any mode shares this essence with every other mode (of a given attribute). Such common essences go no distance toward determining the essence of a singular thing, yet they are necessarily essential features (in the broad sense of necessary but not sufficient features) of all things qua modes of the given attribute. At the other extreme is individual essence, which individuates a singular thing from all others. On this spectrum, species essence is somewhere in the middle. As such, it shares something in common with both common essence and individual essence. Like common essence, it is something that is equally in the part and in the whole of a species. Like the individual essence, it helps to individuate the species in question from all other kinds of entities.

From an epistemological point of view, it is useful to regard individual essence as a kind of limit concept. If we frame individual essence as a limit or goal, then we can think of the path from general common notions, or ideas of common essences, which are equally in the part and in the whole, to less universal notions (i.e., ideas of species essences), in terms of stepping stones on the way to the goal. In this regard, even knowing only very generally that some individual is extended and mobile reveals something about the essence of the thing qua physical entity. In particular, it reveals what I am calling its common essence. As we descend from the most universal notions to specify the object of investigation more and more, we get closer to the essence of the individual.

What would an adequate, Spinozan conception of a biological organism, such as a horse, look like? Obviously, Spinoza did not work out the details of a biology any more than those of a physics.[10] So, specifics are out of the question here. Nevertheless, we do know that he defined individuals by a particular ratio of motion and rest among their constituent parts. What are the parts of a horse? What relations do those parts have to one another? What effects, moreover, follow from the nature of horses considered through the laws of equine nature alone? What sort of lust? What gladness? Perhaps answers to such questions would be the product of an investigation into the functional organization of horses. Perhaps modern genetics provides an alternative (albeit anachronistic) model of the form such an investigation could take. Any and all answers would, of course, remain ever hypothetical. But to the extent that some hypotheses allowed for the understanding of equine behavior better than others, it would be possible to distinguish between more and less effective hypotheses.

It would, in principle, be possible to extend such an investigation beyond horse-hood, in general, to the individual nature of an individual horse, such as Seabiscuit. At the limit of this investigation would lie the discovery of Seabiscuit's essence, that is, an individual essence. The field of

---

[10] While I think no one would object to the claim that Spinoza did not work out the details of a biology, some scholars have justifiably stressed Spinoza's significance and achievement as a proto-biological thinker, nevertheless, drawing attention in particular to the *conatus* doctrine and the modal theory of individuality, which can be understood in functional terms. See Hampshire 2005, xli–xlix; and Jonas 1965. (Diderot's short *Encyclopédie* entry on "*Spinosiste*" is interesting as an early forerunner of biological interpretations of Spinoza (or at least *Spinozism*).)

modern genetics perhaps indicates that the pursuit of such an individual essence is not futile. As already indicated, specifics regarding the form that a Spinozan conception of species essence or individual essence might take in the case of biological organisms are lacking. The suggestions are meant simply to illustrate the idea of investigating species essences and individual essences, respectively.

6.2 Formal Essence, Actual Essence, and Existence

"Essence," in Spinoza, is said in many ways. In addition to the distinction between individual and shared essences (not to mention common essences), Spinoza also qualifies "essence" as "formal" and "actual." The task now is to clarify these latter notions of essence, as well as the sense in which the essences of finite things exist even when the things themselves do not exist in duration. This is relevant to the subject matter of this study in two ways. First, Spinoza uses "formal essence" in defining intuitive knowledge, which we will be looking at in the next chapter. Second, the topic of formal essences came up in Chap. 2, when I discussed objections to my interpretation of genetically conceived ideas of figures as true in form alone. In particular, I limned Don Garrett's view that true ideas of non-durationally existent *possibilia* (which I compared to my own notion of ideas true in form only) correspond to formal essences comprehended in God's attributes. It is now possible to understand more clearly why this would be the case if, as Garrett argues, the formal essences of finite things are infinite modes—we cannot *but* have true ideas of infinite modes, which are among the objects of common notions. If it were the case, it would undercut my distinction between true-in-form and robustly true ideas, since all true-in-form ideas would correspond with a real existent (albeit one not existing in duration), and thus count as robustly true. I said before that I disagreed with Garrett's interpretation of formal essences as infinite modes and on that basis rebuffed the objection to the notion of true-in-form ideas. In what follows, I will explain and defend my own interpretation.

I will argue that the nature of the essences of finite things is best grasped through definitions and that definitions reveal the essences of finite things to be themselves finite (inasmuch as the definitions are individuating) and eternal (inasmuch as the definitions involve neither the coming into nor going out of existence of the finite things). As usual, the epistemological limitations of finite intellects do not determine the mind-independent reality of the objects of knowledge, so the fact that individuating definitions are beyond finite intellectual capacity does not mean that finite things do not have individual essences. The manner in which the essences of things exist non-durationally is best understood, I will argue, as the manner in which such essences eternally follow from God's nature as (finite) components of the mediate infinite mode.

6.2.1 Formal Essences and Existence

E2p8 is the principal source for Spinoza's conception of formal essences as existing independently of the existence of singular things in duration.[11] The proposition reads:

> The ideas of singular things, or of modes, that do not exist must be comprehended in God's infinite idea in the same way as the formal essences of the singular things, or modes, are contained in God's attributes. (G 2:90)

The corollary continues:

> From this it follows that so long as singular things do not exist, except insofar as they are comprehended in God's attributes, their objective being, or ideas, do not exist except insofar as God's infinite idea exists. And when singular things are said to exist, not only insofar as they are comprehended in God's attributes, but insofar also as they are said to have duration, their ideas also involve the existence through which they are said to have duration. (G 2:91)

These lines suggest a distinction between non-durational and durational manners of existing of singular things. Spinoza says that the distinction is "unique," and that he is unable to furnish an example that adequately explains it (E2p8s/G 2:91).[12] I take this to mean that the distinction is

---

[11] See also CM 1.2: "the formal essence neither is by itself nor has been created, for both these presuppose that the thing actually exists. Rather it depends on the divine essence alone, in which all things are contained. So in this sense we agree with those who say that the essences of things are eternal" (G 1:239). Spinoza's claim here that formal essence is contained in the divine essence foreshadows E2p8, but other elements of this text, such as the doctrine of creation, represent elements of Descartes' philosophy, rather than Spinoza's, rendering it problematic for interpreting the latter.

[12] Spinoza tries to illustrate his point with an example anyway, and the example he uses is, notably, geometrical (from Euclid's *Elements*, Book 3, Proposition 35). For discussion of the

also obscure. The obscurity stems, in particular, from Spinoza's parallelism doctrine, according to which the order of ideas is the same as, or mirrors, the order of things. The difficulty regards the manner of being of the formal essences that are the objects of the ideas of non-existing singular things in God's intellect. We might not have too much trouble understanding that a non-existing singular thing could exist *as an idea* in the infinite intellect, but what does it mean to say that it *also* exists—per parallelism—as "comprehended in God's attributes"? According to the foregoing, even if a man does not exist in duration, he nevertheless does exist as "comprehended in God's attributes." What manner of existence is this?

Before proceeding to address these matters, a word about Spinoza's use of the qualifier "formal" in the phrase "formal essence" is in order. As we will see below, there is some basis for contrasting "formal" with "actual" essences (though I will argue that the difference is a small one). The context of Spinoza's use of the qualifier "formal" in *Ethics* Part 2 (and elsewhere) suggests, however, that its chief import lies in contrast not with "actual" but with "objective" essence.[13] The latter distinction is meant to clarify an ambiguity that can arise from the fact that ideas can be viewed in terms of their representational objects or in terms of their own reality. In speaking of the essence of an idea of a tree, we might be referring to the essence of the tree (qua represented in the idea) *or* we might be referring to the mental *thing*, as it were, that is doing the representing. Objective essence designates the former; formal essence designates the latter. (Because non-ideas are also *things*, they all have formal essence in this sense.) The distinction is significant in the context of Spinoza's parallelism doctrine (given in the proposition immediately preceding E2p8). Because ideas are themselves *things* no less than bodies, the order and connection of ideas *qua things* (i.e., as having formal essence) is itself represented (with the same order and connection, but this time as having objective

example, see Viljanen 2011, 25–26.

[13] Spinoza talks of the "formal being of ideas" in E2p5 and invokes the formal/objective distinction in E2p7c, stating, "whatever follows formally from God's infinite nature follows objectively in God from his idea." In these passages, Spinoza appears to be drawing on the distinction that Descartes draws in Meditation Three between the formal and objective reality of ideas (CSM 2:28). (It is generally thought that Suárez's distinction between formal and objective concepts influenced Descartes here.) Spinoza explicitly defends, and appears to endorse, Descartes' distinction between the formal and objective reality of ideas (albeit not using those terms) in Ep. 40 (G 4:198b–99b). See also TIE 35/G 2:15 (which we discussed in Chap. 2).

essence) in the attribute of thought. This generates a number of interpretive complexities that, fortunately, it is unnecessary to get into.[14] The upshot for our purposes is that the qualifier "formal" is meant to clarify an ambiguity attaching to ideas, in particular. It is redundant when discussing the essences of non-ideas, such as bodies. This plausibly explains why Spinoza most often omits the qualifier when discussing the essences of things. With this in mind, we can use what Spinoza says about the essences of finite things in general to attempt to shed light on the questions raised above about their non-durational existence.

6.2.1.1 Essences and Definitions

The notion of essences, or at least, our *understanding* of essences, is closely linked with definitions, for Spinoza. Indeed, true ideas of essences are given through true definitions (TIE 92–5). Thus, on the basis of what Spinoza says about definitions, we can draw inferences about the nature of essences. (Spinoza does this himself, as we will see momentarily.) One such remark, which is very important, is from E1p8s2: "the true definition of each thing neither involves nor expresses anything except the nature of the thing defined" (G 2:50).[15] This might seem somewhat truistic, at first glance, since properly formed definitions are not supposed to express anything beyond their definienda, but Spinoza draws from it an important conclusion: the essence of a thing cannot determine its own destruction, external causes must do so (E3p4/G 2:145). Commentators have raised interesting counterexamples to this claim, such as the tendency of a star or candle to burn itself out.[16] Given that it is a fundamental tenet of Spinoza's philosophy that reality is self-affirming, and the notion of something limiting itself is self-contradictory, however, let us grant this for present purposes.[17]

---

[14] The attribute of thought appears to exhibit a number of peculiar properties of which Spinoza's doctrine of *idea ideae* (ideas of ideas) is one example. One set of interpretive issues concerns reconciling these peculiarities with the parallelism (and parity) of the attributes. I discuss these issues in Homan 2016.

[15] See also CM 1.2: "we can give no definition of anything without at the same time explaining its essence" (G 1:239).

[16] See Della Rocca 1996b, 200–2.

[17] On the absurdity of a thing's self-limitation, see E1p8dem, where Spinoza argues that substances must be infinite because there is nothing else of the same nature to limit them. The tacit implication of Spinoza's argumentation is that substances cannot limit themselves. This is further explicated in the scholium of E1p8: "Since being finite is really, in part, a nega-

It also follows from fundamental aspects of Spinoza's philosophy that just as the essence of a finite thing cannot determine its destruction, so it cannot determine its existence. If a finite thing were to exist through its own nature and essence, it would not depend on anything else for its existence. It would be *causa sui*, like God, unlike a mode. Hence, having said (also in E1p8s2) that there must be a cause for the existence of each thing, Spinoza goes on to note, "this cause, on account of which a thing exists, either must be contained in the very nature and definition of the existing thing (*viz. that it pertains to its nature to exist*) or must be outside it" (G 2:50). Of course, the cause is contained in the very nature and definition only of God, qua substance.[18] Therefore, in the case of finite modes, the cause must be outside the definition.

This appears to clash with what we saw earlier concerning genetic conceptions. Recall Spinoza's insistence upon defining a circle through its cause (as the figure produced by the rotation of a line around a fixed end). This requirement is not restricted to circles, of course; it extends to all definitions—they ought to *include* the cause of their definienda. The tension between the doctrine of E1p8s2, which calls for *excluding* the causes of finite things from their definitions, on the one hand, and the doctrine of genetic definitions, on the other, represents a puzzling interpretive issue.[19]

The simplest and most elegant solution to the problem, in my view, is from Della Rocca. He suggests, "we can say that the essence of x consists in being the effect of a certain cause."[20] That is, even though x—in this case a finite mode—is conceived (or defined) through a cause, it is conceived as the *effect* of the cause, and thus the cause is still excluded from the essence. In this way, it is possible to cognize a thing through its cause, while also respecting the latter's externality to the thing's essence.[21]

---

tion, and being infinite is an absolute affirmation of the existence of some nature, it follows from P7 alone that every substance must be infinite" (G 2:49).

[18] See Ep. 60/G 4:271, where Spinoza characterizes his definition of God in E1d6 as expressive of the efficient cause of God (which in this case is an internal, rather than external, efficient cause).

[19] Schliesser (2014, 13) puts the problem this way: "The apparent paradox looks like this: (i) proximate causes are contained in the definition of a thing; (ii) proximate causes involve extrinsic properties; (iii) definitions include essences; but (iv) extrinsic properties are not involved in the essence."

[20] Della Rocca 1996a, 89.

[21] Schliesser (2014, 12–14) and LeBuffe (2018, 19–37) both give interesting alternative solutions to the tension between the doctrine of definitions and E1p8s2, but ones that are

There is another mitigating consideration worth noting as well. Since the causes of the existence of any finite mode are infinitely complicated, we finite inquirers are not going to run into the problem of formulating a genetic definition that actually provides a blueprint of a thing's generation in all its intricate detail. So, we can cheerfully go about fashioning and utilizing genetic definitions without worrying about rendering a finite entity *causa sui* in the process: the true causal account of any finite thing *must* be outside its definition, since it is necessarily beyond our comprehension. Of course, this is not to say that we cannot engineer artifacts of our own design, defining them to match our idea. Spinoza himself did just this with optical lenses, as we saw in the last chapter. But even Hobbes, the arch constructivist, recognized that "the causes of natural things are not in our power."[22] So, even if we are able to grind glass to elicit refractive properties of our choosing, the glass itself, and the light it refracts, remain natural entities beyond our control (and, thus, beyond our

---

incompatible with fundamental commitments of my interpretation. (Part of my attraction to Della Rocca's solution is its neutrality on substantive metaphysical and epistemological matters.) Schliesser suggests that the essences of things do not exist in space and time, and so, giving a causal explanation of *these* (eternal) objects (which he associates with types as opposed to tokens) does not in fact introduce extrinsic properties (which attach to durational instantiation). I agree with Schliesser's proposal from an epistemological standpoint, insofar as I agree that we finite beings can only ever hope to define what he is calling "types" (i.e., what I have called species essences) not "tokens" (i.e., what I have called individual essences). But from a metaphysical standpoint, this proposal (if I understand it correctly) solves the problem by restricting essences to the species, or "type," level, whereas in my view we must also recognize individual, or "token," essences. Indeed, whereas there is some doubt about the extra-mental reality of species essences or "types" (such as "human") in Spinoza's philosophy, as I discussed at the end of Chap. 4, there is no doubt about the reality of individuals. Whatever the case may be regarding species essences, individual essences (in my view) have an eternal existence in God's attributes and cannot be relegated to space and time alone. I say more about the durational and non-durational existence of essences below when I discuss "actual" essence and *conatus*.

For his part, LeBuffe argues that finite things in fact *are causa sui*, like God; what distinguishes finite things from God is only that their existence may be impeded by external things (unlike God with respect to whom nothing is external). But LeBuffe concedes that while a finite thing has internal reasons, so to speak, for its existence, it also has external reasons (creating the problem under discussion). In response, LeBuffe has recourse to the view that reality and, correlatively, adequacy, admits of degrees. (So, inasmuch as a finite thing is *not causa sui*, it does not exist, and we cannot have an adequate idea of it.) I discussed (critically) the notion of degrees of adequacy at the end of Chap. 4.

[22] Hobbes 1991, 42.

comprehension). All natural phenomena are as Kant's "little blade of grass"—we cannot hope to ever fully understand their generation.[23]

This comports with what we have already seen: the cause included in a genetic definition (of a finite thing) is not an actual cause of anything in nature, but a heuristic.[24] Recall that Spinoza deems it of little importance what causal account is given, so long as it provides a basis for the deduction of the properties of the thing in question (per our discussion of hypotheses in Chap. 4). We will not be able to deduce *all* of the properties of a thing (since they are infinite), but a good genetic definition will explain the properties of interest at any given time (and conceivably also provide for the discovery of unknown others[25]).

For all intents and purposes, therefore, the efficient cause in a genetic definition of a finite thing is not of intrinsic but only of extrinsic value insofar as it provides a basis for the deduction of (some of) a thing's properties. This may explain why Spinoza himself sometimes neglects his causal requirement for grasping a thing's essence. He appears, for instance, to be satisfied that an idea of a triangle as having angles equaling two right angles provides the essence of a triangle, and thus an adequate definition, since he uses this example to illustrate the cognition of the essence of a thing, despite the fact that it has nothing to say about the triangle's generation (E2p49dem/G 2:130). (It is unclear to me how this differs from the Euclidean definition of a circle as a figure in which the lines drawn from the center to the circumference are all equal, which Spinoza rejects

---

[23] Kant 2000, 279.

[24] See also Spinoza's discussion of definitions in Ep. 9 (G 4:42–44), where he distinguishes between definitions of real things (such as "the Temple of Solomon") and definitions of our own creations or conceptions (such as "some temple which I want to build"), saying that only the former need be "true." Spinoza is using "true" here to mean correspondence with an object. As I explained in Chap. 2, he also calls genetically conceived figures "true," despite the fact that they correspond with no object in nature (similar to the imagined temple). My distinction between true-in-form ideas and robustly true ideas is intended to clarify this. In light of this distinction, the definition of the imagined temple need not be robustly true, but it does need to be true in form.

[25] In Ep. 59, Tschirnhaus expresses interest in Spinoza's method of "acquiring knowledge of unknown truths." In reply (Ep. 60), Spinoza says that he has not yet fully worked out the aforementioned method. However, as Goldenbaum (2011, 38–39) discusses, Christian Wolff reports that Tschirnhaus had been impressed by the "Erfindungskunst," or method of discovery, that he had learned from Spinoza, and which was based on Spinoza's theory of definition. This suggests that Spinoza may eventually have divulged more to Tschirnhaus about this method. Unfortunately, any further details are unknown.

in favor of the Hobbesian, genetic definition, but this is not a matter I will pursue further here.[26])

In addition to adopting Della Rocca's suggestion, then, seeing genetic definitions as heuristics for finite knowers—which may be true in form but not robustly true—helps to relax the tension between Spinoza's doctrine of genetic definitions and the doctrine of E1p8s2. Having now addressed this interpretive challenge, let me summarize the argument of this section: essences of things are grasped through definitions. To conceive the essence of a finite thing is not to conceive either its generation or its destruction. The latter are determined by causes external to the nature of the thing, and, therefore, outside the essence. This is not in conflict with the motivations for formulating a definition genetically, as I just argued. These remarks apply to *formal* essences, given what I said about this qualifier above. It is now necessary to examine Spinoza's conception of *actual* essences.

6.2.2 Actual Essences and Existence

According to Spinoza's *conatus* doctrine, "Each thing, as far as it can by its own power, strives to persevere in its being [*in suo esse perseverare conatur*]" (E3p6/G 2:146). Moreover, "The striving [*Conatus*] by which each thing strives to persevere in its being is nothing but the actual essence of the thing" (E3p7/G 2:146). As noted above, Spinoza believes at a fundamental level that if nothing in the nature of a thing can be responsible for limiting or negating it, then everything in its nature instead affirms it. This is why substances are necessarily infinite (E1p8/G 1:49). With nothing external to limit them (since no two substances share an attribute, and thus there is nothing with the requisite commonality to impose limits), substances affirm their own nature absolutely (entailing their infinity). God, as the only substance, with nothing to limit him, affirms his nature absolutely and does whatever follows from his nature. This is what I understand by God's power. Insofar as finite modes follow from and express God's nature, they inherit this fundamental, and absolute,

---

[26] Tschirnhaus presses Spinoza on a similar issue in Ep. 82, proposing that in mathematics, contrary to what Spinoza claims, he is able to infer only one property from a given definition on its own, and in order to infer other properties, the defined thing needs to be related to other things. Spinoza's tentative response—he admits that "perhaps this is correct for very simple things, or beings of reason (under which I include shapes also)" (Ep. 83/G 4:335)—suggests that he might not have been entirely clear on the matter himself.

self-affirmation, or power. Hence, in demonstrating E3p6, Spinoza also cites the fact that finite things are expressions of God's power (E3p6dem/G 2:146). Singular things affirm their own nature, then, insofar as doing so is in the very nature of each singular thing.[27]

In affirming its own nature, a thing also affirms everything that follows from that nature. As Spinoza notes in the demonstration of E3p7: "From the given essence of each thing some things necessarily follow" (G 2:146). To have the essence of a triangle, for example, is to have angles that equal two right angles. If a triangle were not subject to any contrary external forces, it would go on possessing angles equaling two right angles forever. As a finite existent, however, the triangle is always subject to contrary external forces, which threaten to alter its angles, thus destroying it. It is in the face of such contrary, external forces that a thing "strives" to maintain the integrity of its nature.[28] Since what a thing strives to posit is its own nature, we can see why Spinoza identifies the striving with the actual essence of the thing. Since this striving is only necessary (or, we might say, *activated*) in the face of contrary, external forces, or, in other words, when the thing exists in duration, there is an intimate relation between what Spinoza calls "actual essence" and durational existence.

In light of this association between actual essence and durational existence, Garrett argues that the actual essence (or *conatus*) of singular things "exists only so long as the thing itself does, and is not properly contrasted with the thing's existence."[29] In other words, the actual essence of a thing comes into and goes out of existence. On this basis, Garrett argues that there must be a significant difference between actual essence and formal essence, inasmuch as the latter does *not* come in and go out of existence, but is properly contrasted with the thing's durational existence. (In particular, as mentioned earlier, Garrett believes that the formal essence of a singular thing should be identified with an infinite mode.[30] I discuss this view below.)

---

[27] For a fuller discussion of E3p6dem, see Viljanen 2011, 91–104.
[28] See Viljanen 2011, 105–12 for an overview of interpretations of *conatus*. Inertial readings are defined as emphasizing the non-teleological nature of *conatus*. Some have defended contrasting teleological interpretations of *conatus*. (See Viljanen 2011, 112–25.) I do not weigh into this debate here.
[29] Garrett 2009, 286.
[30] Christopher Martin (2008) also defends a view of formal essences as infinite modes and actual essences as finitely existing in duration.

I agree with Garrett that the striving or *conatus* of each thing to persevere in its existence, which Spinoza equates with its actual essence (E3p7/G 2:146), ceases (or begins) to exist when the thing ceases (or begins) to exist in duration. Spinoza implies as much when he says, "The striving by which each thing strives to persevere in its being involves no finite time, but an indefinite time" (E3p8/G 2:147). But I think the sense in which this is the case is relatively trivial. If a triangle comes into existence in duration, then, in a sense, a triangular essence comes into existence in duration, since an existing triangle must *have* a triangular essence. Likewise, when a triangle ceases to exist in duration, then, in a sense, its triangular essence ceases to exist in duration, too. Moreover, since the essence of the thing determines the effects that follow from it, and since to exist is to strive to posit these effects in face of contrary external forces (per the *conatus* doctrine), the essence can be considered as identical with the striving of the thing to persevere in its existence.

All this shows, however, is that existing things *have* essences, and their intrinsic properties and actions are determined by their essences. It does not show that essences themselves are generated and destroyed. In order to think of the generation and destruction of some existing thing, it is necessary to think about external causes responsible for the generation and destruction of the thing. But such external causes have no place in the essence of the thing, which involves neither generation nor destruction, (and play only an extrinsic role in its definition), as we have seen. There is little evidence that Spinoza thinks any differently in this regard about actual, as opposed to formal, essences.[31] Indeed, the fact that definitions

---

[31] A recalcitrant text for my interpretation is the following from the *Short Treatise*: "But our body had a different proportion of motion and rest when we were unborn children, and later when we are dead, it will have still another. Nevertheless, there was before our birth, and will be after our death, an Idea, knowledge, etc., of our body in the thinking thing, as there is now. But it was not, and will not be at all the same, because now it has a different proportion of motion and rest" (KV 2pref; G 1:52). Since a given proportion of motion and rest defines an individual body, and since the definition, as I have argued, gives the essence of a thing, a given proportion of motion and rest should give the essence of an individual body. Moreover, I have argued that that essence is the same whether or not the thing exists in duration. In this passage, however, Spinoza appears to contradict my claim, insofar as he appears to deny that the idea of the motion and rest of an existing individual is the same as that of a non-existing individual. The meaning of the text is not entirely clear, however. It seems paradoxical to speak of the proportion of motion and rest of *my* body *when* I am dead (or *before* I am born), since, presumably, death is precisely the destruction of the proportion of motion and rest that defines my body. One possibility is that Spinoza is referring to the

posit only the thing itself, not external causes (bearing in mind here Della Rocca's solution for reconciling this with genetic definitions), provides the very basis of the *conatus* (or actual essence) doctrine (E3p4dem/G 2:145). So, to the extent that we can think of essences themselves coming into and going out of existence, it is only insofar as it is things *having* essences that do so.

Whether we are thinking of the actual essence of an existing triangle or of the formal essence of a triangle that does not presently exist, we are thinking of the same thing, to wit, the definition of a triangle (or, more precisely, the object of the definition). To express this in general terms, if I_a is a finite individual, and X is the essence of I_a, I understand the difference (or lack thereof) between formal and actual essence as follows:

Formal essence of I_a = X considered as the essence of I_a insofar as I_a does not exist in duration

Actual essence of I_a = X considered as the essence of I_a insofar as I_a exists in duration

The idea is that the difference between formal and actual essence is not, in fact, a difference between how we conceive a given essence itself. Instead, it is a difference in how we conceive an individual with a given essence (i.e., as existing in duration or not). As far as the essence itself is concerned, the difference is purely contextual.

The fault line in Spinoza's essence doctrine, then, does not run between formal essence and non-durational existence, on the one hand, and actual essence and durational existence, on the other. It runs, instead, between essence (whether formal or actual) and durational existence. It is a question of whether we consider the nature of the thing itself and all that

---

particles (or particular bodies) that come together to constitute my body when I am born and proceed to constitute other bodies when I die. In other words, he is speaking of a knowledge of the order of nature that precedes and succeeds my existence. When he says that there is knowledge of *my* body before I am born, he might be referring to the fact that to know the *causes* of my coming into being is a manner of knowing my being. But this raises the issue—discussed earlier—of conflating the external causes of the nature of a thing with the nature of the thing itself. To know the causes of my coming into existence is only knowledge of *me* if it is a manner of grasping *my* proportion of motion and rest. In that case, though, I do not see how the proportion of motion and rest thereby conceived would actually differ from my pre-existence to my existence.

follows from that nature (this is the consideration of its essence) or the thing as it is determined by external forces (this is the consideration of its durational existence).

A statement of this duality is found in E5p29s:

> We conceive things as actual in two ways: either insofar as we conceive them to exist in relation to a certain time and place, or insofar as we conceive them to be contained in God and to follow from the divine nature. But the things we conceive in this second way as true, *or* real, we conceive under a species of eternity, and to that extent they involve the eternal and infinite essence of God (as we have shown in E2p45 and E2p45s). (G 2:298–99)

A similar statement occurs in E2p45s, which Spinoza references at the end of the passage just quoted. E2p45 states, "Each idea of each body, or of each singular thing which actually exists, necessarily involves an eternal and infinite essence of God." Spinoza then proceeds in the scholium to clarify his understanding of existence in this proposition:

> By existence here I do not understand duration, i.e., existence insofar as it is conceived abstractly, and as a certain species of quantity. For I am speaking of the very nature of existence, which is attributed to singular things because infinitely many things follow from the eternal necessity of God's nature in infinitely many modes (see E1p16). I am speaking, I say, of the very existence of singular things insofar as they are in God. For even if each one is determined by another singular thing to exist in a certain way, still the force by which each one perseveres in existing follows from the eternal necessity of God's nature. (G 2:127)

It seems quite clear that in both of these passages (E2p45s and E5p29s) Spinoza has in mind the contrast I have drawn between conceiving something *sub specie durationis*, on the one hand, and conceiving it through its non-durational (i.e., eternal) essence, on the other. When he contrasts the way in which singular things are determined to exist in a certain way by another singular thing, on the one hand, and the "force by which each one perseveres in existing," on the other, in E2p45s, he seems to have in mind the contrast between the externally determined durational existence of a thing, on the one hand, and the *conatus*, or essence, of the thing, on the other. Echoing this contrast, E5p29s confirms that essences are conceived "under a species of eternity." (This is another point the significance of which for the present study will become more fully apparent in the next chapter.) What both passages underscore is the fact that to conceive the essence of things is to conceive them as contained in God and following from the divine nature (as opposed to conceiving them in terms of their agonistic relations to other finite things).

6.2.3 E2p8 Reconsidered

This brings us back, at last, to Spinoza's claim in E2p8 that the formal essences of singular things are "contained in" or "comprehended in" God's attributes whether or not the singular things exist in duration. Since, as we have just seen, essences are eternal, they do not come into and go out of existence depending on whether a singular thing exists in duration or not. Qua eternal, then, the essences must have a form of nondurational existence, and, as such, an ontological home in Spinoza's metaphysics. Since the essences of singular things are essences of finite modes, and modes must exist *in* God's attributes, it is not a surprise that the essences of singular things should be contained in God's attributes.

There is still the question of what these essences *are* that exist in God's attributes, however. According to Garrett, the formal essences of finite things must be infinite modes. His reasoning is that formal essences exist whether or not things exist in duration.[32] In other words, formal essences do not go in and out of existence, but are eternal. Finite things, by contrast, are not eternal and do come into and go out of existence. (We have seen that, for Garrett, this is true of the *actual* essences of things as well.)

In one sense, Garrett's interpretation is consistent with what I said about common essences above. I believe it is quite true to say that the essence of a finite body is motion and rest (the infinite mode) insofar as Spinoza countenances a conception of what I have called "*common essence.*" But finite modes also have an individual essence. The individual essence of a thing is given by its (individuating) definition. As I have argued, however, even if we define a finite thing genetically, its generation and destruction are—strictly speaking—external to it. Thus, to think of an individual essence is not to think of something coming into and going out of existence (any more than it would be in thinking of a common essence). This means that there is no obstacle to viewing the formal essences of things as finite modes. It is surely as finite modes, then, that Spinoza speaks of the formal essences of singular things being comprehended or

[32] See D. Garrett 2009, 289–90.

contained in God's attributes. The infinite modes are also, of course, contained in God's attributes, but it is only in the most minimal sense that they constitute the essence of any singular thing (i.e., as common essence).[33]

Moreover, I think the following passage from *Ethics* Part 5 militates against Garrett's interpretation. Spinoza writes, "it is clear that our Mind, insofar as it understands, is an eternal mode of thinking, which is determined by another eternal mode of thinking, and this again by another, and so on, to infinity; so that together, they all constitute God's eternal and infinite intellect" (E5p40s/G 2:306). In talking about the mind as an eternal mode of thinking in this passage, Spinoza is talking about the essence of the mind. His claim that the essence of the mind is determined by another eternal mode of thinking ad infinitum would seem to suggest that the essence of the mind is not the infinite mode itself, because *that*, presumably, is not determined by eternal modes of thinking ad infinitum.[34] The passage implies instead that the mind's essence is a finite eternal mode of thinking which is determined by its place among infinite other finite eternal modes of thinking that comprise the infinite mode of thought. In any case, any mode that is determined by another of its own kind *must* be finite per Spinoza's definition of finitude in E1d2.[35]

---

[33] In his paper, "Spinoza on the Essence of the Human Body and the Part of the Mind That Is Eternal" (2009), Garrett speaks of formal essences as infinite modes without specifying whether he is talking about *immediate* infinite modes or *mediate* infinite modes. (The same is true in Garrett 2010.) In conversation, however, Garrett clarified to me that he understands the formal essences of things to be *mediate* infinite modes, and, moreover, that there are infinite mediate infinite modes (correlating to infinite formal essences). This means that formal essences can be more specific than would be the case if they were *immediate* infinite modes alone. While I do not think multiple mediate infinite modes are impossible, I interpret E1p22 along with Letter 64 to suggest that there is only a single mediate infinite mode (for each attribute). However, I admit that the text is certainly obscure enough to be open to various interpretations, including Garrett's. In this light, I would appeal to Ockham's razor to support my preference for a single mediate infinite mode along with a single immediate infinite mode. Since the latter includes what is required to individuate modes (i.e., motion and rest) and the former includes the individual existents themselves, I see no need to multiply beings any further. In any case, I will argue below that formal essences should not be identified with the mediate infinite mode (as I interpret it) any more than with the immediate infinite mode.

[34] See the previous note.

[35] E1d2 reads: "That thing is said to be finite in its own kind that can be limited by another of the same nature" (G 2:45). I owe this point to John Grey.

To be sure, both infinite modes and attributes are implicated and involved in the essences of finite things, even when conceived in the strictest sense as individual essences. There is an important relationship between the extremes of the essence spectrum I delineated above. On the one hand, it is impossible to understand the ratio of motion and rest that constitutes the individual essence of a finite body without understanding the motion and rest that comprise the first infinite mode and the attribute of extension from which motion and rest follow (and without which they cannot be conceived). On the other hand, an individual essence is a particular determination of the infinite mode.[36]

I find it helpful to think of the dynamics of the relationship between these extremes in terms of Leibniz's principle of compossibility.[37] We know that, for Spinoza, "infinitely many things in infinitely many modes, (i.e. everything which can fall under an infinite intellect)" follow from God's absolutely infinite nature (E1p16/G 2:60). Recognizing that the existences of certain things are not mutually compatible (or compossible), according to Leibniz's principle, whatever things maximize reality while being mutually compatible will exist.[38] Of course, the difference between Spinoza and Leibniz is that whereas this maximally real set of mutually compatible things follows necessarily from God's nature in Spinoza, Leibniz believes that God freely chooses the optimal set from infinite possible sets (or worlds). But this difference does not alter the fact that in both cases the determination of the maximally real set of mutually compatible things is represented a priori in the infinite intellect of God from first causes.

So, the ratio of motion and rest that defines some finite individual, such as Seabiscuit, is a determination that follows from the attribute of extension and its immediate infinite mode in conjunction with a maximally real set of compatible individuals. This set is the mediate infinite mode.[39] Since

---

[36] This determination is, I take it, what Yovel speaks of in terms of logical (as opposed to mechanical) "cosmic particularization." See Yovel 1991, 92–3.

[37] Leibniz 1989, 169.

[38] See Garrett 1991, 197 for a defense of the attribution of this maximalist proposition to Spinoza.

[39] This interpretation of the logico-causal relationship between the finite modes that comprise the second kind of infinite mode, on the one hand, and the attribute and first kind of infinite mode, on the other, is necessitarian. That is, given the nature of the attribute (and the first kind of infinite mode), the natures of the finite modes comprising the second kind of infinite mode follow by necessity, and therefore are in principle knowable a priori by an

Seabiscuit's essence can only be fully determined in conjunction with the maximally real set of compatible individuals, to understand the essence of Seabiscuit fully it is necessary to understand the entire maximally real set of compatible individuals, or in other words, the particular details of the mediate infinite mode (i.e., "the face of the whole universe"). But I do not think this means that Seabiscuit's essence can be identified with the mediate infinite mode. (In that case, all singular things would share the same essence, and essences would not be individuating as they should be per E2d2.) Still less does it mean that Seabiscuit's essence is identifiable with the attribute or the immediate infinite mode. It does mean, however, that Seabiscuit's individual essence can only be understood by an infinite intellect.

With our limited intellects, we are not able to enjoy a fully wrought idea of individual essence. But we are able to have adequate ideas of the attribute of extension and of the motion and rest that constitutes the first kind of infinite mode. These ideas are our common notions. While they do not constitute the essence of any singular thing, they provide a basis for developing increasingly specific conceptions of the essences of finite modes. Even if a fully wrought conception of individual essence, being infinitely complex, will remain beyond the capacity of finite minds, we can employ universal conceptions of species essence as hypothetical, ever-revisable approximations. I argued in a previous chapter that this process of determination cannot proceed purely a priori for us, but must be informed and guided by experiential data. The fact that the effects produced by a thing are determined by its essence (as we saw with the example of the triangle and the equality of its angles to two right angles) sanctions the use of experience (of effects) in the attempt to ascertain essence. Of course, it is necessary to distinguish between effects that follow from the nature of the thing itself and effects that follow as a result of external forces acting on the thing.[40] The ongoing, methodical refinement of our understanding of this distinction in the case of any individual is possible through the hypothetico-deductive approach I outlined above. As we

---

infinite intellect. While I take this to be more or less the standard way of reading the modality of finite modes, the necessitarian interpretation is not without its detractors. See, in particular, Curley 1988, 47–50. The classic articulation of the necessitarian view is Garrett 1991. For a helpful overview of the issue, see Newlands 2018.

[40] See n. 16 in Chap. 4 for discussion of the distinction between properties that follow from the nature of a thing as opposed to properties that are caused (at least partially) by external things.

have also seen, the fact that our conceptions of the essences of finite modes must be informed by experience does not mean that adequate conceptions are ruled out. While experientially informed adequate conceptions must be hypothetical, they can nevertheless exhibit the form of true ideas. I will have more to say about our knowledge of the essences of things in the next chapter, since it is a major theme in the discussion of intuitive knowledge.

References

Curley, Edwin. 1969. *Spinoza's Metaphysics: An Essay in Interpretation.* Cambridge, MA: Harvard University Press.
———. 1988. *Behind the Geometrical Method: A Reading of Spinoza's Ethics.* Princeton, NJ: Princeton University Press.
Della Rocca, Michael. 1996a. *Representation and the Mind-Body Problem in Spinoza.* New York, NY: Oxford University Press.
———. 1996b. "Spinoza's Metaphysical Psychology." In *The Cambridge Companion to Spinoza*, edited by Don Garrett, 192–266. Cambridge, UK: Cambridge University Press.
Garrett, Don. 1991. "Spinoza's Necessitarianism." In *God and Nature: Spinoza's Metaphysics*, edited by Yirmiyahu Yovel, 191–218. Leiden: E.J. Brill.
———. 2009. "Spinoza on the Essence of the Human Body and the Part of the Mind That Is Eternal." In *The Cambridge Companion to Spinoza's Ethics*, edited by Olli Koistinen, 284–302. Cambridge, UK: Cambridge University Press.
———. 2010. "Spinoza's Theory of *Scientia Intuitiva*." In *Scientia in Early Modern Philosophy*, edited by T. Sorell et al., 99–115. Springer.
Goldenbaum, Ursula. 2011. "Spinoza – Ein toter Hund? Nicht für Christian Wolff." *Zeitschrift für Ideengeschichte* 5(1): 29–41.
Hampshire, Stuart. 2005. *Spinoza and Spinozism.* Oxford, UK: Oxford University Press.
Hobbes, Thomas. 1991. *Man and Citizen* (De Homine *and* De Cive), edited by Bernard Gert. Indianapolis: Hackett Publishing Company.
Homan, Matthew. 2016. "On the Alleged Exceptional Nature of Thought in Spinoza." *Journal of Philosophical Research* 41: 1–16.
Hübner, Karolina. 2016. "Spinoza on Essences, Universals, and Beings of Reason." *Pacific Philosophical Quarterly* 97: 58–88.
Jonas, Hans. 1965. "Spinoza and the Theory of Organism." *Journal of the History of Philosophy* 3(1): 43–58.
Kant, Immanuel. 2000. *Critique of the Power of Judgment.* Translated by Paul Guyer and Eric Matthews. Cambridge, UK: Cambridge University Press.
LeBuffe, Michael. 2018. *Spinoza on Reason.* New York, NY: Oxford University Press.

Leibniz, Gottfried. 1989. *Philosophical Papers and Letters*. Edited and translated by Leroy E. Loemker. Dordrecht: Kluwer Academic Publishers.

Lin, Martin. 2019. *Being and Reason: An Essay on Spinoza's Metaphysics*. New York, NY: Oxford University Press.

Martin, Christopher P. 2008. "The Framework of Essences in Spinoza's *Ethics*." *British Journal for the History of Philosophy* 16(3): 489–509.

Melamed, Yitzhak Y. 2013. *Spinoza's Metaphysics: Substance and Thought*. Oxford, UK: Oxford University Press.

Newlands, Samuel. 2018. "Spinoza's Modal Metaphysics." *The Stanford Encyclopedia of Philosophy*, Edward N. Zalta (ed.), URL https://plato.stanford.edu/archives/falE2p13lem2018/entries/spinoza-modal/.

Schliesser, Eric. 2014. "Spinoza and the Philosophy of Science: Mathematics, Motion, and Being." In The Oxford Handbook of Spinoza, edited by Michael Della Rocca. DOI: https://doi.org/10.1093/oxfordhb/9780195335828.013.020.

Soyarslan, Sanem. 2016. "The Distinction between Reason and Intuitive Knowledge in Spinoza's *Ethics*." *European Journal of Philosophy* 24(1): 27–54.

Viljanen, Valtteri. 2011. *Spinoza's Geometry of Power*. Cambridge, UK: Cambridge University Press.

Yovel, Yirmiyahu. 1991. "The Infinite Mode and Natural Laws in Spinoza." In *God and Nature: Spinoza's Metaphysics*, edited by Yirmiyahu Yovel, 79–96. Leiden: E.J. Brill.

CHAPTER 7

Intuitive Knowledge: The Perfection of Reason

Intuitive knowledge (*scientia intuitiva*), or what Spinoza also calls "knowledge of the third kind," represents the pinnacle of Spinoza's epistemology. Arguably, it also represents the pinnacle of his philosophy more broadly. Consider the following passage from the Appendix of *Ethics* Part 4:

> In life, therefore, it is especially useful to perfect, as far as we can, our intellect, or reason. In this one thing consists man's highest happiness, or blessedness. Indeed, blessedness is nothing but that satisfaction of mind which stems from the intuitive knowledge of God. But perfecting the intellect is nothing but understanding God, his attributes, and his actions, which follow from the necessity of his nature. So the ultimate end of man who is led by reason, that is, his highest desire, by which he strives to moderate all the others, is that by which he is led to conceive adequately both himself and all things which can fall under his understanding. (G 2:267)

Spinoza goes on to identify human blessedness with the intellectual love of God in *Ethics* Part 5, but this is just the satisfaction of mind for which Spinoza says here intuitive knowledge holds the key (E5p36s/G 2:303). A number of other panegyric statements about the third kind of knowledge appear elsewhere in the *Ethics* and other writings, such that its supreme significance is beyond doubt.[1]

---

[1] See, for instance, TIE 29/G 2:13; KV 2.4.9–10/G 1:61; E2p47s/G 2:128.

Despite its unequivocally exalted status, there is lack of clarity about basic aspects of *scientia intuitiva*'s nature and scope. Some of the foremost interpretive issues are on display in the passage quoted above. For instance, when Spinoza speaks of "reason" (*ratio*) there, it is unclear whether he means to invoke the second kind of knowledge (in contrast to the third), or a broader notion of reason that encompasses both the second and third kinds of knowledge. The passage tends to suggest a broader connotation, but either way, it prompts the question of the difference between reason and intuitive knowledge. Do both lead to blessedness? They are, after all, both forms of *adequate* knowledge. But Spinoza seems to imply in this passage, and elsewhere states explicitly, that the third kind of knowledge is superior to the second. Is intuitive knowledge superior because it grants knowledge of a different, loftier object? If so, what are the respective objects of the two kinds of knowledge?

The most important texts for answering these questions pull in different directions. The definitions that Spinoza gives of the kinds of knowledge in the TIE, KV, and *Ethics* suggest that intuitive knowledge and reason have different epistemic content. By contrast, the mathematical example that Spinoza consistently uses in these texts to compare the kinds of knowledge, as well as the non-mathematical example given in E5p36s, suggest different ways of arriving at the same knowledge content. The discrepancy has generated competing interpretations. On the one hand, according to interpretations that emphasize the definitions, reason and intuitive knowledge have different epistemic content. On the other hand, according to interpretations that emphasize the examples, the second and third kinds of knowledge differ only in the method by which they arrive at the same content. I will follow Sanem Soyarslan in referring to the former as the "content interpretation" and the latter as the "method interpretation."[2]

---

[2] Soyarslan 2016. Soyarslan defends a content interpretation. Other adherents of a content interpretation include Curley (1973, 57), Allison (1987, 116–19), Wilson (1996, 117–18), and D. Garrett (2009, 107). Primus (2017) also seems to defend a version of the content interpretation, but unlike the other content interpretations cited, she does not believe that the distinction between reason and intuitive knowledge reflects the difference between knowledge of non-essential properties and knowledge of essences. Instead, Primus argues that whereas reason knows how its objects would be *if* they were formally real, intuitive knowledge adds the certainty *that* its objects are, in fact, formally real. (Allison expresses something similar at one point (1987, 117–18).) Adherents of a method interpretation include Carr (1978), Sandler (2005), and Nadler (2006, 178–85).

Perhaps the biggest issue is getting clear about what intuitive knowledge and reason are supposed to be knowledge *of*. Spinoza consistently says that intuitive knowledge is knowledge of the essences of things, but what kinds of essences? In the last chapter I distinguished three possibilities: common essence, species essence, and individual essence. Is intuitive knowledge supposed to provide knowledge of one of these rather than another? And what about *ratio*?

The interpretive questions I've raised can be boiled down to two primary ones: (1) what is intuitive knowledge *about*, and (2) how does it differ from reason? The questions are obviously interdependent and will be treated as such in what follows. I begin with a preliminary analysis of the principal texts for interpreting the kinds of knowledge—the aforementioned definitions, fourth proportional example, and one or two other pertinent passages—providing fuller exposition of the interpretive issues at stake, and showing why what might seem at first like an open-and-shut case for the content interpretation is subject to serious doubts. The focus will be on Spinoza's discussion of the relevant issues in the *Ethics*, though I will reference the earlier texts as well.

In the second part of the chapter I present what I take to be a prominent and important interpretation of what intuitive knowledge is about, namely, what I called common essences in the last chapter. Although the *common essence interpretation* (as I will call it) of the content of intuitive knowledge captures an important dimension of Spinoza's thought, and may be accurate in some degree, I will argue that intuitive knowledge promises more than knowledge of common essences. To make the case that it can yield knowledge of species essences, if not individual essences, I develop a geometrical variation on Spinoza's fourth proportional example in the third section. A limitation of Spinoza's numerical, fourth proportional example is that it is unhelpful regarding the content of the kinds of knowledge, since numbers, as beings of reason, have no place in Spinoza's ontology. If the argument pressed in previous chapters for (weak) geometrical realism is on track, then a geometrical example will translate into the terms of Spinoza's ontology, promising to be more revealing than a numerical one.

Although my reasons for preferring the method interpretation of the difference between reason and intuitive knowledge will emerge over the course of this chapter, in the fourth section I make a focused case on its behalf. I will articulate my own particular version of the method interpretation, according to which intuitive knowledge is best regarded as the perfection of reason, while also addressing the relevance that Spinoza's notion of *conatus* has for the debate between method and content advocates. I then discuss the connection of intuitive knowledge to the intellectual love of God and account for the superiority of the third kind of knowledge over the second.

7.1 Preliminary Analysis of the Principal Texts

We have already examined the definitions of imagination and reason in previous chapters. Before looking at Spinoza's definition of intuitive knowledge, it will be useful to inspect Spinoza's mathematical example first. Here is the example as presented in the *Ethics*:

> Suppose there are three numbers, and the problem is to find a fourth which is to the third as the second is to the first. Merchants do not hesitate to multiply the second by the third, and divide the product by the first, because they have not yet forgotten what they heard from their teacher without any demonstration, or because they have often found this in the simplest numbers, or from the force of the demonstration of P19 in Book VII of Euclid, namely, from the common property of proportionals. But in the simplest numbers none of this is necessary. Given the numbers 1, 2, and 3, no one fails to see that the fourth proportional number is 6—and we see this much more clearly because we infer the fourth number from the ratio which, in one glance [*uno intuitu*], we see the first number to have to the second. (G 2:122)

The first two ways of solving the fourth proportional problem—applying a formula, the "rule of three," on the recommendation of an external authority, and on the basis of trial and error—correspond to direct and indirect forms of sensory experience, or imagination. Applying the rule of three on the recommendation of a teacher exemplifies indirect sensory experience (i.e., sensory experience of "having heard or read certain words"); applying the rule on the basis of one's own trial and error, on the other hand, exemplifies direct sensory experience.[3] Spinoza provides no

---

[3] See Spinoza's definition of imagination, or the first kind of knowledge, at the beginning of E2p40s2/G 2:122. My distinction between direct and indirect forms of sensory experience, or imagination, reflects Spinoza's distinction between perceiving things and forming universal notions "from singular things which have been represented to us through the senses in a way that is mutilated and confused," on the one hand, and "from signs, e.g., from

direct commentary on the fourth proportional example in the *Ethics*, but in the TIE and KV, he makes plain that the first two ways of solving the problem are uncertain and prone to error (TIE 26–29/G 2:12–13; KV 2.2/G 1:54–55). The epistemic shortcomings of relying on the recommendation of authority are obvious. While the evidence of trial and error may have more to recommend it as a basis of belief, it has the inherent fallibility of any inductive generalization.

The third way of solving the problem corresponds to the second kind of knowledge. This way involves the same formula (of multiplying the second and third numbers and dividing by the first) employed in the first two ways. However, this time the application of the formula is based not on what was learned from a teacher or trial and error, but on mathematical proof.[4]

Finally, the fourth way of solving the problem corresponds, of course, to the third kind of knowledge. It stands out from the other ways in eschewing any formula. In certain cases—involving the simplest numbers—it is possible to see the solution "in one glance." Given the numbers 1, 2, and 3, one sees intuitively that the fourth proportional number is 6 simply by apprehending the ratio that obtains between the first two numbers and inferring the fourth proportional number on the basis of that intuited ratio. Like the third way of solving the problem, it is "without danger of error" (TIE 29/G 2:13). Knowledge of both the second and third kinds, unlike the first, is "necessarily true" (E2p41/G 2:122) and "teaches us to distinguish the true from the false" (E2p42/G 2:123).

Overall, the fourth proportional example distinguishes the three kinds of knowledge along two main fault lines. First, there is the certainty/uncertainty or adequacy/inadequacy division, where the first two ways of solving the problem represent uncertain and inadequate forms of knowledge while the third and fourth ways represent certain and adequate forms. Second, there is the distinction between the three ways of solving the problem that use the rule of three, on the one hand, and the fourth way, which uses no rule or formula, on the other. We might think of this as a mediated/unmediated or indirect/direct distinction: while the first and second kinds of knowledge generate solutions to problems or conclusions from premises in a mediated or indirect fashion—interposing

---

the fact that, having heard or read certain words, we recollect things, and for certain ideas of them, which are like them, and through which we imagine the things," on the other.

[4] For a helpful analysis of the relevant demonstration in Euclid, see Matheron 1986.

between problem and solution the application of a formula—the third kind of knowledge is direct or unmediated—the solution is seen in one glance.

Although the fourth proportional example successfully illustrates distinctions between all three (or four, if we count the two subdivisions of imagination) kinds of knowledge, it seems especially geared toward distinguishing intuitive knowledge from the other two kinds. This is suggested by Spinoza's presentation of the example itself. He groups together the first three ways of solving the problem in a long disjunctive sentence, then turning to the climax of the example: "But in the simplest numbers none of this [i.e., bothering with the rule of three] is necessary." This accented shift is also apparent in Spinoza's presentation of the definitions of the kinds of knowledge. Once again, he groups together the first two kinds of knowledge as ways in which "we perceive many things and form universal notions" (E2p40s2/G 2:122). Then, when he introduces the third kind of knowledge, it is set apart: "In addition to these two kinds of knowledge, there is (as I shall show in what follows) another" (E2p40s2/G 2:122).

Moreover, Spinoza's commentaries on the fourth proportional example in the *Short Treatise* and TIE stress the special status of intuitive knowledge. In the former text, Spinoza says that intuitive knowledge "goes far beyond the others" (in the quality of the knowledge it yields) (KV 2.2/G 1:55), and in the latter, he concludes that it is "what we must chiefly use" (TIE 29/G 2:13). What is it about the third kind of knowledge that makes it so special compared with imagination and reason?

In the *Short Treatise*, Spinoza provides the following characterization of the difference between the second and third kinds of knowledge (which he refers to there as "belief" and "clear knowledge," respectively):

> We call the second belief, because the things we grasp only through reason, we do not see, but know only through a conviction in the intellect that it must be so and not otherwise.
>
> But we call that clear knowledge which comes not from being convinced by reasons, but from being aware of and enjoying the thing itself. (KV 2.2.2/G 1:55)

Spinoza's point here is that the third kind of knowledge is more penetrating than the second. It allows us to access "the thing itself," whereas the second kind of knowledge affords only a more superficial, albeit accurate, grasp of the object. He goes on a little later to say that the second kind of knowledge "teaches us only what it belongs to the thing to be" whereas the third gets at "what it is" (KV 2.4.2/G 1:59).

The KV's rather vague distinctions between the second and third kinds of knowledge are generally echoed in the TIE, albeit with a bit more definition. Spinoza is clear there that only the fourth mode of perceiving (which is the TIE's analogue of intuitive knowledge) "comprehends the adequate essence of the thing" (TIE 29/G 2:13). The third (i.e., the TIE's analogue of reason), by contrast, is "the perception that we have when the essence of a thing is inferred from another thing, but not adequately (*sed non adequate*)" (TIE 19/G 2:10). This is a bit confusing, since inadequate knowledge is a cause of error (in the *Ethics*, at least), whereas Spinoza says that the third mode of perceiving is without danger of error in the TIE. Does the third mode have the essence of a thing as its object, but perceive it inadequately? Or does it have the properties of a thing as its object and perceive *those* adequately (while failing to perceive the essence of the thing adequately)?[5]

Whether or not the analogues of reason in the KV and TIE, respectively, have as their object the essence of a thing or only *propria*, and whether or not they are characterizable as adequate, what is certain is that reason, in these texts, does not consist in an adequate cognition of essence, whereas intuitive knowledge does.

In the *Ethics*, too, Spinoza defines the third kind of knowledge as a knowledge of essences. The definition reads there as follows: "this kind of knowing proceeds from an adequate idea of the formal essence of certain attributes of God to the adequate knowledge of the essence of things" (G 2:123). Spinoza glosses this definition in E5p25dem, and in the gloss the notion of "*formal* essence" drops out to leave a knowledge "which proceeds from an adequate idea of certain attributes of God to an adequate knowledge of the essence of things" (G 2:296).[6] In both cases, intuitive

---

[5] Cf. D. Garrett (2009, 109): "Although [Spinoza] indicates that this inference may not proceed 'adequately,' this does not entail that the resulting ideas are themselves inadequate and false ones in his later technical sense; since he claims in the *Ethics* that all ideas constituting reason are adequate and true, he presumably means only that the inference fails to show exactly what the essence of the cause is and *how* that essence produces the effect." Garrett's appeal to the *Ethics*' notions of reason and adequacy assumes that Spinoza's account of reason (and adequacy) does not change from the TIE to the *Ethics*—an assumption about which I raise some doubts below.

[6] As a number of commentators have noted, the phrase "formal essence of certain attributes" is puzzling, since attributes are themselves expressions of divine essence, so 'the for-

knowledge *proceeds from an adequate idea of certain attributes of God to an adequate knowledge of the essence of things.*

Does reason, by contrast, *not* yield knowledge of essences, then? One difference between the *Ethics* and the earlier texts is that reason is unambiguously considered an adequate form of knowledge in the *Ethics*. If the earlier texts are a guide, and only intuitive knowledge can be an adequate knowledge of essences, then this implies that if reason is adequate, it must have as its object the properties of things, not their essences. This appears to be borne out, for in the *Ethics*, Spinoza says that the second kind of knowledge proceeds from "common notions and adequate ideas of the properties of things" to the formation of other "universal notions." If by "properties" and "universal notions," Spinoza has in mind properties that are true of something, but do not constitute the essence of the thing, then Spinoza's definition of reason would seem to reflect the distinction between reason and intuitive knowledge in the early texts. That is, while reason yields knowledge about something that is true (and thus, without danger of error), it does not constitute knowledge of the essence of anything (at least not *adequate* knowledge of essence). If this is right, then the question of the difference between reason and intuitive knowledge would be unproblematic: reason and intuitive knowledge differ *both* in terms of method, insofar as intuitive knowledge consists in an immediate grasp of its object, whereas reason grasps its object only in a mediated or discursive fashion; *and* in terms of content, insofar as intuitive knowledge consists in knowledge of essences, whereas reason does not. The content interpretation, in this case, would be right: intuitive knowledge differs in both method and content, and not just in method, *pace* the method interpretation.

---

mal essence of certain attributes' sounds like 'the formal essence of certain essences' (i.e., as Garrett puts it, "seemingly redundant" (2009, 105)). It will be recalled that in Chap. 6 I suggested that the qualifier "formal" contrasts with "objective" in certain contexts (à la Suárez and Descartes) and with "actual" in others. In the present context, I suspect that the contrast must be with "objective," since there can be no formal-actual distinction for attributes (since that distinction depends on the durational existence of finite modes). In that case, Spinoza may have wished to emphasize that in beginning with a knowledge of attributes, intuitive knowledge begins not with knowledge of how attributes are perceived by us (i.e., merely as objective essences), but as they are in themselves (i.e., as formal). This suggestion is, admittedly, speculative. In any case, the elision of the phrase "formal essence" in E5p25dem suggests that probably not much rides on it.

There is reason to doubt, however, that Spinoza's understanding of the distinction between reason and intuitive knowledge in the *Ethics* mirrors his understanding of the distinction in the earlier texts as the foregoing line of interpretation assumes. There are, for one thing, significant discontinuities between the early texts and the *Ethics*. For instance, there is little sign in either the TIE or the *Short Treatise* of the concept of "common notions." Since the common notions are the basis of the second kind of knowledge, if they represent a new development since the earlier texts, then reason is very likely itself understood differently in the *Ethics* than in the earlier texts.[7] I suggested above that the earlier texts are ambiguous with regard to whether reason is an adequate form of knowledge or not. There is some evidence that in the earlier texts reason was, in fact, not adequate. Spinoza says in the TIE, "a thing is perceived through its essence alone when, from the fact that I know something, I know what it is to know something" (TIE 22/G 2:11). An adequate idea is supposed to be one that is transparently true, however. In other words, it is supposed to be clear that one knows something when one has an adequate idea. The passage just quoted suggests that only knowledge of essence is adequate. Since Spinoza is talking about the equivalent of intuitive knowledge in this passage, the implication is that only intuitive knowledge is adequate. Contrast this with the fact that reason is unambiguously an adequate form of knowledge in the *Ethics*. Moreover, it has the crucial feature just mentioned: "Knowledge of the second and third kinds, and not of the first kind, teaches us to distinguish the true from the false" (E2p42/G 2:123). Reason, then, no less than intuitive knowledge makes it clear what it means to know something in the *Ethics* whereas its analogue in the TIE did not. In these ways, then, there is ground for thinking that reason's epistemic star has risen from the time of the earlier texts to the *Ethics*.

What is more, on the basis of the examples that Spinoza gives of the difference between reason and intuitive knowledge, it is unclear, at least prima facie, why an unmediated, non-discursive mode of knowing is able to provide access to an essential content that remains inaccessible to a mediated, discursive mode of knowing. Furthermore, if the fourth proportional example successfully captures the relevant differences between the kinds of knowledge, the content interpretation looks to be in trouble,

---

[7] According to Deleuze (1988, 56), the theory of common notions, which does not appear before the *Ethics*, "transforms the entire Spinozan conception of Reason, and defines the status of the second kind of knowledge."

since the content yielded by each of the ways of solving the fourth proportional problem appears to be the same. In each case, all that seems to be discovered is the numerical value of the fourth proportional, which happens to be 6 in the version that Spinoza gives.

Perhaps the fourth proportional example is ill-suited to illustrate differences in content between the kinds of knowledge, since it is numerical, and, as we have seen, numbers are beings of reason *sans* object in Spinoza's ontology. The example may well simply not have been designed to capture all of the differences between the kinds of knowledge. Perhaps it was intended only to capture the differences in the method by which they respectively proceed (without that meaning that differences of method are the only differences).

Fortunately, the fourth proportional problem is not the only example that Spinoza gives to illustrate the distinction between the second and third kinds of knowledge. In *Ethics* Part 5, he compares knowing that the mind depends upon God with respect to both its essence and its existence on the basis of intuitive knowledge, on the one hand, and on the basis of reason, on the other:

> I thought this worth the trouble of noting here, in order to show by this example how much the knowledge of singular things I have called intuitive, or knowledge of the third kind (see E2p40s2), can accomplish, and how much more powerful it is than the universal knowledge I have called knowledge of the second kind. For although I have shown generally in Part I that all things (and consequently the human Mind also) depend on God both for their essence and their existence, nevertheless, that demonstration, though legitimate and put beyond all chance of doubt, still does not affect our Mind as much as when this is inferred from the very essence of any singular thing which we say depends on God. (E5p36s/G 2:303)

In this case, there is no question of dealing with beings of reason rather than real beings. The knowledge of the mind's relation to God is knowledge of real things if anything is. However, like the fourth proportional example, it is unclear from this example how the knowledge yielded by the second and third kinds of knowledge respectively differ in content. Spinoza appears to be comparing two ways of gaining the same knowledge content, namely, the dependence on God of the mind's essence and existence. Moreover, the distinction he appears to be emphasizing is, in fact, one neither of content nor of method, but of how much the different ways of knowing "affect our Mind."

I will discuss the significance of affective discrepancies between intuitive knowledge and reason later. It is necessary first to clarify whether reason and intuitive knowledge in fact produce different knowledge content or not. The evidence of the two examples that Spinoza gives to illustrate the differences between the two throws into doubt what seemed to be a straightforward case for the content interpretation.

7.2 The Content of Intuitive Knowledge: The Common Essence Interpretation

Let us look more closely at Spinoza's definition of intuitive knowledge. Here it is, again, a kind of knowledge "*which proceeds from an adequate idea of certain attributes of God to an adequate knowledge of the essence of things*" (G 2:296, italics added). (I have used the version in which the phrase "formal essence" is elided.) The definition can be divided into two parts: (1) that from which intuitive knowledge proceeds: "*an adequate idea of certain attributes of God*"; and (2) that in which intuitive knowledge terminates: "*an adequate knowledge of the essence of things.*" As Spinoza makes clear in a number of places (such as E5p24 and E5p25), when he says "things" here he means "singular things." So intuitive knowledge terminates in an adequate knowledge of the essence of *singular* things. As we know, singular things are finite, determinate modes.[8]

What is the essence of singular things? Recall the essence spectrum from the last chapter. At one extreme is the essence constitutive of the attribute (and that of the immediate infinite mode). All modes of any given attribute share the attribute (and immediate infinite mode) as their common essence. So, my body as a mode of the attribute of extension is essentially extended just as the body of a mouse and the body of a rock are essentially extended. According to one possible interpretation, intuitive knowledge is just the knowledge that for any mode of a given attribute, its

---

[8] Commentators have wondered if the termination of intuitive knowledge in the knowledge of singular things per the definition rules out intuitive knowledge of non-singular things, such as attributes and infinite modes. (See D. Garrett 2009, 110.) I addressed the question of the kind of knowledge (reason or intuitive knowledge) responsible for our knowledge of common notions and attributes in a note to a previous chapter. See n. 27 in Chap. 4.

essence is determined by the attribute of which it is a mode. Thus, to know a rock intuitively would be the same as to know a human body intuitively—in both cases, I would know that, as modes of the attribute of extension, they are both essentially extended things. Of course, as the attributes are expressions of divine essence, an important aspect of this knowledge is knowing that the essence of a given mode is divine.[9] I will call this the *common essence interpretation* of the content of intuitive knowledge.

The common essence interpretation would accord nicely with what Spinoza says in E5p36s. In this scholium, as we saw, Spinoza uses the example of knowing that the mind follows from the divine nature with respect to both essence and existence to illustrate the difference between reason and intuitive knowledge. He derives this truth about the mind from the fact that "the essence of our Mind consists only in knowledge [*in sola cognitione*], of which God is the beginning and foundation" (E5p36s/G 2:303). By "knowledge" (*cognitio*), here, Spinoza does not mean anything unique to the human mind.[10] "Knowledge" is being used expansively to encompass the characteristic of all modes of thinking, including those that constitute the minds of mice and rocks. (By Spinoza's parallelism doctrine, even rocks can be said to have minds in some sense.[11])

---

[9] One problem this raises is: what to make of the difference between a Spinozist's grasp of the nature of a rock as essentially extended and, say, a Cartesian's, for whom extension is not a divine attribute (at least not formally)? The answer, I think, is that the difference is very significant indeed. As we saw in Chap. 5, Spinoza forcefully rejects the Cartesian understanding of extension on the grounds that it lacks the immanent causal power of a divine essence, and thus fails to explain the individuation of extended modes. This suggests that to have even a minimal adequate understanding of an extended mode such as a rock *as* essentially extended requires an adequate understanding of extension, which, in turn, requires an adequate understanding of God. In other words, it requires an understanding of some of the most basic aspects of Spinoza's monistic philosophy. This should come as little surprise, however, given what we have already discussed regarding the foundational role of God in Spinoza's methodology in Chap. 2. All knowledge (of the robust kind) in Spinoza depends upon an adequate understanding of God (as self-caused, absolutely infinite, etc.). I return to this point in Sect. 7.4 of this chapter.

[10] In order for there to be knowledge unique to the human mind, there would have to be (among other things) a discrete (shared) human essence, but I cast doubt on this possibility in Chap. 4. In any case, I think it is clear that in talking about the "knowledge" (*cognitio*) that constitutes the essence of our mind, Spinoza is talking about the fact that the human mind consists of ideas, which are modes of God's attribute of thought (as he states explicitly in E2p11dem). All minds, however (not just human), consist of ideas.

[11] See E2p13s/G 2:96–7.

Thus, when he speaks of the essence of the mind qua singular thing in E5p36s, he seems to refer only to the fact that the mind is a thinking thing.

In addition to fitting with E5p36s, the common essence interpretation has a few other points in its favor as well. In the first place, it could help to explain Spinoza's parsimonious use of examples. If, as the common essence interpretation holds, intuitive knowledge has the same content in all cases (at least within an attribute) regardless of the individual nature of the singular thing in question, then there is little need for Spinoza to proliferate examples of intuitive knowledge. Adherents of the common essence interpretation might also point to those places where Spinoza emphasizes knowledge of the union that things have with God, particularly knowledge of the union that the mind has with God, as of supreme epistemic and ethical value. In the opening sections of the TIE, Spinoza calls "the knowledge of the union that the mind has with the whole of Nature" the "highest good" (TIE 13/G 2:8). If the third kind of knowledge is knowledge of the union that the mind (and other things) has with God (or Nature), in the sense that the mind is a mode of the divine attribute of thought, and if knowledge of the union between mind and God is the highest good, then the common essence interpretation can easily explain Spinoza's claim that intuitive knowledge is the key to human blessedness.

Against the common essence interpretation, it might be objected that surely there is more to intuitive knowledge than simply the knowledge of the mode-attribute relation, or, in other words, the knowledge of the union of things with God. It might be objected, that is, that on this interpretation the knowledge yielded by *scientia intuitiva* is too thin. I think there is something to this objection, as I will explain shortly, but there is one sense in which the objection is clearly off the mark. In particular, it misses just how counter-intuitive, not to mention disturbing, Spinoza's assertion of the union of things with God was in the seventeenth century. After stating in E2p11c, for instance, that "the human Mind is a part of the infinite intellect of God," Spinoza adds a placatory scholium, stating, "Here, no doubt, my readers will come to a halt, and think of many things which will give them pause. For this reason I ask them to continue on with me slowly, step by step, and to make no judgment on these matters until they have read through them all" (G 2:95). Indeed, if the main thrust of Spinoza's *Ethics* could be distilled to a single tenet, it would likely be the union of all things with God. So, for these reasons, it would be a mistake to regard this claim as too epistemically exiguous to explain Spinoza's enthusiasm for the third kind of knowledge.

The common essence interpretation of intuitive knowledge captures an important dimension of Spinoza. As a result, a number of scholars have embraced, in one way or another, this interpretation of the content of intuitive knowledge.[12] Sometimes this side of Spinoza is associated with mysticism,[13] though I do not see much mysticism in Spinoza, even when focusing on his doctrine of the union of things with God. He proves the union through painstaking argumentation, after all, though perhaps Gueroult's notion of a "*mystique sans mystère*"[14] reflects Spinoza's peculiar blend of rationalism and spirituality (if that is the right word). In any case, it is certainly fair to emphasize a side of Spinoza that seems far more interested in attaining freedom and blessedness than, say, in natural philosophy, or what we nowadays call science. Even in *Ethics* Part 2, the part of the *Ethics* in which Spinoza goes further into matters of natural science than anywhere else, Spinoza's short preface promises to explain only those things "that can lead us, by the hand, as it were, to the knowledge of the human Mind and its highest blessedness" (G 2:84). If Spinoza's focus is a kind of spiritual freedom, it makes sense for him to embrace as the pinnacle of wisdom the realization that all is one.

But even if the common essence interpretation captures an important dimension of Spinoza, one which is quite prominent in *Ethics* Part 5, it is not the only dimension. Importantly, it is not the only dimension relevant to interpreting the nature and scope of intuitive knowledge. There is, on the other hand, the Spinoza who *is* interested in natural philosophy. Much of this study has focused on the scientific (as opposed to the ethical) side of Spinoza. We have seen that Spinoza outlines a methodology of scientific investigation in both the TTP and the TIE. In these texts, he makes the following two things quite clear: (1) scientific investigation ideally leads to a knowledge of the essences of singular things; and (2) this knowledge is more specific than knowledge of things as modes of one or another attribute. In the TTP, for instance, Spinoza characterizes the result of the method of interpreting nature as the inference of "the definitions of natural things" (TTP 7.7/G 3:98). Since we've seen that definitions provide the essences of things, this is a way of saying that the interpretation of

---

[12] Sandler 2005 is a good example, I think, of the common essence interpretation. He argues that the third kind of knowledge yields only *knowledge that* the essences of singular things follow from (or form part of) God's nature, but does not yield any *knowledge of* the essences of singular things, since *knowledge of* is beyond our cognitive capacities (2005, 88–90).

[13] See De Dijn 1990, 151–55.

[14] Gueroult 1968, 9.

nature culminates in the knowledge of the essences of things. But we know also that Spinoza says that this knowledge results from a deduction of less universal things from universal things in conjunction with experiential input. So, the knowledge of the essences of things is not simply the knowledge that they are modes of one or another attribute. That would be to abandon the investigation before the process of deducing less universal things has even begun.

In the TIE, moreover, Spinoza says of the "fixed and eternal things," which are presumably the attributes or the infinite modes or a combination of both: "because of their presence everywhere, and most extensive power, they will be to us like universals, or genera of the definitions of singular, changeable things, and the proximate causes of these things" (TIE 101/G 2:37). Spinoza's talk of the "fixed and eternal things" in the TIE is obscure, but it arises in the context of a discussion of an adequate, scientific approach to gaining knowledge of the essences of singular things (as discussed already in Chap. 5). The scientific tenor of the discussion comes out in subsequent paragraphs where Spinoza speaks à la Bacon about "aids" and experiments (TIE 103/G 2:37). As with the TTP, there would be no need to grapple with the complexities introduced by experiment and experience if the knowledge of the connection between singular things and the fixed and eternal things was the extent of the knowledge sought.

So the discussions of scientific method in the TTP and TIE indicate that Spinoza intended, at any rate, to find a way of generating knowledge of the essences of singular things that goes beyond the minimal knowledge envisioned by the common essence interpretation, with its focus on the ethical side of Spinoza. The essence spectrum that I introduced in the last chapter can help to clarify the options. I have just argued that the knowledge of common essence is not all we are able to know of singular things, and thus not all that intuitive knowledge is capable of. At the other extreme is essence as given by the individuating definition of a singular thing. I argued previously that knowledge of the essences of things to this level of specificity is beyond the capacity of finite intellects, although it serves well as an ideal toward which we can hope to continually progress. Even if knowledge of completely individuating essences is beyond the capacity of finite intellects, we can do better, nevertheless, than attaining the minimal knowledge envisioned by the common essence interpretation. In particular, we should expect to be able to gain knowledge of the sorts of essences that lie somewhere in the middle of the essence spectrum, which I called species essences, with the expectation that we can improve in the direction of individual essences over time.

It might be objected that in the texts on scientific method I have referenced in arguing against the common essence interpretation of intuitive knowledge, Spinoza has in the mind the sort of discursive, deductive approach to deriving knowledge of things that is characteristic of the second kind of knowledge rather than the third. Furthermore, one might argue, the second kind of knowledge does not produce knowledge of essences. For these reasons, the points I have made are misdirected. They apply to reason, but not intuitive knowledge. It is reason that can progress ever further toward a knowledge of individual essences without ever getting there. Intuitive knowledge, by contrast, promises a direct, unmediated path to knowledge of essences. This objection implies the content interpretation of the difference between intuitive knowledge and reason outlined above. I will argue below for the method interpretation over the content interpretation. In doing so, I will answer this objection. First, it is necessary to look more closely at the prospects for intuitive knowledge of essences that goes beyond the common essence interpretation.

Before turning to these prospects, I want to clarify that in rejecting the common essence interpretation of intuitive knowledge, I do not deny that knowledge of the union of a singular thing with God can count as intuitive knowledge. I deny simply that it is all that can be hoped for from intuitive knowledge. I also do not deny that Spinoza's emphasis in the *Ethics* may well be on this relatively minimal knowledge of essences. It may be, indeed, that this minimal knowledge is just as good for affective-therapeutic and, therefore, ethical purposes as a more refined knowledge of essences. And it may be that the fact that Spinoza's emphasis in the *Ethics* is on ethical over purely epistemological concerns explains the apparent plausibility of the common essence interpretation. But even if Spinoza's emphasis in the *Ethics* is on ethical rather than epistemological concerns, an inquiry into Spinoza's epistemology is perfectly justified in focusing on the latter. Finally, if epistemology is our focus, then, my argument is, there is more to say about intuitive knowledge and its prospects than the common essence interpretation would suggest.

7.3 Beyond the Common Essence Interpretation

Even with Spinoza's two examples—one mathematical and one non-mathematical—of the distinction between intuitive knowledge and reason, we are still left with basic questions about the nature of intuitive knowledge and what distinguishes it from reason. I think the situation might be improved if we can introduce a different kind of example from either of the ones Spinoza gives. It will be ideal to have an example that preserves the structure of the fourth proportional example, which is nicely designed to highlight the differences between the three kinds of knowledge, while being couched in terms more amenable to those of Spinoza's ontology than the numerical fourth proportional example. In light of what I just argued regarding the common essence interpretation, we will want an example of knowledge of the essences of things that is more specific than the sort of minimal knowledge envisioned by the common essence interpretation. In particular, it will be useful to have an example that fits with the analysis of Spinozan science laid out in previous chapters.

In theory it would be possible to adapt one of the examples we looked at in discussing Spinoza's optical letters. In the opening paragraphs of the *Optics*, Descartes contrasts the discovery of the telescope "through experiment and good fortune" with the demonstrative deduction of the nature and properties of telescopes that he sets out over the course of that work (DM, 65). It would not be difficult to distinguish non-discursive intuitions from discursive demonstrations in the many insights and arguments that Descartes presents in his pioneering optical treatise. But a simpler example is preferable, and simplicity is, of course, the virtue of mathematical examples, and a chief reason why Spinoza so often employs them.

A geometrical example would be ideal. If my case for geometrical figures in the earlier chapters of this book is tenable, then a geometrical example has all the benefits of the clarity of mathematical examples, while also (unlike Spinoza's numerical fourth proportional example) being translatable into the terms of Spinoza's ontology.[15] Instead of Proposition

---

[15] Cf. Matheron 1986, 139. Matheron entertains the possibility of alternatives to the fourth proportional example, including the "algebraic resolution of a geometrical problem." While he seems to concede that alternative mathematical examples might be less trivial (as he says) than the fourth proportional example, he does not appear to consider that they might better illuminate the kinds of knowledge by being translatable into the terms of Spinoza's ontology. I suspect this is because Matheron adopts the common essence interpretation of the content of intuitive knowledge, which is, as discussed, a minimal epistemic achievement,

19 in Book VII of Euclid, Spinoza might have used Proposition 12 from Book VI, which is a version of the fourth proportional problem using lines instead of numbers. Heath calls it the "geometrical equivalent of the 'rule of three.'"[16] I am not certain of Spinoza's motivations for latching on to the numerical version, though I suspect it was favored for its simplicity. It is (slightly) easier to intuit the solution "in one glance" in the case of the numerical version, and, recall, the main purpose of the example is to illustrate the nature and merits of this kind of intuition.

But even if Spinoza had employed the geometrical rule of three, it would still be possible and useful to formulate an example more easily translatable into the scheme of Spinozan science elaborated above. I have found that the isoperimetric problem works nicely in this regard. While Spinoza does not himself discuss the problem, it is one with which he would have been familiar, since Descartes references it in the *Rules for the Direction of the Mind* (CSM 1:27/AT X:390).

7.3.1 A Geometrical Alternative to the Fourth Proportional Example: The Isoperimetric Problem

Here is the isoperimetric problem, modeled as closely as possible on Spinoza's presentation of the fourth proportional example for purposes of clarity and simplicity:

> Which of all plane figures with the same perimeter has the greatest area? One way to solve the problem would be through trial and error: one could draw several different kinds of plane figures – a triangle, a square, a pentagon, a circle – all with the same perimeter, and measure which one has the greatest area. Or, one could simply ask a mathematician or other authoritative figure for the answer or other authoritative figure. To solve the problem in these ways is to use the first kind of knowledge, or imagination. Next, one could set about solving the problem mathematically. Jakob Steiner, for example, published several proofs in 1842 showing that a circle is the solution to the isoperimetric problem.[17] To solve the problem discursively, with mathematical proofs, is to use the second kind of knowledge. Finally, one can simply see in one glance that the circle is the solution to the problem. To solve the

---

and for which the fourth proportional example suffices. On this last point, see Matheron 1986, 149.

[16] Heath 1956, Vol. 2, 215.
[17] Steiner 1842.

problem this way, in one glance, is to use the third kind of knowledge, *scientia intuitiva*.

As we can see, it is not hard to differentiate ways of solving the isoperimetric problem, and to match these up with the different ways of solving the problem of the fourth proportional in Spinoza's example, and with the three kinds of knowledge. To solve the problem by trial and error, that is to say, by drawing several different kinds of shape with the same perimeter and measuring which has the greatest area, may well generate the correct solution to the problem, but one could not be certain of one's solution, because there is no reason to be sure that other, untested shapes would not accommodate greater areas. Needless to say, the same uncertainty attaches *a fortiori* to deferring to authority. This is all in line with what we should expect with the first kind of knowledge. For its part, the mathematical solution of the isoperimetric problem has a long, interesting, and complicated history, which I will not get into here.[18] The main point is simply that a mathematical proof is one way of solving the isoperimetric problem, which has the characteristics of discursivity and adequacy to be expected with the second kind of knowledge. Finally, the intuitive solution to the problem also has all the tell-tale signs we should expect. The solution is seen "in one glance," that is, *non*-discursively; it is certain and adequate; and, because it is able to eschew discursivity, it is seen "much more clearly," as Spinoza says in the fourth proportional example, than with the second kind of knowledge. I will say more about how exactly the solution is grasped intuitively, but if, reading along, you are able to intuit that a circle is the solution to the problem, the distinctiveness of the intuitive grasp of the solution should be evident.

To see better how this might work in practice, imagine assigning to a child what has come to be known in mathematics as Dido's Problem on the basis of its appearance in Virgil's *Aeneid*. The task is to enclose the greatest area of space with a piece of string. In order to motivate the child, you might evenly distribute M&M's over a table, and tell her that she can have as many pieces of candy as she is able to enclose with the piece of string (which is, say, two feet long).[19] It is reasonable to assume that the child will not solve the isoperimetric problem with a mathematical proof

---

[18] For the evolution of mathematical approaches to the problem, see Blåsjö 2005.
[19] This example is supposed to provide only a rough illustration, and I ignore the issue that would arise if the string is laid over only a part of one of the lens-shaped candies.

in her head—Steiner, after all, takes over 100 pages for his set of proofs—so we can discount the second way of solving the problem for the purposes of this example. That leaves the first and third ways of solving the problem, corresponding to the first and third kinds of knowledge. Consider how the child might solve the problem by means of the first kind of knowledge. Recall that both authoritative testimony and trial and error are different ways of solving the problem via imagination. Let us discount the uninteresting appeal to authority, and focus instead on the method of trial and error. We can imagine the child first counting the M&M's enclosed by a very elliptical shape, and comparing that with the M&M count in the case of a more circular shape. We can imagine the child proceeding in this way with a few other ways of shaping the string—say a rectangular shape and a triangular shape—and announcing as "the solution" of the problem the one which yielded the highest M&M's count. It may be that the child happened upon the solution to the problem, because she happened to try a circle, and that shape yielded the most M&M's. But in that case, the solution is arrived at haphazardly, and, most importantly, the child does not know *why* the winning shape won. As such, the solution to the problem is, to use Spinoza's language, inadequate, even if true by happenstance.

Alternatively, the child might manage to solve the problem using the third kind of knowledge as follows. At first, as in the case just discussed, the child tries a few different shapes. In so doing, it is possible that the child will start to understand the *relationship* between the shape of the perimeter of the string and the area enclosed. The child may come to *see* that the more circular she makes the string, the more M&M's are enclosed. In this case, the eureka moment should be soon to come and the child will realize that a perfect circle encloses the greatest number of M&M's. In this case, the child will have solved the problem intuitively. She will have grasped the relationship between perimeter and area enclosed just as someone might grasp the relationship (i.e., ratio) between two numbers, as in Spinoza's fourth proportional number example. What is important here is that the child comes to see *why* (to the extent that it is ever possible to grasp *why* something is the case) the circle is the solution to the problem by means of seeing *how* the different areas get *generated*. The child grasps, for instance, how in moving from a more rectangular to a more circular shape, the enclosure of area becomes more efficient—less space is wasted in corners and angles.

To be sure, Dido's problem is a product of human contrivance and does not necessarily count as knowledge of finite bodies themselves. However, the kind of generative grasp of the solution displayed in the example just examined is easily applied to finite bodies. Consider, for instance, Aristotle's contrast between the doctor's knowledge *that* circular wounds heal more slowly (which would stem from Spinoza's first kind of knowledge) and the geometer's knowledge *why* (which, I take it, would be quite the same as knowing why a circle solves the isoperimetric problem).[20] Knowing that a sphere is the figure which maximizes the ratio of volume to surface area (to cast the problem in three dimensions), moreover, allows us to understand why, given surface tension, bubbles are spherical. Packing snowballs provides another example.[21] When you pick up a bunch of snow and start packing it, it forms a ball, since packing the snow tighter and tighter minimizes the surface area. Once again, we see how a child could intuit the relationship between surface area and volume by actually packing the snow and seeing how it changes, how the sphere takes shape.[22]

7.3.2 *The Isoperimetric Example and Spinoza's Definition of Intuitive Knowledge*

Recall that Spinoza defines intuitive knowledge as a kind of knowing that proceeds from an adequate knowledge of the attributes to the adequate knowledge of the essences of things. The intuitive solution to the isoperimetric problem can help to illuminate this definition. Let me start with the knowledge of attributes. There can be no doubt that an adequate knowledge of extension is involved in and presupposed by the solution to the isoperimetric problem. As Spinoza argues in E2pp45–47, an adequate knowledge of extension is involved in *every* idea of body that we have (and, more generally, an adequate knowledge of God's essence is involved in the idea of each singular thing). This is because a mode is a mode *of* an attribute, so to have an idea of a mode is to have an idea of an attribute as

---

[20] Aristotle 1984, Vol. 1, 129.
[21] This example is taken from Blåsjö 2005.
[22] Presumably, the child could be more or less aware of her grasp of the relationship between surface area and volume. Colloquially, when we say, for example, "Sally has a good intuition about these things," we mean to imply that she naturally grasps these relationships without being fully aware of what she is grasping. Spinoza himself does not distinguish between degrees of awareness, and I think it best to leave this distinction to the side, assuming that for Spinoza one has to be aware of the relationship to count as knowing it adequately.

expressed in a certain, determinate way. To have an idea of a body, then, just is to have an idea of extension as determined in a certain way. It is, then, of course, impossible to have an idea of a body without also having an idea of extension.[23]

Spinoza proceeds in E2p46 to argue that the knowledge of an attribute (i.e., "God's infinite and eternal essence") that each idea involves is "adequate and perfect" (G 2:127):

> whether the thing is considered as a part or as a whole, its idea, whether of the whole or a part (by 2p45), will involve God's eternal and infinite essence. So what gives knowledge of an eternal and infinite essence of God is common to all, and is equally in the part and in the whole. And so (by 2p38) this knowledge will be adequate, q.e.d. (E2p46dem/G 2:127–8)

Since an idea of the relevant attribute is involved in the idea of any finite mode, it is involved whether the thing is considered as a part or as a whole. Hence, an idea of an attribute is "equally in the part and in the whole" of each idea of a singular thing (and "common to all"). The fact that Spinoza's argument for E2p46 relies on the argument for the adequacy of common notions in E2p38 suggests that ideas of attributes are common notions. This makes sense given that the attribute is common to all of the modes that modify that attribute, and that while the attribute constitutes the essence of all of its modifications in general, it does not constitute the (individual) essence of any singular thing, since it does not individuate singular things.[24]

---

[23] This, again, raises the question of the extent to which cognition of extension is explicitly or only implicitly involved in all cognition of bodies. On this, see previous note.

[24] Cf. Deleuze 1988, 57. Deleuze rejects the notion that the idea of God is a common notion, citing E2p47s in which Spinoza explicitly distinguishes between the idea of God and common notions. The relevant passage reads: "But that men do not have so clear a knowledge of God as they do of the common notions comes from the fact that they cannot imagine God, as they can bodies, and that they have joined the name *God* to the images of things which they are used to seeing" (G 2:128). This passage raises a number of interpretive difficulties. For instance, it might be read to imply that common notions can be imagined. This would conflict with Spinoza's claim that common notions can only be conceived adequately. I have already addressed this difficulty in Chap. 4 and I discuss it further in Sect. 7.4 of this chapter. I think Deleuze's point can be accepted, so long as a distinction (which Deleuze seems to elide) between the idea of God and the idea of an attribute is borne in mind. It is true that the common notions are not equivalent to the idea of God, if the idea of God is an idea of a substance consisting of infinite attributes. However, the common notions can be equivalent to a given attribute of God, such as extension.

The implication of E2p46dem that our ideas of attributes are common notions is significant for understanding the relationship between the second and third kinds of knowledge. Since we already know that common notions form the basis of the second kind of knowledge, the fact that our adequate ideas of attributes (which provide the basis for the third kind of knowledge) are common notions implies that the second and third kinds of knowledge begin from the same knowledge content.[25] (This is a strong point in favor of the method interpretation.[26] I will come back to the question of the relation between reason and intuitive knowledge in the next section. At that time, I will address an objection to my claim that reason and intuitive knowledge begin from the same knowledge content.)

---

[25] A text that appears to contradict this claim is the following from E5p20s: "From what we have said, we easily conceive what clear and distinct knowledge – and especially that third kind of knowledge (see IIP47S), whose foundation is the knowledge of God itself – can accomplish against the affects" (G 2:294). Since it is contrasted with the third kind of knowledge, "clear and distinct knowledge" here is seemingly the same as reason, or the second kind of knowledge. The passage appears to suggest that being based in "the knowledge of God itself" is a distinguishing feature of intuitive knowledge, thus contradicting my claim that reason and intuitive knowledge have the same basis. A closer inspection of the context of the comment mitigates its contradictory force, however. According to E5p4, we can form a "clear and distinct concept" of any affection of the body, due to our common notions of all corporeal objects. (This is the basis of the power that "clear and distinct knowledge," or reason, has over the affects.) According to E5p14, by contrast, "The mind can bring it about that all the body's affections, or images of things, are related to the idea of God." As far as I can tell, this is the main referent of Spinoza's mention in E5p20s of what the third kind of knowledge, "whose foundation is the knowledge of God itself," can accomplish against the affects. That is, by conceiving affects as related to God, and thus, via the third kind of knowledge, we neutralize their power over us. However, when we look at the demonstration of E5p14, we find that the basis of our ability to "relate" (*referre*) affections to the idea of God is simply our ability to form some clear and distinct idea of them (and here we are referred back to E5p4). Although Spinoza does not reference E2pp45–47 in E5p14dem, he does reference E2p47s in E5p20s, as we saw above. In any case, E2pp45–47, which explains that all ideas are related to God, appears to be the most plausible basis of the connection between clear and distinct ideas and God that is affirmed in E5p14. If this is right, rather than contradicting my reading of E2p46dem, E5p20s simply brings us back to where we started.

[26] Cf. Sandler 2005. Sandler defends a method interpretation, but affirms a distinction between the common notions and ideas of God's attributes as the respective bases of the second and third kinds of knowledge. Sandler's version of the method interpretation centers on a rejection of a difference in the content *yielded* by the second and third kinds of knowledge. Insofar as my version of the method interpretation rejects a difference in content at both the starting and end points of the second and third kinds of knowledge, it is distinct from Sandler's.

Solving the isoperimetric problem not only involves and presupposes adequate knowledge of the attribute of extension by virtue of pertaining to bodies. The same can also be said for adequate knowledge of motion. Intuiting the solution to the isoperimetric problem is a matter of intuiting how surface area changes with perimeter shape (or how volume changes with surface shape in the three-dimensional version). This involves and presupposes knowledge of motion, since the shape of a body can only form through motion, and changes in the shape of a body can only happen through motion. Ideas of motion, like ideas of extension, are common notions, and, as such, can only be conceived adequately. We have seen that motion and rest constitute the immediate infinite mode of extension. Thus, it makes sense that in "proceeding" from the adequate knowledge of the attribute of extension to an adequate knowledge of the essence of a finite body, the mind proceeds also from the adequate knowledge of the infinite mode of motion and rest.

What about the termination of intuitive knowledge in the adequate knowledge of the essence of things? Can the isoperimetric example help illuminate this aspect of Spinoza's definition of intuitive knowledge as well? I believe it can, so long as we clarify what to expect by way of illumination. We know that Spinoza defines the essence of an individual body in terms of a ratio of motion and rest, but it's not clear what this really means. I presume that in the case of a relatively simple physical individual, such as a soap bubble, the definition of the thing would have to include such known features as sphericity and surface tension, but I am not sure how Spinoza might have envisioned those features being expressed in a ratio of motion and rest.

I want to approach the question of the knowledge of essences involved in the solution to the isoperimetric problem from a different angle, by first establishing that the intuitive solution to the problem is adequate, or at least true in form. Recall the key features of adequate understanding. The mind is active, internally determined in its search for understanding, rather than passively affected by external forces. In being active and internally determined, the mind searches for explanations or causes of phenomena. Given the need to rely on experiential data in investigating the nature and properties of singular things, I said, adequate, causal explanations must be considered as hypotheses subject to revision in light of further experience. In the case of physical phenomena, adequate explanations will take the form of understanding things in terms of the most general laws and principles governing the physical world, and in terms of what follows from those most general laws and principles. Such explanations can be considered causal insofar as the attribute and immediate infinite mode can be considered the causes of all finite bodies (as argued in the last section of the previous chapter).

The intuitive solution of the isoperimetric problem exhibits these features of adequate understanding. I argued that we can think of the intuitive solution as the result of understanding how area changes with perimeter shape through seeing how different areas get generated (by changes in perimeter shape). I also said that the solution to the problem involves and presupposes adequate understanding of the attribute of extension and the infinite mode of motion and rest. While in the case of the purely geometrical version of the problem, the causal solution is provided by the intuitive grasp of the relationship between area and perimeter shape alone, in the case of natural phenomena, such as the formation of bubbles, additional factors, such as the hypothesis of surface tension, must be introduced. But surface tension, in this latter case, serves as a hypothetical causal explanation of experiential data. Thus, while hypothetical, it exhibits the same formal features of adequacy as the apprehension of the area-perimeter relationship in the purely geometrical version of the problem.

In sum, in descending from an adequate knowledge of attribute and infinite mode to a causal understanding of the relationship between area and perimeter shape, the intuitive solution of the isoperimetric problem (whether understood purely geometrically or applied to natural phenomena) exhibits the features of adequate understanding. I said I wanted to approach the question of the knowledge of essences involved in the solution to the isoperimetric problem by first establishing that the intuitive solution to the problem is adequate, or at least true in form. Having established the latter, how does this bear on the question of essences? What I would like to suggest is that *all adequate ideas are ideas of essences*—at least at some point on the essence spectrum. That is to say, while not all adequate ideas are ideas of individual essences, all adequate ideas are ideas of essences of some sort, recalling the fact that Spinoza countenances common essences and species essences in addition to individual essences.

We have already seen (in Chap. 6) that the essence of a singular thing involves neither existence nor duration (E1p24c). Rather, to understand the essence of a singular thing is to conceive it *sub specie aeternitatis*. Is the converse also true? Is it the case that when we conceive an object under a species of eternity the object is an essence? Spinoza does not say so explicitly, but I think it can be shown to be the case. Doing so will provide a way of showing that adequate understanding is understanding of essences.

First, to understand something adequately is to understand it under a species of eternity. This is implied by Spinoza's famous statement in E2p44c, "It is of the nature of Reason to perceive things under a certain species of eternity" (G 2:126). Although Spinoza speaks here explicitly of "Reason," not of adequate understanding, more generally, which includes both reason and intuitive knowledge, I think that Spinoza is using the term "reason" in the broader sense entertained at the beginning of this chapter, which encompasses both forms of adequate knowledge. This is suggested by a passage from *Ethics* Part 5, where Spinoza states: "The Mind's essence consists in knowledge (by 2p11); therefore, the more the Mind knows things by the second and third kind of knowledge, the greater the part of it that remains (by 5p23 and 5p29)" (E5p38dem/G 2:304). As E5p23 and E5p29 make clear, the human Mind "remains," or is eternal, insofar as its object is eternal. Thus, in knowing things by the second and third kinds of knowledge, the object of the human mind's cognition is eternal.

Second, the eternal object of the human mind in conceiving things by the second and third kinds of knowledge is, according to E5p29, the essence of the human body (conceived under a species of eternity) (G 2:298). Given that Spinoza defines the mind as the idea of the body, in having any idea the mind must have an idea either of the durational existence of the body or of its eternal essence. The fact that the mind has an idea of the eternal essence of the human body in conceiving things by the second and third kinds of knowledge strongly suggests that the mind *must* have an essence as its object in conceiving things adequately (since it has no immediate object apart from its body). It should be noted that the fact that the mind's object in conceiving things adequately is its body conceived under a species of eternity does not mean, of course, that its knowledge is limited to the human body. We already know that the mind has an idea of God just by virtue of having an idea of anything, and Spinoza goes on to explain that on the basis of the mind's idea of the human body (under a species of eternity) it can also form adequate ideas of God and of everything that follows from God (i.e., of anything else) (E5p31dem/G 2:299).[27]

So, adequate knowledge is knowledge of an object under a species of eternity, and knowledge of an object under a species of eternity is knowledge of essences. The third kind of knowledge, then, is knowledge of essences just insofar as it is adequate knowledge. The only caveat that must be added to this statement is that, given the limits of the human intellect, and its need to rely on experience, in venturing beyond knowledge of essence qua attribute, intuitive knowledge is true only in form, and, correlatively, the knowledge of essences that it yields is only knowledge of species essences, which, like the genetic figures of the TIE, are beings of reason (albeit *true* beings of reason).

At the very limit of any hypothetico-deductive inquiry into the nature of a singular thing is the knowledge of its fully individuating essence. This would theoretically involve a specification of the precise ratio of motion and rest constituting a finite body. Some commentators have interpreted intuitive knowledge as yielding knowledge of the fully individuating essences of things.[28] This interpretation, which might be called the *individual essence interpretation*, is the opposite of the common essence interpretation discussed above. As I have said before, knowledge of individual essences is beyond the capacity of a finite intellect, so I do not see how it would be possible for human beings to know anything intuitively, as Spinoza thinks we can, if the individual essence interpretation were correct. Nevertheless, I do think individual essences should be regarded as an epistemic ideal toward which scientific inquiry can always strive, and hope, to progress. In this sense, the individual essence interpretation can be reconciled with the interpretation I am developing here. I see it as a strength of my interpretation that it can accommodate both the common essence interpretation and the individual essence interpretation (at least as an ideal) by locating essences on a spectrum.

---

[27] It may be, nevertheless, that since our ideas of all things are mediated through ideas of our bodies, self-knowledge has a certain priority in Spinoza. On this, see Soyarslan 2016, 42–46; and A. Garrett 2003, 197–223.

[28] Steinberg 2009, 154–55; and Curley 1973, 56–59.

7.4 The Difference Between Reason and Intuitive Knowledge: A Method Interpretation

The argument I just gave for the termination of the third kind of knowledge in a knowledge of essences works just as well for the second kind of knowledge. Since all adequate knowledge is knowledge of essences, according to the foregoing, and since reason is, of course, one of the forms of adequate knowledge, then reason too terminates in knowledge of essences. It is true that, according to Spinoza's definition of reason, the second kind of knowledge provides a way of forming "universal notions" (E2p40s2/G 2:122). It is also true that universal notions are not individual essences. However, even if the second kind of knowledge cannot terminate in individual essences, it can very well terminate in common essences or species essences and must do so, if it is adequate, for the reasons just given.

It has often been thought that what differentiates the second and third kinds of knowledge is that whereas the former does not yield knowledge of essences, the latter does. This common reading falters, however, upon close inspection of Spinoza's doctrine of essences. It is impossible that human beings would be able to have intuitive, adequate knowledge of the individual essences of finite things, since such individual essences are infinitely complicated and require an infinite intellect to be comprehended. Yet Spinoza is quite insistent that human beings can have intuitive knowledge of the essences of singular things. Let me concede here that it is, of course, possible that Spinoza thought that we could have adequate knowledge of the *individual* essences of things. Perhaps, too, he thought that the third kind of knowledge is uniquely capable of this feat. I do not pretend to fully understand his intentions in this regard. The tensions in the relevant texts that I have highlighted in this chapter suggest to me that, at the very least, he struggled with the issue. Whatever the case may be regarding Spinoza's intentions, however, the only way I am able to make sense of Spinoza's claim that human beings can have intuitive knowledge of the essences of singular things is to see it as applying to non-individual essences, that is, common essences or species essences. As we have seen, Spinoza's only non-mathematical example of intuitive knowledge bears this reading out, since the intuitive knowledge of the human mind's relation to divine essence is only the knowledge of the essence of the mind qua mode of the attribute of thought—a minimal epistemic achievement from the perspective of the essence spectrum, and one that Spinoza explicitly affirms is available to reason. So, knowledge of essences does not, in the end, serve to differentiate intuitive knowledge from reason.

What is more, I argued that reason and intuitive knowledge both begin with common notions (i.e., knowledge of the most common essences). Despite the fact that Spinoza defines reason, on the one hand, as beginning with common notions and adequate ideas of the properties of things and intuitive knowledge, on the other hand, as beginning with an adequate idea of God's attributes, I argued, on the basis of E2p46, that adequate ideas of God's attributes *are* common notions, and thus, my claim was that the starting points of reason and intuitive knowledge turn out to be the same.

This claim might be objected to in two ways. First, I just said that both reason and intuitive knowledge start from common notions. But what about the option for reason to start from the "adequate ideas of the properties of things"? Could this not differentiate it from intuitive knowledge? I do not think so. The phrase "adequate ideas of the properties of things" could refer to either (1) universal common notions (UCNs) or (2) peculiar common notions (PCNs).[29] The objection stalls on either construal. If it refers to UCNs, then the phrase "adequate ideas of the properties of things" does not differentiate reason from intuitive knowledge, since, as I am arguing, they both start from UCNs. If it refers to PCNs, on the other hand, this runs into the issue of adequacy we discussed in Chap. 4. Recall that while PCNs can be true in form, they cannot be robustly true. On the assumption that reason can generate robustly true ideas from UCNs, it would be strange if what differentiated it from intuitive knowledge is that it is *also* capable of generating (merely) true-in-form ideas in another way.[30] If reason has this capacity, why shouldn't intuitive knowledge, as well? After all, our examples of genetically conceived figures seem like plausible prospective candidates for intuitive, true-in-form ideas.

Putting the "adequate ideas of the properties of things" to the side, then, and returning the focus to my claim that both reason and intuitive knowledge begin from (universal) common notions, it might be objected that here I am guilty of an intensional fallacy: conceiving extension, for example, *as* a common property of bodies, is not the same as conceiving

---

[29] See n. 22 in Chap. 4.

[30] A different line of objection rejects this assumption and argues that *all* of reason's deliverances are merely true in form (i.e., those stemming *both* from PCNs *and* from UCNs). I address this alternative tack below.

extension *as* an expression of God's essence. This is an important objection.[31] In response, one point to clarify right away is that when we are talking about the *common notion* of extension as the common property of bodies, we are not talking about the inadequate conception of extension that we initially derive from the senses. As we know, common notions are inherently adequate ideas, and, thus, cannot be the same as inadequate sensory ideas. So, inasmuch as reason starts with common notions, it starts with *adequate* ideas, in this case, an adequate idea of extension. This clarification on its own does not answer the objection completely, since the objector might attempt to distinguish even the *adequate* idea of extension as a common property of bodies from an adequate idea of extension as an expression of God's essence: arguably, the latter idea is explicitly *about* God (in some sense) whereas the former is not. I want to say two things in response to this subtler form of the objection.

First, I do not think it is clear from Spinoza's definition of intuitive knowledge that its starting point must have God as an explicit object. All the definition says is that intuitive knowledge starts from an adequate idea of God's attributes. This seems consistent with the starting point being an adequate idea of extension simpliciter (i.e., not conceived explicitly *as* an attribute of God). By the same token, I do not think it is clear that reason's starting point is *not about* God (in some sense). The only relevant example Spinoza gives of reason in E5p36s has for its starting point the proposition that *all things depend on God for both essence and existence*. This suggests that the starting point of reason certainly *can* be a proposition explicitly about God.

The fact of the matter is, Spinoza is just not very clear himself about when God is or is not contained in the content of a thought. On the one hand, he says that we "cannot imagine God" (E2p47s/G 2:128), suggesting that God is absent from all inadequate ideas. On the other hand, E2pp45–46 suggest that *all* ideas involve an adequate idea of God. Perhaps the way to resolve these claims is to infer that *only* adequate ideas involve an adequate idea of God. If this is right, do *all* adequate ideas involve an adequate idea of God? This is, of course, precisely the question. What I want to say is that it is far from obvious what the answer is, and the ambiguity is a feature of Spinoza's philosophy, not one that my interpretation fallaciously exploits.

---

[31] I am grateful to Sanem Soyarslan for pressing me on this objection.

A second response I want to make to the objection recalls a point from Chap. 2. That is, we cannot be sure that our true-in-form ideas are *robustly* true in the sense of corresponding with a real object in nature until we have attained the adequate idea of God qua ground and cause of all things. A system of adequate Spinozan knowledge is a system of ideas grounded in and related to the idea of God. The objection proposes that while adequate ideas derived from intuitive knowledge *are* related to the (adequate) idea of God, those derived from reason are *not*. As I see it, however, relation to an adequate idea of God is not a feature that distinguishes intuitive knowledge from reason. Instead, it distinguishes *robustly* adequate ideas, on the one hand, from inadequate ideas and those which are merely true in form, on the other. In order to see the relation to God as a feature that distinguishes intuitive knowledge from reason, it would be necessary to insist that only ideas known intuitively are *robustly* true, whereas adequate ideas of reason are only *true in form*.[32] The problem I see with this tack is the following: either intuitive knowledge would have to be able to proceed discursively or discursive knowledge could never be robustly true (because it is not intuitive knowledge). Neither option seems plausible to me. Spinoza goes out of his way in the fourth proportional example and in E5p36s to show that intuitive knowledge does *not* proceed discursively. If we know one thing about intuitive knowledge it is surely that. On the other hand, I see no reason why a discursive procedure should inherently fail to yield robustly true ideas. This point will become clearer, I think, when I come to discuss the fluidity of the distinction between discursive and non-discursive knowledge (at the end of Sect. 7.5 of this chapter) later.

At this point, I take myself to have motivated my contention that the second and third kinds of knowledge begin and end with the same epistemic content and defended it against some important objections. I will address other objections below and, going forward, I hope to further motivate my position. If I am right that the second and third kinds of knowledge begin and end with the same epistemic content, this suggests that what differentiates reason and intuitive knowledge lies in the process by which they arrive at knowledge of the essences of things from common notions, as the method interpretation would have it. Spinoza's example of our knowledge of the human mind's relation to divine essence in E5p36s illustrates well the procedural distinction between reason and intuitive

---

[32] Primus (2017) appears to accept such a distinction between intuitive knowledge and reason.

knowledge, as I have noted. Reason proceeds toward the conclusion discursively via a middle term as follows: *All things depend on God for both essence and existence. The human mind is a thing. Therefore, the human mind depends on God for both essence and existence.* Knowing the relation between the human mind and God intuitively, by contrast, involves knowing it without any intermediary term or syllogistic reasoning process.[33]

The difference between intuitive knowledge and reason is vanishing, however, when the demonstration characteristic of reason is a simple syllogism. Since the mind can encompass easily at once the entire syllogism, it is as if the relationship between the human mind and God can be seen "in one glance" as in the case of intuitive knowledge. Descartes distinguishes intuition from deduction in the *Rules* "on the grounds that we are aware of a movement or a sort of sequence in the latter but not in the former, and also because immediate self-evidence is not required for deduction, as it is for intuition."[34] On the method interpretation, Spinoza's distinction between intuitive knowledge and reason is comparable to Descartes' distinction between intuition and deduction. It may be that one is aware "of a movement or a sort of sequence" even in the case of a simple syllogism of which one is not aware when the conclusion is intuited. So, it may be that the distinction between reason and intuitive knowledge obtains even in cases where only a simple syllogism is necessary to grasp something via reason. Even so, the distinction between reason and intuitive knowledge is much more evident when the conclusion is removed from the first principle (from which the reasoning begins) by many intermediary steps, such that it is impossible (or very difficult) to keep all of the steps in mind at once.[35] In this light, the distinction is clearer when we

---

[33] As many commentators have observed, the fact that *scientia intuitiva* is non-discursive or unmediated does not mean that it is non-inferential, contrary to what the received notion of "intuition" might lead one to think. Inasmuch as the third kind of knowledge *proceeds* from knowledge of God's attributes to knowledge of the essences of singular things, there is, as it were, a movement of thought, though, as Bennett put it (1984, 364–65), it is more akin to an intellectual step than a walk. See Parkinson 1954, 183–84; Carr 1978, 245–46; and Melamed 2013, 110–13.

[34] CSM 1:15.

[35] Cf. Manzini 2011, 68–70. Manzini argues against connecting Spinoza's distinction between intuitive knowledge and reason with Descartes' distinction between intuition and deduction in the *Rules for the Direction of the Mind*. Manzini's chief argument is that whereas Descartes opposes intuition to deduction, for Spinoza, intuitive knowledge is a form of deduction, insofar as it is inferential. However, intuition can be inferential for Descartes as well, so long as the inference is encompassed in a single act of mind. I agree, nevertheless,

consider all the steps that go into Spinoza's demonstration of substance monism in *Ethics* Part 1 and compare following the first 14 propositions of *Ethics* Part 1, including demonstrations, with grasping the relation between the mind and God intuitively. Spinoza's fourth proportional example and the isoperimetric example elaborated above also illustrate the distinction well, since in both cases the demonstration of the solution is quite involved, contrasting starkly with the immediacy of intuition.

7.4.1   Can Conatus *Save the Content Interpretation?*

In light of the foregoing, the case for the method interpretation is, I think, quite strong. Something remains, nevertheless, to be said on behalf of the content interpretation. Since the beginning and end points of the second and third kinds of knowledge are the same, if there is a difference in epistemic content between the two kinds of knowledge it must emerge in the respective manners in which they proceed. A case can be made that a difference in epistemic content does emerge by virtue of the different procedures of the two kinds of knowledge. Consider again the knowledge of the human mind's dependence on God for both existence and essence. When this knowledge is ascertained by the second kind of knowledge, it is the result of a syllogism: *All things depend on God for their essence and existence. The human mind is a thing. Therefore, the human mind depends on God for its essence and existence.* The result is spit out, as it were, as the product of computation. It is true, we are sure that it is true, and we know why it is true. Nevertheless, in a sense, the actual dependence of the mind's existence and essence on God is not *seen*. It is ascertained through reason *that* it is so. Still, there is something arguably lacking, namely, the apprehension of what Spinoza calls in *Ethics* Part 2 "the force [*vis*] by which each [thing] perseveres in existing," which "follows from the eternal

---

that Spinoza's distinction is not identical to Descartes'—even in form. (There are obvious differences in content, since Descartes does not define his distinction in terms of metaphysical categories like Spinoza does.) The primary contrast in Spinoza is between discursivity and non-discursivity (i.e., in the presence or absence of a middle term), rather than between encompassing an object in a single thought or not. As noted above, I see no reason why it would not be possible to encompass a discursive reasoning process in a single thought, for Spinoza, without that counting as intuitive knowledge. Nevertheless, a discursive reasoning process grasped in a single thought is presumably *very close* to being a *non*-discursive cognition (perhaps on the verge of so being), and the similarity here seems more important than any difference.

necessity of God's nature" (E2p45s/G 2:127). Elsewhere, Spinoza uses the term *conatus* to refer to this force (*vis*) of persevering in existing. Thus, it can be argued that in grasping the human mind's dependence on God intuitively, we are able to apprehend also the force by which the human mind perseveres *through* God's power as part of the intuition. By contrast, when the fact of the human mind's dependence on God is demonstrated discursively and indirectly via middle terms, the apprehension of this force or power to exist is lacking.

Something similar can be seen in comparing the ways in which the isoperimetric problem can be solved by intuitive knowledge and by reason, respectively. In intuiting the solution to the isoperimetric problem, one grasps the relation between perimeter shape and area by seeing how changes of shape generate increases or decreases in area. In applying the solution of the isoperimetric problem to understanding real phenomena, such as the sphericity of soap bubbles in light of surface tension, it is perhaps not far-fetched to say that one could apprehend, as part of one's intuition, the striving of the soap bubble for sphericity in the process of formation, and the striving to persevere in a spherical shape (through its precarious wobbles) once formed. Although I did not provide a demonstration of the isoperimetric problem, we should expect that such an apprehension of striving would be absent in the laborious process of demonstrating the solution from first principles.

This does not mean that reason is unable to demonstrate that each thing strives to persevere in its being or that the striving by which each thing strives to persevere is the essence of the thing. This is, of course, precisely what Spinoza himself does in the demonstrations to E3p6 and E3p7. Even if reason is able to demonstrate *that* these things are so, however, this line of argument suggests that something is lacking in these demonstrations, nevertheless, namely, the apprehension of the striving itself.

Arguably, then, even though reason and intuitive knowledge begin and end with the same knowledge content, intuition is able to grasp the force or power (Spinoza uses *vis* and *potentia* interchangeably in places[36]) of a thing to persevere in existing *in* intuiting the essence of a thing. By contrast, whereas reason arrives equally at adequate knowledge of the essence of a thing, its more circuitous, discursive path forecloses the grasp of *conatus* available to intuition. A difference in content thus emerges as a result

[36] E4p6/G 2:214; E5pref/G 2:280. See Viljanen 2011, 64.

of the methodological differences between the two kinds of knowledge. Call this the *attenuated* content interpretation.[37] If the attenuated content interpretation is right, it would help to explain why the inference through reason that the human mind depends for its essence and existence "does not affect our Mind as much as when this is inferred from the very essence of any singular thing which we say depends on God" (E5p36s/G 2:303), that is, when this is inferred through the third kind of knowledge. The affective superiority of intuitive knowledge over reason would be explained by the fact that in intuiting the essence of something, one intuits also the force of its power to exist.[38]

There are, however, some reasons to doubt the attenuated content interpretation. According to the argument sketched above on its behalf, while it is possible to demonstrate through reason that a singular thing strives to persevere in its being, the demonstration nevertheless fails to apprehend the striving itself, which can only be grasped intuitively. But it is less than clear what precisely is lacking in the demonstration of *conatus* that is present in intuition. I have already acknowledged that in the case of long demonstrations (such as that of the solution to the isoperimetric problem), it can be impossible to encompass the entire demonstration in thought at once. But this cannot be the explanation of what is allegedly left out according to the attenuated content interpretation. We have

---

[37] Soyarslan's version of the content interpretation appears to draw on the line of reasoning I have laid out in this section, and thus may be an example of what I am calling the attenuated content interpretation. See Soyarslan 2016, 44.

[38] It is interesting in this connection to consider Thomas Nagel's contention that there is something missing from the objective apprehension of one's own death through the syllogism, "Everyone dies; I am someone, so I will die," namely, "the internal fact that one day this consciousness will black out for good and subjective time will simply stop. My death as an event in the world is easy to think about; the end of my world is not" (1986, 225). An adherent of the attenuated content interpretation might wish to compare Nagel's distinction between the objective (or external) and subjective (or internal) apprehensions of one's own death and Spinoza's distinction between the intuitive and rational apprehensions of one's own dependence upon God. In both cases (the attenuated content advocate could argue), the external, syllogistic procedure fails to get at an intrinsic aspect of its object (despite the object being the same in both cases). The problem with this Nagelian interpretation is that it would push Spinoza's third kind of knowledge in the direction of a peculiar kind of self-knowledge. While I have admitted that there may be some priority to self-knowledge in Spinoza (see n. 27 of this chapter), and while some commentators (referenced below in n. 44 of this chapter) have interpreted intuitive knowledge as a peculiar kind of self-knowledge, the interpretation is bedeviled by Spinoza's clear indication that many things besides the self can be apprehended intuitively, as I argue later.

already seen that some demonstrations are short enough that it *is* possible to encompass everything in a single glance. (Furthermore, the extent to which this is possible in the case of any given demonstration is both relative to the power of a given mind and can change over time even for the same individual. I develop this important point in the next section.) To compare apples with apples, then, we need to compare a relatively short demonstration (i.e., one that can be encompassed in thought all at once) of *conatus* with an intuition of *conatus*. It is in this case that I doubt one could show that anything *is* lacking in the demonstration. One might, of course, *define "conatus"* (or "force" or "power") as accessible only to intuition, but this would beg the question.

Another point against the attenuated content interpretation is textual. Recall that Spinoza uses the qualifier "actual" in speaking of the essence of a thing constituted by its *conatus*. If knowledge of *conatus* were in fact the distinguishing feature of the third kind of knowledge, then, we would expect Spinoza to use the language of "actual essence" in the definition of intuitive knowledge. Instead, Spinoza says that intuitive knowledge terminates in an adequate knowledge of the *formal* essence of singular things.[39]

Finally, while the subtle difference in content posited by the attenuated content interpretation provides a convenient explanation of Spinoza's claim of the affective superiority of intuitive knowledge, this particular subtle difference is not necessary to explain Spinoza's claim, at least in cases where the demonstration is complex. It strikes me as quite plausible that an intuitive grasp of some truth would affect the mind differently than a complex demonstrative proof of the same truth *just by virtue of being simpler and easier to apprehend*. It is not at all clear that one understands anything more about the fourth proportional problem or the

[39] The qualifier "formal," at any rate, appears in the *Nagelate Schriften*. The important point is less the presence of the qualifier "formal" and more the absence of the qualifier "actual." Although I argued in the last chapter that the difference between formal and actual essence is just a question of whether the thing (whose essence is under consideration) is considered as existing durationally or not, the qualifier "actual" is nevertheless clearly associated with the *conatus* of a mode existing in duration, so if Spinoza had meant to stress the knowledge of a thing's *conatus* in defining intuitive knowledge, we would expect to see the use of the qualifier "actual" in this context. Cf. D. Garrett 2009, 111–12. Referring to the language in the *Opera posthuma* rather than the *Nagelate Schriften*, Garrett discusses why Spinoza might have refrained from qualifying the kind of essences known through intuitive knowledge, proposing that even if knowledge of actual (and formal) essences is not possible for human minds, it is possible for God. (I explained my disagreement with Garrett's interpretation of the formal essence/actual essence distinction in the last chapter.)

isoperimetric problem when one grasps its solution intuitively rather than demonstratively. Nevertheless, it makes sense that there would be a greater "satisfaction of mind" in understanding the solution intuitively. "[A] directly established truth is as preferable to a truth established by a proof as spring water is to piped water," as Schopenhauer evocatively puts it.[40] Since the intuition allows one to see everything together, as it were, there is a sense in which it is more perfect than a cumbersome demonstration. I will develop this point further in turning now to discuss the affective dimension of intuitive knowledge, and, in particular, its connection to the intellectual love of God.

7.5 *Amor Dei Intellectualis* and the Supremacy of Intuitive Knowledge

In the second part of *Ethics* Part 5, Spinoza emphasizes the power and value of the third kind of knowledge in a series of propositions that culminate in its association with the intellectual love of God, the attainment of which Spinoza identifies with human salvation, blessedness, and freedom. These propositions convey the impression of something uniquely special about *scientia intuitiva*, so they warrant a closer examination.

Let us consider first Spinoza's claim in E5p27, "The greatest satisfaction of mind there can be arises from this third kind of knowledge" (G 2:297). The reasoning behind this is fairly straightforward. It relies primarily on two premises: (1) the mind's highest good is knowing God; and (2) the more one knows things by the third kind of knowledge, the more one knows God. The second premise, in turn, relies on Spinoza's claim that the more we understand singular things, the more we understand God (E5p24/G 2:296), coupled with the fact that intuitive knowledge is a knowledge of singular things. What remains unclear from this line of reasoning (which seems straightforward enough per se) is why Spinoza singles out the third kind of knowledge, making no mention of the second kind. Doesn't knowledge of *anything* provide knowledge of God, after all? And isn't knowledge of the second kind a form of genuine knowledge? Why shouldn't it also lead to great satisfaction of mind?

Before addressing these questions, I want to turn to Spinoza's claim about the connection between the third kind of knowledge and the

---

[40] Schopenhauer 1969, 64.

intellectual love of God, since it raises similar questions. This is what Spinoza says:

> From the third kind of knowledge, there necessarily arises an intellectual Love of God. For from this kind of knowledge there arises (by 5p32) Joy, accompanied by the idea of God as its cause, i.e. (by defaff6), Love of God, not insofar as we imagine him as present (by 5p29), but insofar as we understand God to be eternal. And this is what I call intellectual love of God [*amor Dei intellectualis*]. (E5p32c/G 2:300)

This remarkable passage describes the ineluctable unfolding of a sequence of causes set off by intuitive knowledge. Intuitive knowledge first leads to joy, along with the idea of God as the cause of one's joy. The idea of God as the cause of one's joy then leads to the love of God as the cause of one's joy. There is actually one step missing in Spinoza's presentation of the causal sequence in this corollary. As Spinoza explains in E5p32dem, intuitive knowledge first leads to joy, along with the idea of *oneself* as the cause of the joy. *Then*, insofar as the idea of any singular thing involves the idea of God as cause (as we have discussed), the idea of *oneself* as the cause of joy leads to the idea of God as the cause of one's joy.

The few references to past propositions that Spinoza includes in his explication of the intellectual love of God in E5p32c do not do justice to the complex argumentative edifice on which the corollary rests. While it would take us too far afield to go into all the details, I want to say a bit more by way of paraphrase about what is behind Spinoza's reasoning. When we adequately understand something, we act in the sense that the understanding follows from our own nature (E3p1/G 2:140), and we are also aware of the fact that we understand (E2p43/G 2:123). When we are aware of our own activity, we feel joy and our power of acting increases (E3p11s/G 2:149; E3p53/G 2:181). In addition, we are aware of ourselves as the cause of the joy (insofar as it is our actions that cause the joy), and this leads us to feel self-satisfaction (*acquiescentia in se ipso*[41]) or self-

---

[41] Whereas Curley translates *acquiescentia in se ipso* as "self-esteem," I have opted for "self-satisfaction" in order to preserve its resonance with "*acquiescentia animi*" (E4app/G 2:267) and "*acquiescentia mentis*" (E5p27/G 2:297), both of which Curley translates as "satisfaction of mind." For an excellent discussion of *acquiescentia in se ipso*, see Carlisle 2017. Carlisle draws attention to the translation difficulties to which Spinoza's multifarious uses of "*acquiescentia*" give rise, stressing, in particular, the distinction between *vana* (vain, empty) and *vera* (true) forms of *acquiescentia* (Carlisle 2017, 213, 232). The former relates to the

love (E3p55s/G 2:182–83; E3defaff25/G 2:196). Love, according to Spinoza, is the feeling of joy accompanied by the idea of an external cause (E3p13s/G 2:151), but the phenomenon of self-love shows that love does not have to be directed to an external cause. It is at this point in the cognitive-affective causal mechanism described in E5p32c that the idea of ourselves as the cause of joy prompts, in addition, the idea of God as the cause of joy. On the basis of Spinoza's definition of love, this idea of God as the cause of joy leads to love of God. It remains to add that this love of God is intellectual, insofar as it derives from an understanding of God as eternal, not from an image of God as present to the senses.[42]

As noted above, Spinoza proceeds from here to argue that the intellectual love of God is that "wherein our salvation, or blessedness, or Freedom, consists" (E5p36s/G 2:303). The aspects of *Ethics* Part 5 concerned with human salvation and blessedness raise notorious paradoxes about the relationship between the eternal aspect of our minds and our existence in duration. Since this terrain is beyond the purview of a study of Spinoza's epistemology, I will not venture into it.[43] For our purposes, it suffices to note that, for Spinoza, there is a direct line from the achievement of intuitive knowledge to the achievement of the highest human good.

The tight connection that Spinoza draws between the third kind of knowledge and the intellectual love of God in *Ethics* Part 5 has led some commentators to think that intuitive knowledge is peculiarly *about* the relationship between the mind and God.[44] This would be to interpret the content of intuitive knowledge even more narrowly than the common

---

imagination and is caused by external factors, in particular, the praise of others. The latter, by contrast, follows from adequate understanding. It is the latter, of course, that is relevant to the cognitive-affective causal mechanism that leads to intellectual love of God. Carlisle goes further and also distinguishes forms of *acquiescentia* relating to reason and intuitive knowledge, respectively (such that there is a form of *acquiescentia* for each of the three kinds of knowledge). She bases this latter distinction on a content interpretation of the difference between reason and intuitive knowledge. Since I embrace the method interpretation, I do not agree with distinguishing two different kinds of *acquiescentia* for reason and intuitive knowledge. On my reading, while the affects related to intuitive knowledge can differ from those related to reason, it is only insofar as the latter do "not affect our mind as much" (E5p36s). The difference is a question of strength, then, in my view, not quality.

[42] For a more nuanced discussion of the distinction between intellectual and other kinds of love of God than I am able to provide here, see Nadler 2018, 302–8.

[43] For discussion of Spinoza's claim of the mind's eternity, see Jaquet 2018 and Bennett 1984, 357–63.

[44] De Dijn 1990; Yovel 1990; Hubbeling 1986, 228.

essence interpretation of intuitive knowledge adumbrated above. Just as Spinoza's claim in the opening sections of the TIE that the knowledge of the mind's union with the whole of nature is the highest human good can be appealed to in support of the common essence interpretation, so it also might seem to support the narrower interpretation of intuitive knowledge as knowledge of the mind's union with God. However, this interpretation is contradicted by texts in which Spinoza indicates that many things can be known intuitively (E2p47s/G 2:128; E5p25dem/G 2:296). Whatever pride of place the knowledge of the mind's union with *Deus sive Natura* might occupy in Spinoza's system, it remains an *instance* of intuitive knowledge, and should not be mistaken for its peculiar content.

As we have seen from the foregoing analysis of E5p32c, the intellectual love of God "necessarily arises" from intuitive knowledge. Attention to the mechanism by which this happens indicates that intuitive knowledge of *anything* could equally prompt the feeling of joy, which is accompanied by the idea of God as the cause of one's joy, leading, finally, to the intellectual love of God. This is because the joy is not connected with understanding one particular thing or another. Instead, it is connected with the *activity* of understanding. If this is right, it raises the following question: if it is simply the activity of understanding which sets off the chain reaction leading to intellectual love of God, why must the understanding take the form of intuitive knowledge rather than reason? After all, reason yields adequate understanding just as intuitive knowledge does, and it is in having adequate ideas that the mind acts, not in having adequate ideas via one kind of knowledge or another.

As we know, according to Spinoza, intuitive knowledge leads to the intellectual love of God and the greatest satisfaction of mind there can be. Although this gives the impression that intuitive knowledge uniquely holds the key to the highest human good, in examining Spinoza's arguments, we have seen no reason to privilege the third kind of knowledge over the second. What, then, explains Spinoza's seemingly unwarranted silence about the second kind of knowledge in the second part of *Ethics* Part 5?

Somewhat ironically, it may be that the similarities between the second and third kinds of knowledge explain *both* Spinoza's silence about the second kind of knowledge *and* the fact that the logic of his arguments on behalf of the virtues of intuitive knowledge apply equally to reason. In order to see this, it is first necessary to look more closely at the similarity between Spinoza's distinction between reason and intuitive knowledge, on the one hand, and Descartes' distinction between intuition and deduction, on the other.

If the method interpretation (or at least the version articulated here) is correct, then, as noted above, the distinction between reason and intuitive knowledge is akin to Descartes' distinction between intuition and deduction (notwithstanding important differences between Descartes' and Spinoza's respective epistemologies, which I will discuss in the concluding chapter). A notable aspect of Descartes' distinction is its fluidity. For Descartes, we intuit something when we can grasp the truth of the thing in a single mental act. We deduce something, by contrast, when we cannot fit it into a single act of apprehension, but must proceed through a series of steps, or mental motions, from one act of comprehension to another. It may be that when we first encounter a proof, we do not understand it as a whole in a single act of apprehension, but must proceed step by step from premises to conclusion. Through continuous study of the proof, however, we can come to intuit it as a whole. Hence, on Descartes' understanding of the distinction between intuition and deduction, what is at one time a deduction can become at another time intuited.[45]

I submit that something similar can be said about Spinoza's second and third kinds of knowledge. That is, what is known at first (or at one time) discursively by reason, can come to be known (at another time) non-discursively by intuitive knowledge. Evidence that this was Spinoza's view is provided by the comment with which he prefaces the Appendix to *Ethics* Part 4:

> The things I have taught in this part concerning the right way of living have not been so arranged that they could be seen at one glance [*ut uno aspectu videri possint*]. Instead, I have demonstrated them at one place or another, as I could more easily deduce one from another. So I have undertaken to collect them here and bring them under main headings. (G 2:266)

Curley is astute to join the *uno aspectu* of this passage with the *uno intuitu* of the fourth proportional example under the common translation, "in one glance," since the Appendix to Part 4 no less than the fourth proportional example appears to invoke the hallmark of *scientia intuitiva*: non-discursivity. The passage suggests that whereas the propositions comprising *Ethics* Part 4 were demonstrated discursively, according to the second kind

---

[45] See the first paragraph of Rule 7 of Descartes' *Rules* (CSM 1:25).

of knowledge, for organizational reasons, the Appendix, by contrast, is an attempt to facilitate an intuitive understanding of the right way of living. We know, moreover, from E5p28 (one of the few mentions of the second kind of knowledge in the latter part of *Ethics* Part 5) that "The striving, or desire, to know things by the third kind of knowledge cannot arise from the first kind of knowledge, but can indeed arise from the second" (G 2:297). The Cartesian interpretation of the distinction between reason and intuitive knowledge makes this proposition easy to understand. Since intuitive knowledge is just the capacity to know something non-discursively, in one glance, it makes sense that the desire for such penetrating insight would be stimulated by the relatively laborious process of understanding something discursively through reason.[46]

If this Cartesian reading of Spinoza's distinction between reason and intuitive knowledge is right, then the distinction between reason and intuitive knowledge is fluid in the sense that what is known at one time through reason can be known at another time intuitively. In a sense, the two kinds of knowledge are really the same—they are both forms of adequate knowledge, and adequate knowledge is, as it were, adequate knowledge—except for the fact that the third kind of knowledge can be viewed as the perfection of the second kind.[47] This would explain Spinoza's apparent conflation

---

[46] Although Spinoza proclaims that E5p28 is evident through itself, the demonstration that he goes on to give is not terribly clear. He says "the ideas which are clear and distinct in us, or which are related to the third kind of knowledge (see E2p40s2), cannot follow from the mutilated and confused ideas, which (by E2p40s2) are related to the first kind of knowledge; but they can follow from adequate ideas, or (by E2p40s2) from the second and third kind of knowledge" (E5p28dem/G 2:298). Spinoza's talk of ideas "which are related to" the first and third kinds of knowledge respectively is vague and confusing. Nevertheless, I take him to be expressing a view he has expressed elsewhere: adequate (or clear and distinct) ideas are productive of other adequate ideas (but inadequate ideas are not productive of adequate ideas) (Ep. 37/G 4:188a). If so, then Spinoza is simply saying that since the second kind of knowledge consists of adequate ideas, and since adequate ideas can produce other adequate ideas, then the second kind of knowledge can produce the third kind of knowledge, which also consists of adequate ideas. If this is all he is saying, then we can see why he would say that the proposition is self-evident. But, it is hard to see how this could be true unless the content of reason and intuitive knowledge is interchangeable. So, as confusing as the demonstration of this proposition is, I think it is ultimately consistent with the Cartesian reading of the distinction between reason and intuitive knowledge.

[47] Cf. Malinowski-Charles 2004. Malinowski-Charles interprets reason and intuitive knowledge as "in reality the same knowledge, but simply under two different modalities" (2004, 142). Her interpretation of the sameness of reason and intuitive knowledge, if I understand it correctly, is, however, different from mine. She sees reason and intuitive knowl-

of reason and intuitive knowledge in the passage from the Appendix of *Ethics* 4 which I quoted at the beginning of this chapter, the first part of which reads: "In life, therefore, it is especially useful to perfect, as far as we can, our intellect, or reason. In this one thing consists man's happiness, or blessedness. Indeed, blessedness is nothing but that satisfaction of mind which stems from the intuitive knowledge of God." The apparent conflict between Spinoza's claim that blessedness consists in the perfection of reason and also in the satisfaction of mind stemming from intuitive knowledge is resolved if intuitive knowledge *is* the perfection of reason.

It is no mystery why Spinoza might view the third kind of knowledge as the perfection of the second, if all that distinguishes the former from the latter is its eschewal of discursivity: when one is able to see something *uno intuitu*, in one glance, one sees it more clearly, indeed, as clearly as possible. If this is the case, it explains why Spinoza would not bother mentioning the second kind of knowledge when speaking of the mind's greatest satisfaction and the intellectual love of God, even if reason can also produce great satisfaction and, indeed, intellectual love of God. In these sections of *Ethics* Part 5, Spinoza is speaking of the highest human good. He makes it plain that the highest human good is achieved through knowledge. But the third kind of knowledge is our highest form of knowledge. So in discussing the highest human good achievable through knowledge, he speaks of our highest form of knowledge, to wit, *scientia intuitiva*.

Intuitive knowledge is the perfection of reason, then, but not in the sense of yielding a more refined or loftier knowledge content. Instead, reason finds its perfection in intuitive knowledge when a discursive train of reasoning is distilled in a single act of mental vision. It is in this sense, I think, that we should take Spinoza's oracular dictum, "the eyes of the mind, by which it sees and observes things, are the demonstrations themselves" (E5p23s/G 2:296).

---

edge as different moments in one process of adequate understanding. In particular, she proposes that the end point of reason is identical to the starting point of intuitive knowledge. Her reading provides a compelling explanation of how intuitive knowledge might arise out of reason, but it has trouble making sense of the examples of the distinction between reason and intuitive knowledge that Spinoza gives, in particular, the fourth proportional example and the example in E5p36s, which suggest parallel epistemic pathways, rather than complementary aspects of a single pathway. Malinowski-Charles recognizes this, but attributes it to a problem of coherence in Spinoza's texts (2004, 161).

7.6 Intuitive Knowledge in Spinozan Science

In concluding this chapter, I would like to notice briefly how intuitive knowledge might feature in Spinozan science. This is not hard to see on the interpretation I have defended. As the perfection of reason, intuitive knowledge will sometimes be achieved after careful study of demonstrative reasoning, as we saw, for instance, in the case of the propositions of *Ethics* Part 4. However, this is not necessary, as is readily manifest in the case of Spinoza's fourth proportional example. Euclid's proof *might* help prepare the way for an intuitive grasp of the solution of the problem, but in practice, this is implausible, since the solution is so easy. Intuitive knowledge, then, is possible with or without the ladder of reason.

Thanks to the isoperimetric example, it is possible to see how intuitive knowledge would pertain to and function in a wide range of practical scenarios. In studying soap bubbles and in designing aerostats, scientists and engineers undoubtedly rely on an intuitive grasp of the relationship between surface area and volume enclosed. In studying all manner of natural phenomena and in designing all manner of technologies, scientists and engineers employ the three kinds of knowledge in combination, collecting data, consulting manuals, and conducting trials with the first kind of knowledge; making law-based predictions and proving theorems with the second kind of knowledge; and intuiting relationships *uno intuitu* with the third.

Like reason, moreover, intuitive knowledge must incorporate the data of experience into its judgments if the latter are to engage with the world of things. Even the minimal knowledge of the mind's dependence upon God depends on the experiential knowledge of the *cogito* itself. Reliance on experience poses no problems when making minimal epistemic claims about common essences, but in the case of claims about species essences, the price for having to rely on experience is the fact that even intuitive judgments, no less than those of reason, are hypothetical, true only in form.

References

Allison, Henry E. 1987. *Benedict de Spinoza: An Introduction*. Revised Edition. New Haven: Yale University Press.

Aristotle. 1984. *The Complete Works of Aristotle*. 2 vols., edited by Jonathan Barnes. Princeton, NJ: Princeton University Press.

Bennett, Jonathan. 1984. *A Study of Spinoza's* Ethics. Indianapolis, IN: Hackett.
Blåsjö, Viktor. 2005. "Evolution of...The Isoperimetric Problem." *American Mathematical Monthly* 112: 526–566.
Carlisle, Clare. 2017. "Spinoza's *Acquiescentia*." *Journal of the History of Philosophy* 55(2): 209–236.
Carr, Spencer. 1978. "Spinoza's Distinction Between Rational and Intuitive Knowledge." *The Philosophical Review* 87(2): 241–252.
Curley, Edwin. 1973. "Experience in Spinoza's Theory of Knowledge." In *Spinoza: A Collection of Critical Essays*, edited by Marjorie Grene, 25–59. Notre Dame, IN: University of Notre Dame Press.
De Dijn, Herman. 1990. "Wisdom and Theoretical Knowledge in Spinoza." In *Spinoza: Issues and Directions*, edited by Edwin Curley and Pierre-François Moreau, 147–56. Leiden: E.J. Brill.
Deleuze, Gilles. 1988. *Spinoza: Practical Philosophy*. Translated by Robert Huxley. San Francisco: City Lights Books.
Garrett, Aaron V. 2003. *Meaning in Spinoza's Method*. Cambridge, UK: Cambridge University Press.
Garrett, Don. 2009. "Spinoza on the Essence of the Human Body and the Part of the Mind That Is Eternal." In *The Cambridge Companion to Spinoza's* Ethics, edited by Olli Koistinen, 284–302. Cambridge, UK: Cambridge University Press.
Gueroult, Martial. 1968. *Spinoza I: Dieu (Éthique, I)*. Paris: Aubier-Montaigne.
Heath, Thomas L. 1956. *The Thirteen Books of Euclid's Elements*. Vol 2. Commentary. New York: Dover Publications, Inc.
Hubbeling, H. G. 1986. "The Third Way of Knowledge (Intuition) in Spinoza." *Studia Spinozana* 2: 219–32.
Jaquet, Chantal. 2018. "Eternity." In *The Oxford Handbook of Spinoza*, edited by Michael Della Rocca, 370–76. New York, NY: Oxford University Press.
Malinowski-Charles, Syliane. 2004. "The Circle of Adequate Knowledge: Notes on Reason and Intuition in Spinoza." *Oxford Studies in Early Modern Philosophy* 1: 139–64.
Manzini, Frédéric. 2011. "D'où vient la connaissance intuitive? Spinoza devant l'aporie de la connaissance des singuliers." In *Spinoza et ses scolastiques: Retours aux sources et nouveaux enjeux*, edited by Frédéric Manzini, 67–84. Paris: PUPS.
Matheron, Alexandre. 1986. "Spinoza and Euclidean Arithmetic: The Example of the Fourth Proportional." In *Spinoza and the Sciences*, edited by Marjorie Grene and Debra Nails, 125–150. Boston: D. Reidel.
Melamed, Yitzhak Y. 2013. "Mapping the Labyrinth of Spinoza's *Scientia Intuitiva*." In *Übergänge – diskursiv oder intuitiv? Essays zu Eckart Försters Die 25 Jahre der Philosophie*, edited by Johannes Haag and Markus Wild, 99–116. Frankfurt, Kostermann.
Nadler, Steven. 2006. *Spinoza's* Ethics: *An Introduction*. Cambridge, UK: Cambridge University Press.

———. 2018. "The Intellectual Love of God." In *The Oxford Handbook of Spinoza*, edited by Michael Della Rocca, 295–313. New York, NY: Oxford University Press.

Nagel, Thomas. 1986. *The View from Nowhere*. New York: Oxford University Press.

Parkinson, G.H.R. 1954. *Spinoza's Theory of Knowledge*. London: Oxford University Press.

Primus, Kristin. 2017. "*Scientia Intuitiva* in the *Ethics*." In *Spinoza's* Ethics: *A Critical Guide*, edited by Yitzhak Y. Melamed. Cambridge, UK: Cambridge University Press.

Sandler, Ronald. 2005. "*Intuitus* and *Ratio* in Spinoza's Ethical Thought." *British Journal for the History of Philosophy* 13(1): 73–90.

Schopenhauer, Arthur. 1969. *The World As Will and Representation*. Vol. 1. Translated by E. F. J. Payne. New York: Dover Publications.

Soyarslan, Sanem. 2016. "The Distinction between Reason and Intuitive Knowledge in Spinoza's *Ethics*." *European Journal of Philosophy* 24(1): 27–54.

Steinberg, Diane. 2009. "Knowledge in Spinoza's *Ethics*." In *The Cambridge Companion to Spinoza's* Ethics, edited by Olli Koistinen, 140–66. Cambridge, UK: Cambridge University Press.

Steiner, Jakob. 1842. "Sur le maximum et le minimum des figures dans le plan, sur la sphere, et dans l'espace en générale. Premier mémoire," *Journal für die reine und angewandte Mathematik* 24: 93–162; 189–250.

Viljanen, Valtteri. 2011. *Spinoza's Geometry of Power*. Cambridge, UK: Cambridge University Press.

Wilson, Margaret D. 1996. "Spinoza's theory of knowledge." In *The Cambridge Companion to Spinoza*, edited by Don Garrett, 89–141. Cambridge, UK: Cambridge University Press.

Yovel, Yirmiyahu. 1990. "The Third Kind of Knowledge as Salvation." In *Spinoza: Issues and Directions*, edited by Edwin Curley and Pierre-François Moreau, 157–75. Leiden: E.J. Brill.

CHAPTER 8

Conclusion

The portrait of Spinoza's epistemology that I have sketched in this book exhibits, among other things, the following two salient, and controversial, characteristics: it is more epistemically optimistic and sanguine than pessimistic and skeptical (especially regarding knowledge of the physical realm), and it is more Cartesian than anti-Cartesian (or un-Cartesian).[1] Inasmuch as Descartes' epistemic outlook might be regarded as optimistic and sanguine, these two characteristics are interrelated. As goes without saying, Spinoza's epistemology has been and could be interpreted very differently than I have done here. It is possible, for instance, to view Spinoza as epistemically pessimistic and anti-Cartesian. One version of the mathematical antirealist interpretation of Spinoza exemplifies such an outlook. In closing, I want to address directly both of the salient, controversial characteristics of my interpretation. First, I will make some final remarks in defense of the epistemically sanguine cast of my interpretation against the pull of a more skeptical reading. Second, I want to address explicitly some points about the relationship between Spinoza's epistemology as I have portrayed it and that of Descartes. In particular, having

---

[1] My interpretation of Spinoza's epistemology has not been *all* epistemic optimism. In Chap. 4, I poured cold water on the idea that peculiar common notions, or our ideas of properties common to only a subset of things, can be "adequate in the human mind," if, by this, we mean robustly true. At best, I argued, such ideas can be true-in-form hypotheses.

generally stressed similarities between the two over the course of this book, I will highlight a notable difference.

8.1 Spinoza's Epistemic Outlook

According to the version of mathematical realism I have argued for, geometrical figures exist as the determinations of finite bodies. However, this does not mean that our knowledge of geometrical figures is straightforwardly "real" in the sense of directly corresponding to extra-mental objects. Any correspondence between our geometrical ideas and the actual properties of natural bodies is complicated by our need to rely on distortive sensory experience for knowledge of such bodies. This, I argued, is where Spinoza's scientific methodology comes into play, and I advanced an interpretation of this methodology as hypothetico-deductive in relation to the knowledge of finite things. (I add the qualification "in relation to the knowledge of finite things," because, I have contended, Spinoza regards our knowledge of the most general laws of nature as apodictic, not hypothetical.) This hypothetico-deductive reading of Spinozan scientific method nicely accommodates the notion of true-in-form geometrical ideas as beings of reason within a broadly mathematical realist framework. Since the imaginative ideas of the geometrical properties of natural bodies derived from sensory experience are inadequate, if we are to have adequate conceptions of geometrical objects, these need to be constructed. As constructions, they are beings of reason, but may serve as heuristics for interpreting and better understanding nature. If we are able to deduce and predict the actual properties of natural objects using our adequate conceptions, the latter are thereby confirmed in reflecting reality, at least provisionally and approximately. As heuristics (or approximations), our adequate conceptions are ever-revisable in light of further experience and experiment. True-in-form geometrical conceptions are *able* to serve as heuristics and are *useful* as such, because geometrical figures are among the properties of finite bodies. Hence, I say, true-in-form geometrical conceptions are beings of reason within a broadly mathematical realist framework. In my view, this interpretation provides a compelling reconciliation of the antirealist and realist tendencies of Spinoza's treatment of geometrical entities.

There is, however, another response to the challenge posed by the need to rely on distortive sensory experience for knowledge of finite bodies besides the one I have defended in terms of hypothetico-deduction. I said that the need to rely on distortive sensory experience complicates the correspondence between our geometrical ideas and the geometrical properties of things, but one might argue that, in fact, it *undermines* the correspondence and renders it impossible. After all, as we have seen, what makes sensory experience distortive is the fact that it represents only the way our bodies are affected by external things, not the things themselves. It represents a small part of a larger whole, the vast majority of which is external to our minds. Even this, arguably, misstates the situation, since what is external to our minds is not simply a larger whole, but infinite. How could the finite human mind ever make progress in untangling an infinitely complex object? "What," Pascal queried, "is a man in the infinite?"[2] Even if the hypothetico-deductive picture of ever-revisable, approximative heuristics may concede that the task of interpreting nature is an infinite one, perhaps it is better characterized as a futile one, and nature a dark labyrinth, after all.

This epistemically pessimistic attitude about the human predicament points toward the skeptical reading of Spinoza that I mentioned in the Introduction. As I acknowledged then, there is some basis for this reading. A kind of Pascalian vertigo before the infinite is evoked in Spinoza's famous depiction in Letter 32 of the worm living in the blood. The worm observes and explains the interactions among the particles of blood in its vicinity in terms of their natures and properties, but in doing so treats the particles of blood as wholes when in fact they are parts of the blood as a whole, determined in their interactions not only by their own natures and properties but also by the universal nature of the blood. The blood itself, however, has the same relation to greater wholes as the particles of blood have to it, and such is the case for all bodies, which, Spinoza says, "must be considered as a part of the whole universe....And since the nature of the universe is not limited, as the nature of the blood is, but is absolutely infinite, its parts are regulated in infinite ways by this nature of the infinite power, and compelled to undergo infinitely many variations" (Ep. 32/G 4:173a)—all of which is, of course, beyond the comprehension of a finite intellect. Recall the remark from TTP 4 that I quoted earlier: "we are completely ignorant of the order and connection of things itself, i.e., of how things are really ordered and connected" (TTP 4.4/G 3:58).

The infinite complexity of nature is not in dispute. The question is what it portends for human inquiry. Does it render it an infinite task or a fool's

---

[2] Pascal 1995, 60.

errand? Referring to the infinitely small and the infinitely vast—both of which lie beyond our middling, finite grasp—Pascal writes, "Because they failed to contemplate these infinities, men have rashly undertaken to probe into nature as if there were some proportion between themselves and her."[3] In lieu of presumptuous investigation into nature, Pascal instead advises silent contemplation of our predicament. (This is what I had in mind when, in the Introduction, I spoke of Pascalian renunciation.) This, I take it, is the tendency of the skeptical response to the infinite complexity of nature. However, it is not, in my view at least, Spinoza's response.

We have already seen that Spinoza's comment in TTP 4 regarding our ignorance of the order and connection of things is followed not by a gesture of renunciation, but instead by the provision to "consider things as possible," or in other words, as I argued above, to deploy true-in-form adequate conceptions as part of a hypothetico-deductive approach. There is equally no reason to interpret the lesson of Letter 32's worm-in-the-blood analogy to be the futility of investigating the natural world, as a look at the context in which Spinoza disclaims knowledge of the relationship between the parts and whole of nature shows. In his previous letter to Oldenburg (Ep. 30), Spinoza had addressed the ongoing war between the Dutch and English, remarking,

> these turmoils move me, neither to laughter nor even to tears, but to philosophizing and to observing human nature better. For I do not think it right for me to mock nature, much less to lament it, when I reflect that men, like all other things, are only a part of nature, and that I do not know how each part agrees with the whole to which it belongs, and how it coheres with the other parts. And I find, simply from the lack of this knowledge, that certain things in nature, which I perceive in part and only in a mutilated way, and which do not agree at all with our philosophic mind, previously seemed to me vain, disorderly and absurd, whereas now I permit each to live according to his own mentality. Surely those who wish to die for their good may do so, so long as I am allowed to live for the true good. (G 4:166/5)

In this passage (which perfectly exhibits Spinoza's signature blend of passion and dispassion), Spinoza describes a shift in his own thinking from a less philosophical to a more philosophical mindset. In his less philosophical mindset, he explains, he was wont to find certain things in nature, such as human beings' proclivity for warfare, "vain, disorderly and absurd." He

---

[3] Pascal 1995, 61.

attributes this attitude to a lack of knowledge regarding how each part of nature agrees with the whole. I think, in fact, that the misguided attitude is due not just to a lack of knowledge of the relationship between part and whole but, more fundamentally, to mistaking parts for wholes. So, what Spinoza means is that he previously ignored the fact *that* each thing is part of a whole, not merely *how* each thing coheres with the whole. The more philosophical mindset that he came to adopt, according to his telling, consists in grasping this fact, and in seeing things as parts of, and determined by, a greater whole. This explains why in both his less philosophical and more philosophical mindsets he is equally ignorant of *how* the parts cohere with the whole, and yet, he comes to understand something important in attaining the more philosophical standpoint.

Does this mean that when, at the beginning of the passage, Spinoza says that the turmoils move him neither to laughter nor to tears but to philosophizing, he has in mind simply the contemplation of the "bigger picture," and a kind of Stoic apathy vis-à-vis whatever takes place? If so, this is reminiscent of the common essence interpretation of intuitive knowledge discussed in the last chapter, according to which intuitive knowledge consists in the grasp of the union of things with God—a minimal achievement from an epistemic standpoint, albeit one of great ethical import. Now, as then, I think this line of interpretation captures an important part of what is going on, but not the whole picture. If all Spinoza meant by "philosophizing" was contemplating the *fact* of things' infinitely complex determination by the whole of nature, there would be little reason for him to add that the turmoils also prompt him to "observing human nature better." This suggests a positive program of investigating human nature for which recognition of the fact that human nature is determined by general laws is merely a prerequisite. To be sure, no productive inquiry into human nature is possible in the absence of understanding that man is not an *imperium in imperio* insulated from natural laws. But this understanding is just the beginning, not the end, of inquiry. Spinoza's attention to the method of interpreting nature suggests as much.

One might argue that Spinoza's scientific method is designed for utility or power instead of truth. This is certainly the case with Hobbes, for instance, for whom science is the generation of effects from causes (and vice versa) and the "end of knowledge is power."[4] In Spinoza's case, we know that a true-in-form adequate idea is one that provides a basis for

---

[4] Hobbes 2005, 7.

predicting the properties of a thing. The need to rely on distortive sensory experience in the formation of even our true-in-form adequate ideas, moreover, coupled with the infinite complexity of nature, means that no robustly true idea of a finite thing is attainable for finite minds. So, perhaps it makes sense to understand Spinozan knowledge of finite things in terms of power, not truth, à la Hobbes. Spinozan science would, then, be instrumentalist, in the sense in which instrumentalism contrasts with realism.

It is wrongheaded to conflate Spinoza with Hobbes in this way, however (even if there are important points of contact and probable influence). Unlike Hobbes, Spinoza does not think our only access to the natural world is through the senses. Spinoza's common notions constitute adequate ideas—immune to sensory distortion and true, not just in form, but robustly—about the most general features of nature. The most general laws of nature count, moreover, among the common notions. This means that the Spinozan scientific enterprise is grounded in a clear knowledge of reality in a way that Hobbes' fails to be. Because Spinoza's system touches ground, as it were, at its foundation, the task of Spinozan science is an infinite one, but not a futile one. In this regard, a much better comparison is with neither Pascal nor Hobbes, but Descartes. As I am urging is the case with Spinoza, Descartes, too, has ambitions for a positive program of scientific inquiry rooted in his belief that human beings are able to attain assured knowledge of scientific foundations, but he must confront the task of reconciling these ambitions with the need to rely on distortive sensory perception for knowledge of particulars. Like Spinoza, he does so via hypothetico-deductive methodology. These parallels between Spinoza and Descartes now warrant final analysis.

8.2 Spinoza Vis-à-Vis Descartes (and Galileo)

Throughout this study I have made frequent reference to Descartes. This is standard practice in Spinoza scholarship, since Descartes is Spinoza's most important influence. While mentioning one or two contrasts along the way, most often I have highlighted similarities between the two philosophers. In Chap. 2, I highlighted the Cartesian aspects of Spinoza's response to skepticism. In particular, I argued that while true-in-form mathematical ideas can get the method going in the right direction, it is not complete (and, therefore, nor is the response to the skeptic) until an idea is found that is not true merely in form, but robustly true. As for

Descartes, I argued, so, for Spinoza, this idea must be an idea of God *qua ens realissimum*.

In the central chapters (Chaps. 3, 4, and 5) on the status of geometrical figures and the role of geometry in Spinozan science I noted an array of parallels with Descartes' treatment of the issues. Perhaps most important for my agenda was the model that Descartes provides for handling the ambiguity of geometrical entities. While recognizing the abstractness of figures when considered independently of bodies, Descartes has no trouble making sense of the mathematization thesis, so long as figures are considered not independently of bodies, but among the properties of bodies. I suggested we handle the ambiguity of geometrical entities in Spinoza in just this way. The upshot is that geometry has a central role to play in Spinozan as in Cartesian science. Spinoza and Descartes, moreover, make analogous concessions to the need to rely on sensory experience for knowledge of finite things, even while affirming the ideal of deducing consequences from first principles a priori. The result, for both, is a hypothetico-deductive approach to natural knowledge of finite things.

Finally, in Chap. 7, I argued that the fluidity of Descartes' distinction between deduction and intuition provides a model for thinking about the relationship between reason and intuitive knowledge in Spinoza as part of my case for the method interpretation of the distinction between the second and third kinds of knowledge.

These are only the most prominent points of overlap I have highlighted over the course of the study. Indeed, the portrait of Spinoza's epistemology that I have sketched could certainly be considered substantially Cartesian. Highlighting certain similarities between Spinoza and Descartes has been part of my strategy, since Descartes is one of the philosophers most closely associated with a mathematized conception of nature, and an important objective of this study has been to emphasize the way in which Spinoza also embraces mathematization. While my strategy has led me to stress similarities, this does not mean, of course, that there are no important differences between the epistemologies of Spinoza and Descartes. An adequate treatment of these differences would require a study in its own right,[5] but I would like to discuss one difference, in particular, in bringing this study to a close.

---

[5] Curley (1988) provides an excellent comparative analysis of Spinoza and Descartes, though the emphasis is on metaphysical and ethical issues, rather than epistemological ones.

What is especially profound in Spinoza's philosophy is the identity between the human mind and God. The human mind is not identical to God qua infinite, but Spinoza tells us that God constitutes the essence of the human mind nevertheless, insofar as the latter is a mode of God's infinite intellect. Thus, when the human mind has one idea or another, it is correct to say that God has one idea or another (E2p11c). The only question is whether the idea in the human mind is a fragment of a more complex idea in God's mind or is in fact identical with an idea in God's mind without qualification. Our inadequate ideas are fragments of the divine mind, but our adequate ideas are themselves divine, we might say, inasmuch as they are identical with ideas in the divine intellect. There is, then, absolutely no reservation regarding the truth of our adequate ideas (E2p34).

The situation is very different in Descartes. The Cartesian *res cogitans* is not part of the divine intellect, but a separate substance altogether. The comparative distance between the human and divine in Descartes has epistemological ramifications. This is seen in what Descartes says himself about adequate knowledge in the Fourth Replies:

> if a piece of knowledge is to be *adequate* it must contain absolutely all the properties which are in the thing which is the object of knowledge. Hence only God can know that he has adequate knowledge of all things.
>
> A created intellect, by contrast, though perhaps it may in fact possess adequate knowledge of many things, can never know it has such knowledge unless God grants it a special revelation of the fact. In order to have adequate knowledge of a thing all that is required is that the power of knowing possessed by the intellect is adequate for the thing in question, and this can easily occur. But in order for the intellect to know it has such knowledge, or that God put nothing in the thing beyond what it is aware of, its power of knowing would have to equal the infinite power of God, and this plainly could not happen on pain of contradiction. (CSM 2:155)

In this passage, Descartes is saying that although we can have adequate knowledge—indeed, "this can easily occur"—we cannot know that we have adequate knowledge. The reason for this is that we cannot be sure that God has not put something into the thing beyond what we are aware of. Descartes' reasoning here is curious, since, were God to put something in the idea beyond what we are aware of, it would smack of deception. But Descartes rules out the possibility of divine (or demonic) deception in proving God to be a being whose perfection is inconsistent with guile. So, it is not immediately clear how Descartes' point about adequate knowledge can be squared with what he claims to establish about God.[6]

Whether or not Descartes is entitled to his stance on adequate knowledge, and whatever the grounds might be in case he is, there is a clear contrast to be drawn with Spinoza either way. There is no question that, for Spinoza, to know something adequately is also to know that we know it adequately, or, as Spinoza puts it in the *Ethics*, "He who has a true idea at the same time knows that he has a true idea, and cannot doubt the truth of the thing" (E2p43/G 2:123). For Spinoza, every true idea is adequate and vice versa, so Spinoza's statement about true ideas applies equally to adequate ideas. There is no possibility, moreover, of Spinoza talking about something different from Descartes. He clarifies that "to have a true idea means nothing other than knowing a thing perfectly, or in the best way" (E2p43s/G 2:124). While Descartes' commentary on adequate knowledge does not disqualify us from perfect knowledge, in one sense, it does disqualify us from being sure that we know something perfectly. It is this disconnect between knowledge and certainty that Spinoza rejects. It is clear that the basis of his rejection is the mind's participation in the divine intellect. Spinoza reasons as follows: "our Mind, insofar as it perceives things truly, is part of the infinite intellect of God (by E2p11c); hence, it is as necessary that the mind's clear and distinct ideas are true as that God's ideas are" (E2p43s/G 2:124–25). So, because our minds are part of the divine intellect, when we have true ideas, we know that we know something perfectly, or adequately. In the case of Descartes, by contrast, because of the separation of the human mind from God, we can never be sure that our knowledge is perfect, even when our ideas are true.

---

[6] One possible explanation is that Descartes' famous, but shadowy, doctrine of the creation of the eternal truths is lurking in the background. That is, perhaps God's absolute omnipotence makes it impossible to ever be sure of anything at a certain level. Frankfurt's article on this subject (1977) is superb. Goldenbaum (2016, 286) makes the further, complementary suggestion that Descartes' approach was one of caution:

> Descartes was as aware as anyone of the theological concerns regarding Galileo. Therefore, in spite of his enthusiastic statements about the certainty of deduction and intuition (both of which are available to us) in his early writings, especially in the *Rules*, he has to backpedal and grant that God could have made the world in a way that would be completely incomprehensible to us, in opposition even to what we hold to be mathematically necessary.

I argued in Chap. 2 that the robust truth of our clear and distinct or true-in-form ideas cannot be taken for granted at the outset. It is only once a true idea of God is attained, and the participation of the human mind in the divine intellect is established, that Spinoza's claim in E2p43 that we can be certain that our true-in-form ideas are actually (or robustly) true is secure. Once the relation between the human mind and God is established, however, there is no longer any reservation about the perfection of our true ideas. They are, after all, identical with the ideas in the divine intellect.

To be sure, the notion of an idea true in form but not true robustly is not rendered obsolete, even after the participation of the human mind in the divine intellect is established. On the contrary, true-in-form ideas have an integral role to play in providing provisional conceptions of the species essences (and perhaps individual essences) of singular things in Spinoza's hypothetico-deductive scientific method. Nevertheless, although ideas of species essences can only aspire to the form of true ideas, they exist on a spectrum anchored by ideas that are true in the robust sense. On the one hand, our ideas of common essences are adequate and perfect. On the other hand, while adequate ideas of individual essences may be forever out of reach for finite minds, we see that concessions to the limitations of finite minds, such as Descartes makes, are joined, in Spinoza, with affirmations of the capacity for perfect knowledge despite our finitude. Even with concessions to finitude, then, Spinoza's identification of the human mind with ideas in the divine intellect makes possible what, for Descartes, is impossible: the knowledge that we have (at least some) adequate, or perfect knowledge.

On this score, Spinoza is closer to Galileo, the other lion of mathematization. Consider the following statement by Salviati from Galileo's *Dialogo*:

> I say that the human intellect does understand some [propositions] perfectly, and thus in these it has as much absolute certainty as Nature itself has. Of such are the mathematical sciences alone; that is, geometry and arithmetic, in which the Divine intellect indeed knows infinitely more propositions, since it knows all. But with regard to those few which the human intellect does understand, I believe that its knowledge equals the Divine in objective

certainty, for here it succeeds in understanding necessity, beyond which there can be no greater sureness.[7]

Simplicio's response to Salviati reads: "This speech strikes me as very bold and daring." What strikes Simplicio, of course, is Salviati's contention that in its knowledge of mathematical propositions, the human intellect equals the intellect of God—the same thing that Spinoza knew would give his readers pause after E2p11c, when he announced the participation of the human mind in God's intellect.[8]

Spinoza would not entirely agree with Salviati's statement here (which seems to represent Galileo's own thinking). In the first place, Spinoza would disagree that the mathematical sciences *alone* afford absolute certainty, since we can have adequate knowledge of God's attributes, among other metaphysical categories and propositions. Indeed, for Spinoza, our knowledge of foundational metaphysics is a better example of what we can be absolutely certain of than mathematics. Arithmetic, I argued, is unequivocally concerned with beings of reason, for Spinoza. While our ideas about numbers can exhibit the form of truth, they cannot be true in a robust sense. Our geometrical ideas can be robustly true, by contrast, insofar as they are ideas about the determinations of finite bodies, though I have argued that our capacity to achieve absolute certainty about such matters is limited by our need to rely on sensory experience in deriving knowledge about finite particulars. Geometrical knowledge that is independent of finite particulars is, like arithmetic, abstract. While Spinoza would therefore disagree with the particulars of Salviati's statement, I think he would applaud its spirit nevertheless, insofar as it recognizes the human capacity for absolute certainty, that is, perfect cognition. Unlike Galileo, of course, Spinoza elaborates a metaphysical framework that makes sense of the "very bold and daring" claim to the capacity for understanding equal to God's by identifying the human intellect with a part, however minor, of God's intellect. In this, he distinguishes himself from Galileo, Descartes, and, indeed, just about everyone else.

---

[7] Galileo 1967, 103.
[8] For an insightful discussion of seventeenth- and eighteenth-century theological concerns stemming from geometrical method and the notion of adequate ideas, see Goldenbaum 2016.

References

Curley, Edwin. 1988. *Behind the Geometrical Method: A Reading of Spinoza's Ethics*. Princeton, NJ: Princeton University Press.

Frankfurt, Harry. 1977. "Descartes on the Creation of the Eternal Truths." *Philosophical Review* 86(1): 36–57.

Galileo, Galilei. 1967. *Dialogue Concerning the Two Chief World Systems*. Translated by Stillman Drake. Berkeley, CA: University of California Press.

Goldenbaum, Ursula. 2016. "The Geometrical Method as the New Standard of Truth, Based on the Mathematization of Nature." In *The Language of Nature: Reassessing the Mathematization of Nature in the Seventeenth Century*, edited by Geoffrey Gorham et al., 274–307. Minneapolis, MN: University of Minnesota Press.

Hobbes, Thomas. 2005. *The English Works of Thomas Hobbes of Malmesbury*. Vol. 1. Translated by William Molesworth. London: John Bonn, 1839. Replica edition, Elbiron Classics.

Pascal, Blaise. 1995. *Pensées*. London: Penguin Books.

REFERENCES

Allison, Henry E. 1987. *Benedict de Spinoza: An Introduction*. Revised Edition. New Haven: Yale University Press.

Ariew, Roger. 2016. "The Mathematization of Nature in Descartes and the First Cartesians." In *The Language of Nature: Reassessing the Mathematization of Natural Philosophy in the Seventeenth Century*, edited by Geoffrey Gorham et al., 112–134. Minneapolis, MN: University of Minnesota Press.

Aristotle. 1984. *The Complete Works of Aristotle*. 2 vols., edited by Jonathan Barnes. Princeton, NJ: Princeton University Press.

Balaguer, Mark. 2009. "Realism and Antirealism in Mathematics." In *Philosophy of Mathematics*, edited by Andrew D. Irvine, 35–102. Burlington, MA: North Holland.

Barbone, Steven. 2002. "What Counts as an Individual for Spinoza?" In *Spinoza: Metaphysical Themes*, edited by Olli Koistinen and John Biro, 89–112. New York: Oxford University Press.

Barnes, Jonathan. 2000. "Introduction." In *Outlines of Scepticism* by Sextus Empiricus, edited by Julia Annas and Jonathan Barnes, xi–xxxi. Cambridge, UK: Cambridge University Press.

Bennett, Jonathan. 1984. *A Study of Spinoza's Ethics*. Indianapolis, IN: Hackett.

Blåsjö, Viktor. 2005. "Evolution of…The Isoperimetric Problem." *American Mathematical Monthly* 112: 526–566.

Bolton, Martha. 1985. "Spinoza on Cartesian Doubt." *Noûs* 19: 379–395.

Carlisle, Clare. 2017. "Spinoza's *Acquiescentia*." *Journal of the History of Philosophy* 55(2): 209–236.

Carr, Spencer. 1978. "Spinoza's Distinction Between Rational and Intuitive Knowledge." *The Philosophical Review* 87(2): 241–252.

Carriero, John Peter. 1995. "On the Relationship between Mode and Substance in Spinoza's Metaphysics." *Journal of the History of Philosophy* 33(2): 245–73.

Charles, Syliane. 2002. "Le salut par les affects: le rôle de la joie comme moteur du progrès éthique ches Spinoza." *Philosophiques* 29(1): 73–87.

Chisholm, Roderick. 1973. *The Problem of the Criterion*. Milwaukee, WI: Marquette University Press.

Cook, J. Thomas. 1998. "Spinoza and the Plasticity of Mind." *Studia Spinozana* 14: 111–36.

Curley, Edwin. 1969. *Spinoza's Metaphysics: An Essay in Interpretation*. Cambridge, MA: Harvard University Press.

———. 1973. "Experience in Spinoza's Theory of Knowledge." In *Spinoza: A Collection of Critical Essays*, edited by Marjorie Grene, 25–59. Notre Dame, IN: University of Notre Dame Press.

———. 1988. *Behind the Geometrical Method: A Reading of Spinoza's Ethics*. Princeton, NJ: Princeton University Press.

De Dijn, Herman. 1990. "Wisdom and Theoretical Knowledge in Spinoza." In *Spinoza: Issues and Directions*, edited by Edwin Curley and Pierre-François Moreau, 147–56. Leiden: E.J. Brill.

Delahunty, R. J. 1985. *Spinoza*. London: Routledge & Kegan Paul.

Deleuze, Gilles. 1988. *Spinoza: Practical Philosophy*. Translated by Robert Huxley. San Francisco: City Lights Books.

———. 1990. *Expressionism in Philosophy: Spinoza*. Translated by Martin Joughin. New York: Zone Books.

Della Rocca, Michael. 1994. "Mental Content and Skepticism in Descartes and Spinoza." *Studia Spinozana* 10: 19–42.

———. 1996a. *Representation and the Mind-Body Problem in Spinoza*. New York, NY: Oxford University Press.

———. 1996b. "Spinoza's Metaphysical Psychology." In *The Cambridge Companion to Spinoza*, edited by Don Garrett, 192–266. Cambridge, UK: Cambridge University Press.

———. 2007. "Spinoza and the Metaphysics of Skepticism." *Mind* 116: 851–74

———. 2008. *Spinoza*. New York, NY: Routledge.

Di Bella, Stephano, and Schmaltz, Tad M. 2017. "Introduction to Universals in Modern Philosophy." In *The Problem of Universals in Early Modern Philosophy*, edited by Stephano di Bella and Tad M. Schmaltz, 1–13. New York, NY: Oxford University Press.

Doney, Willis. 1975. "Spinoza on Philosophical Skepticism." In *Spinoza: Essays in Interpretation*, edited by Eugene Freeman and Maurice Mandelbaum, 139-57. La Salle, Il: Open Court.

Fløistad, Guttorm. 1973. "Spinoza's Theory of Knowledge in the Ethics." In *Spinoza: A Collection of Critical Essays*, edited by Marjorie Grene, 101–127. Notre Dame, IN: University of Notre Dame Press.

Frankfurt, Harry. 1977. "Descartes on the Creation of the Eternal Truths." *Philosophical Review* 86(1): 36–57.

Franklin, James. 2009. "Aristotelian Realism." In *Philosophy of Mathematics*, edited by Andrew D. Irvine, 103–156. Burlington, MA: North Holland.

Frege, Gottlob. 1980. *The Foundations of Arithmetic*. Translated by J. L. Austin. Evanston, IL: Northwestern University Press.

Gabbey, Alan. 1996. "Spinoza's natural science and methodology." In *The Cambridge Companion to Spinoza*, edited by Don Garrett, 142–191. Cambridge, UK: Cambridge University Press.

Galileo, Galilei. 1967. *Dialogue Concerning the Two Chief World Systems*. Translated by Stillman Drake. Berkeley, CA: University of California Press.

———. 2008. *The EssentialGalileo*. Translated by Maurice A. Finocchiaro. Indianapolis, IN: Hackett Publishing Company.

Garber, Daniel. 1992. *Descartes' Metaphysical Physics*. Chicago, IL: University of Chicago Press.

———. 2001. *Descartes Embodied: Reading Cartesian Philosophy through Cartesian Science*. Cambridge, UK: Cambridge University Press.

———. 2015. "Superheroes in the History of Philosophy: Spinoza, Super-Rationalist." *Journal of the History of Philosophy* 53(3): 507–21.

Garrett, Aaron V. 2003. *Meaning in Spinoza's Method*. Cambridge, UK: Cambridge University Press.

Garrett, Don. 1979. "Spinoza's 'Ontological' Argument." *Philosophical Review* 88(2): 198–223.

———. 1990. "Truth, Method and Correspondence in Spinoza and Leibniz." *Studia Spinozana* 6: 13–43.

———. 1991. "Spinoza's Necessitarianism." In *God and Nature: Spinoza's Metaphysics*, edited by Yirmiyahu Yovel, 191–218. Leiden: E.J. Brill.

———. 2009. "Spinoza on the Essence of the Human Body and the Part of the Mind That Is Eternal." In *The Cambridge Companion to Spinoza's Ethics*, edited by Olli Koistinen, 284–302. Cambridge, UK: Cambridge University Press.

———. 2010. "Spinoza's Theory of *Scientia Intuitiva*." In *Scientia in Early Modern Philosophy*, edited by T. Sorell et al., 99–115. Dordrecht: Springer.

Gaukroger, Stephen. 1980. "Descartes' Project for a Mathematical Physics." In *Descartes: Philosophy, Mathematics and Physics*, edited by Stephen Gaukroger, 97–140. Sussex, U.K.: Harvester Press.

Gilead, Amihud. 2000. "The Indispensability of the First Kind of Knowledge." In *Spinoza on Knowledge and the Human Mind*, edited by Yirmiyahu Yovel and Gideon Segal, 209–222. Leiden: Brill.

Goldenbaum, Ursula. 2004. "The Affects as a Condition of Human Freedom in Spinoza's *Ethics*." In *Spinoza on Reason and the 'Free Man,'* edited by Yirmiyahu Yovel and Gideon Segal, 149–161. New York: Little Room Press.
———. 2011. "Spinoza – Ein toter Hund? Nicht für Christian Wolff." *Zeitschrift für Ideengeschichte* 5(1): 29–41.
———. 2016. "The Geometrical Method as the New Standard of Truth, Based on the Mathematization of Nature." In *The Language of Nature: Reassessing the Mathematization of Nature in the Seventeenth Century*, edited by Geoffrey Gorham et al., 274–307. Minneapolis, MN: University of Minnesota Press.
Gorham, et al., eds. 2016. *The Language of Nature: Reassessing the Mathematization of Natural Philosophy in the Seventeenth Century*. Minneapolis, MN: University of Minnesota Press.
Gorham, Geoffrey, Hill, Benjamin, and Slowik, Edward. 2016. "Introduction." In *The Language of Nature: Reassessing the Mathematization of Natural Philosophy in the Seventeenth Century*, edited by Geoffrey Gorham et al., 1–28. Minneapolis, MN: University of Minnesota Press.
Grey, John. 2013. "'Use Them at Our Pleasure': Spinoza on Animal Ethics." *History of Philosophy Quarterly* 30: 367–388.
Gueroult, Martial. 1968. *Spinoza I: Dieu (Éthique, I)*. Paris: Aubier-Montaigne.
———. 1974. *Spinoza II: L'Âme (Éthique, II)*. Paris: Aubier-Montaigne.
Hampshire, Stuart. 2005. *Spinoza and Spinozism*. Oxford, UK: Oxford University Press.
Hegel, Georg Wilhelm Friedrich. 1995. *Lectures on the History of Philosophy*, Vol. 3. Translated by E.S. Haldane and Frances H. Simson. Lincoln, NE: University of Nebraska Press.
Hobbes, Thomas. 1991. *Man and Citizen* (De Homine *and* De Cive), edited by Bernard Gert. Indianapolis: Hackett Publishing Company.
———. 2005. *The English Works of Thomas Hobbes of Malmesbury*. Vol. 1. Translated by William Molesworth. London: John Bonn, 1839. Replica edition, Elbiron Classics.
Homan, Matthew. 2014. "Spinoza and the Problem of Mental Representation." *International Philosophical Quarterly* 54: 75–87.
———. 2016. "On the Alleged Exceptional Nature of Thought in Spinoza." *Journal of Philosophical Research* 41: 1–16.
———. 2018a. "Memory Aids and the Cartesian Circle." *British Journal for the History of Philosophy* 26: 1064–1083.
———. 2018b. "Geometrical Figures in Spinoza's Book of Nature." *Journal of the History of Philosophy*. 56(3): 455–476.
Hubbeling, H. G. 1986. "The Third Way of Knowledge (Intuition) in Spinoza." *Studia Spinozana* 2: 219–32.

Hübner, Karolina. 2015. "Spinoza on Negation, Mind-Dependence, and the Reality of the Finite." In *The Young Spinoza: A Metaphysician in the Making*, edited by Yitzhak Y. Melamed, 221–237. Oxford, UK: Oxford University Press.

———. 2016. "Spinoza on Essences, Universals, and Beings of Reason." *Pacific Philosophical Quarterly* 97: 58–88.

Iltis, Carolyn. 1971. "Leibniz and the Vis Viva Controversy." *Isis* 62: 21–35.

Jalobeanu, Dana. 2016. "'The Marriage of Physics with Mathematics': Francis Bacon on Measurement, Mathematics, and the Construction of a Mathematical Physics." In *The Language of Nature: Reassessing the Mathematization of Natural Philosophy in the Seventeenth Century*, edited by Geoffrey Gorham et al., 51–80. Minneapolis, MN: University of Minnesota Press.

James, Susan. 2011. "Creating Rational Understanding: Spinoza as a Social Epistemologist." *Proceedings of the Aristotelian Society Supplementary Volume* 85(1): 181–199.

Jaquet, Chantal. 2005. "Le problème de la différence entre les corps" in *Les expressions de la puissance d'agir chez Spinoza*. doi :https://doi.org/10.4000/books.psorbonne.151. Publications de la Sorbonne.

———. 2018. "Eternity." In *The Oxford Handbook of Spinoza*, edited by Michael Della Rocca, 370–76. New York, NY: Oxford University Press.

Jonas, Hans. 1965. "Spinoza and the Theory of Organism." *Journal of the History of Philosophy* 3(1): 43–58.

Kant, Immanuel. 2000. *Critique of the Power of Judgment*. Translated by Paul Guyer and Eric Matthews. Cambridge, UK: Cambridge University Press.

Kenny, Anthony. 1970. "The Cartesian Circle and the Eternal Truths." *Journal of Philosophy* 67: 685–700.

Klever, W.N.A. 1986. "Axioms in Spinoza's Science and Philosophy of Science." *Studia Spinozana* 2: 171–95.

———. 1988. "Moles in Motu: Principles of Spinoza's Physics." *Studia Spinozana* 4: 165–95.

———. 1990. "Anti-Falsificationism: Spinoza's Theory of Experience and Experiments." In *Spinoza: Issues and Directions. The Proceedings of the Chicago Spinoza Conference*, edited by E. M. Curley and Pierre-François Moreua, 124–135. Leiden: E. J. Brill.

Koyré, Alexandre. 1978. *Galileo Studies*. Translated by John Mepham. Atlantic Highlands, NJ: Humanities Press.

Lachterman, David R. 1978. "The Physics of Spinoza's *Ethics*." In *Spinoza: New Perspectives*, edited by Robert W. Shahan and J. I. Biro, 71–112. Norman: University of Oklahoma Press.

Laerke, Mogens. 2011. "Spinoza's Cosmological Argument in the *Ethics*." *Journal of the History of Philosophy* 49(4): 439–462.

Lear, Jonathan. 1982. "Aristotle's Philosophy of Mathematics." *The Philosophical Review* 91(2): 161–192.

LeBuffe, Michael. 2009. "The Anatomy of the Passions." In *A Cambridge Companion to Spinoza's Ethics*, edited by Olli Koistinen, 188–222. New York, NY: Cambridge University Press.

———. 2018. *Spinoza on Reason*. New York, NY: Oxford University Press.

Lecrivain, André. 1986. "Spinoza and Cartesian Mechanics." In *Spinoza and the Sciences*, edited by Marjorie Grene and Debra Nails, 15–60. Dordrecht: D. Reidel.

Leibniz, Gottfried. 1989. *Philosophical Papers and Letters*. Edited and translated by Leroy E. Loemker. Dordrecht: Kluwer Academic Publishers.

Lin, Martin. 2005. "Memory and Personal Identity in Spinoza." *Canadian Journal of Philosophy* 35(2): 243–268.

———. 2019. *Being and Reason: An Essay on Spinoza's Metaphysics*. New York, NY: Oxford University Press.

LoLordo, Antonia. 2017. "Gassendi on the Problem of Universals." In *The Problem of Universals in Early Modern Philosophy*, edited by Stephano di Bella and Tad M. Schmaltz, 13–40. New York, NY: Oxford University Press.

Malinowski-Charles, Syliane. 2004. "The Circle of Adequate Knowledge: Notes on Reason and Intuition in Spinoza." *Oxford Studies in Early Modern Philosophy* 1: 139–64.

Manning, Richard. 2016. "Spinoza's Physical Theory," *The Stanford Encyclopedia of Philosophy*. Edward N. Zalta (ed.), URL = https://plato.stanford.edu/archives/win2016/entries/spinoza-physics/.

Manzini, Frédéric. 2011. "D'où vient la connaissance intuitive? Spinoza devant l'aporie de la connaissance des singuliers." In *Spinoza et ses scolastiques: Retours aux sources et nouveaux enjeux*, edited by Frédéric Manzini, 67–84. Paris: PUPS.

Marshall, Eugene. 2008. "Adequacy and Innateness in Spinoza." *Oxford Studies in Early Modern Philosophy* 4: 51–88.

———. 2013. *The Spiritual Automaton: Spinoza's Science of the Mind*. New York, NY: Oxford University Press.

Martin, Christopher P. 2008. "The Framework of Essences in Spinoza's *Ethics*." *British Journal for the History of Philosophy* 16(3): 489–509.

Mason, Richard V. 1993. "Ignoring the Demon? Spinoza's Way with Doubt." *Journal of the History of Philosophy* 31: 545–64.

Matheron, Alexandre. 1986. "Spinoza and Euclidean Arithmetic: The Example of the Fourth Proportional." In *Spinoza and the Sciences*, edited by Marjorie Grene and Debra Nails, 125–150. Boston: D. Reidel.

McRae, Robert. 1965. "'Idea' as a Philosophical Term in the Seventeenth Century." *Journal of the History of Ideas* 26: 175–90.

Melamed, Yitzhak Y. 2000. "On the Exact Science of Nonbeings: Spinoza's View of Mathematics." *Iyyun, The Jerusalem Philosophical Quarterly* 49: 3–22.

———. 2010. "Acosmism or Weak Individuals?: Hegel, Spinoza, and the Reality of the Finite." *Journal of the History of Philosophy* 48: 77–92.

———. 2013a. *Spinoza's Metaphysics: Substance and Thought.* Oxford, UK: Oxford University Press.

———. 2013b. "Mapping the Labyrinth of Spinoza's *Scientia Intuitiva.*" In *Übergänge – diskursiv oder intuitiv? Essays zu Eckart Försters Die 25 Jahre der Philosophie*, edited by Johannes Haag and Markus Wild, 99–116. Frankfurt, Kostermann.

———. 2018. "The Building Blocks of Spinoza's Metaphysics: Substance, Attributes, and Modes." In *The Oxford Handbook of Spinoza*, edited by Michael Della Rocca, 84–113. New York, NY: Oxford University Press.

Miller, Jon. 2004. "Spinoza and the *a priori.*" *Canadian Journal of Philosophy* 34(4): 555–590.

Moreland, J. P. 2001. *Universals.* Montreal, CA: McGill-Queen's University Press.

Morrison, John. 2015. "Restricting Spinoza's Causal Axiom." *Philosophical Quarterly* 65(258): 40–63.

Mueller, Ian. 1970. "Aristotle on Geometrical Objects." *Archiv für Geschichte der Philosophie* 52(2): 156–171.

Nadler, Steven. 2006. *Spinoza's* Ethics: *An Introduction.* Cambridge, UK: Cambridge University Press.

———. 2018. "The Intellectual Love of God." In *The Oxford Handbook of Spinoza*, edited by Michael Della Rocca, 295–313. New York, NY: Oxford University Press.

Nelson, Alan. 2015. "The Problem of True Ideas in Spinoza's *Treatise on the Emendation of the Intellect.*" In *The Young Spinoza: A Metaphysician in the Making*, edited by Yitzhak Y. Melamed, 52–65. Oxford, UK: Oxford University Press.

Newlands, Samuel. 2011. "More Recent Idealist Readings of Spinoza." *Philosophy Compass* 6(2): 109–19.

———. 2015. "Spinoza's Early Anti-Abstractionism." In *The Young Spinoza: A Metaphysician in the Making*, edited by Yitzhak Y. Melamed, 255–71. Oxford, UK: Oxford University Press.

———. 2018. "Spinoza's Modal Metaphysics." *The Stanford Encyclopedia of Philosophy,* Edward N. Zalta (ed.), URL https://plato.stanford.edu/archives/falE2p13lem2018/entries/spinoza-modal/.

Nolan, Lawrence. 1997. "The Ontological Status of Cartesian Natures." *Pacific Philosophical Quarterly* 78: 169–194.

———. 1998. "Descartes' Theory of Universals." *Philosophical Studies* 89: 161–180.

Osler, Margaret J. 2008. "Descartes' Optics: Light, the Eye, and Visual Perception." In *A Companion to Descartes*, edited by Janet Broughton and John Carriero, 124–141. Malden, MA: Blackwell Publishing.

Palmerino, Carla Rita. 2016. "Reading the Book of Nature: The Ontological and Epistemological Underpinnings of Galileo's Mathematical Realism." In *The*

Language of Nature: Reassessing the Mathematization of Natural Philosophy in the Seventeenth Century, edited by Geoffrey Gorham et al., 29–50. Minneapolis, MN: University of Minnesota Press.

Parkinson, G.H.R. 1954. *Spinoza's Theory of Knowledge*. London: Oxford University Press.

———. 1973. "Language and Knowledge in Spinoza." In *Spinoza: A Collection of Critical Essays*, edited by Marjorie Grene, 73–100. Notre Dame, IN: University of Notre Dame Press.

Perler, Dominik. 2017. "Spinoza on Skepticism." In *The Oxford Handbook of Spinoza*, edited by Michael Della Rocca, 220–39. Oxford University Press.

Peterman, Alison. 2012. "Spinoza on the 'Principles of Natural Things'." *The Leibniz Review* 22: 37–65.

———. 2015. "Spinoza on Extension." *Philosopher's Imprint* 15: 1–23.

Petry, M.J. (ed.) 1985. *Spinoza's Algebraic Calculation of the Rainbow and Calculation of Chances*. Dordrecht: Martinus Nijhoff Publishers.

Popkin, Richard. 2003. *The History of Scepticism from Savonarola to Bayle*. Oxford, UK: Oxford University Press.

Primus, Kristin. 2017. "*Scientia Intuitiva* in the *Ethics*." In *Spinoza's Ethics: A Critical Guide*, edited by Yitzhak Y. Melamed. Cambridge, UK: Cambridge University Press.

Ribe, Neil M. 1997. "Cartesian Optics and the Mastery of Nature." *Isis* 88(1): 42–61.

Sabra, A. I. 1967. *Theories of Light: From Descartes to Newton*. New York, NY: American Elsevier Publishing Company, Inc.

Sandler, Ronald. 2005. "*Intuitus* and *Ratio* in Spinoza's Ethical Thought." *British Journal for the History of Philosophy* 13(1): 73–90.

Savan, David. 1986. "Spinoza: Scientist and Theorist." In *Spinoza and the Sciences*, edited by Marjorie Grene and Debra Nails, 95–123. Dordrecht: D. Reidel.

Schliesser, Eric. 2014. "Spinoza and the Philosophy of Science: Mathematics, Motion, and Being." In *The Oxford Handbook of Spinoza*, edited by Michael Della Rocca. DOI: https://doi.org/10.1093/oxfordhb/9780195335828.013.020.

Schmaltz, Tad M. 1991. "Platonism and Descartes' View of Immutable Essences." *Archiv für Geschichte der Philosophie* 73: 129–170.

———. 1999. "Spinoza on the Vacuum." *Archiv für Geschichte der Philosophie* 81(2): 174–205.

———. 2020. *The Metaphysics of the Material World: Suárez, Descartes, Spinoza*. New York, NY: Oxford University Press.

Schneider, Daniel. 2016. "Spinoza's Epistemological Methodism." *Journal of the History of Philosophy* 54: 573–599.

Schopenhauer, Arthur. 1969. *The World As Will and Representation*. Vol. 1. Translated by E. F. J. Payne. New York: Dover Publications.

Sepkoski, David. 2007. *Nominalism and Constructivism in Seventeenth-Century Mathematical Philosophy*. New York, NY: Routledge.

Soyarslan, Sanem. 2016. "The Distinction between Reason and Intuitive Knowledge in Spinoza's *Ethics*." *European Journal of Philosophy* 24(1): 27–54.

Steinberg, Diane. 1993. "Spinoza, Method, and Doubt." *History of Philosophy Quarterly* 10: 211–24.

———. 1998. "Method and the Structure of Knowledge in Spinoza." *Pacific Philosophical Quarterly* 79: 152–69.

———. 2009. "Knowledge in Spinoza's *Ethics*." In *The Cambridge Companion to Spinoza's Ethics*, edited by Olli Koistinen, 140–66. Cambridge, UK: Cambridge University Press.

Steiner, Jakob. 1842. "Sur le maximum et le minimum des figures dans le plan, sur la sphere, et dans l'espace en générale. Premier mémoire," *Journal für die reine und angewandte Mathematik* 24: 93–162; 189–250.

Striker, Gisela. 1990. "The Problem of the Criterion." In *Epistemology* (Companions to Ancient Thought 1), edited by S. Everson, 143–160. Cambridge, UK: Cambridge University Press.

Suárez, Francisco. 1995. *On Beings of Reason: Metaphysical Disputation LIV*. Translated by John P. Doyle. Milwaukee, WI: Marquette University Press.

Vermij, Rienk, and Atzema, Eisso. 1995. "Specilla circularia: an Unknown Work by Johannes Hudde." *Studia Leibnitiana* 27: 104–121.

Vermij, Rienk. 2013. "Instruments and the Making of a Philosopher. Spinoza's Career in Optics." *Intellectual History Review* 23: 65–81.

Viljanen, Valtteri. 2011. *Spinoza's Geometry of Power*. Cambridge, UK: Cambridge University Press.

Von Duuglas-Ittu, Kevin. 2008a. "Spinoza's Blunder and the Spherical Lens." *Frames/sing* (blog). Posted June 21, 2008. Available at: https://kvond.wordpress.com/2008/06/21/spinozas-blunder-and-the-spherical-lens/

———. 2008b. "Deciphering Spinoza's Optical Letters." *Frames/sing* (blog). Posted August 17, 2008. Available at: https://kvond.wordpress.com/2008/08/17/deciphering-spinozas-optical-letters/

———. 2008c. "Spinoza: Not As Abused as Is Said." *Frames/sing* (blog). Posted September 14, 2008. Available at: https://kvond.wordpress.com/2008/09/14/spinoza-not-as-abused-as-is-said/

Williams, Michael. 1999. "Skepticism." In *The Blackwell Guide to Epistemology*, edited by John Greco and Ernest Sosa, 35–69. Oxford, UK: Blackwell Publishers.

Wilson, Margaret D. 1991. "Spinoza's Causal Axiom (*Ethics* I, Axiom 4)." In *God and Nature: Spinoza's Metaphysics*, edited by Yirmiyahu Yovel, 133–60. Leiden: E.J. Brill.

———. 1996. "Spinoza's theory of knowledge." In *The Cambridge Companion to Spinoza*, edited by Don Garrett, 89–141. Cambridge, UK: Cambridge University Press.

———. 1999. "'For They Do Not Agree in Nature with Us': Spinoza on the Lower Animals." In *New Essays on the Rationalists*, edited by Rocco Gennaro and C. Huenemann, 336–52. Oxford, UK: Oxford University Press.

Wolfson, Harry Austryn. 1934. *The Philosophy of Spinoza: Unfolding the Latent Process of His Reasoning*. Volume 1. Cambridge, MA: Harvard University Press.

Yovel, Yirmiyahu. 1990. "The Third Kind of Knowledge as Salvation." In *Spinoza: Issues and Directions*, edited by Edwin Curley and Pierre-François Moreau, 157–75. Leiden: E.J. Brill.

Index

A

Abstraction/abstract, 7, 11n28, 12, 24, 31, 32n11, 33n12, 34–36, 44, 48, 52, 57n7, 60, 65, 70, 71, 71n25, 72n26, 79n35, 82, 93, 117n54, 137, 142, 157n7, 237
Acosmism, 62, 68, 69, 138
Activity, 103, 104n32, 218, 220
Adequate, *see* Idea; Knowledge
Affects, 11, 73, 81, 92, 93, 100, 103, 103n29, 103n31, 107, 117, 120n57, 156, 190, 191, 203n25, 215, 216, 219n41
Antirealism, 8n20, 11, 11n28, 51–84
  mathematical antirealism, 10, 16
A posteriori, 90, 123
A priori, 10, 36, 46, 47, 90, 91, 93, 99, 116, 116n51, 118–120, 123, 133–136, 134n19, 145, 146, 159, 177, 177n39, 178, 233
Aristotle/Aristotelian, 8n20, 71, 71n25, 72, 102, 103n28, 138n23, 201
Arithmetic, 72, 83, 83n42, 84, 236, 237
Attribute, 13–14n34, 17, 43–45, 45n26, 55, 69, 75, 77, 80, 91, 93, 96, 96n16, 96–97n17, 97, 97n18, 101–102n27, 102, 108n39, 111, 116, 116n51, 117, 123, 124, 140n25, 142, 146, 153, 154–155n1, 155n2, 158–161, 160n9, 163–166, 166n14, 168n21, 170, 175–178, 176n33, 177n39, 181, 187, 187–188n6, 188, 191–195, 191n8, 192n9, 192n10, 201–205, 202n24, 203n26, 207–210, 212n33, 223n47, 231, 237

B

Bacon, Francis, 12n30, 76, 89n3, 107, 195
Being of imagination, 52, 53, 58
Being of reason, 31, 52–54, 53n1, 62, 65, 66, 70, 84, 115n48, 132
Bennett, Jonathan, 3n5, 12, 12n31, 80n36, 92n6, 108n39, 120n57, 139, 139–140n25, 212n33
Blessedness, 2, 16, 18, 181, 193, 194, 217, 219, 223
Boyle, Robert, 75, 76, 108n38

C

Causal axiom, 45, 63–64n13
Cause
  adequate, 64n14
  immanent, 146
Certainty, 26, 27, 42n21, 47n29, 56, 84, 116, 119, 182n2, 185, 235–237, 235n6
Cognitio, 1, 1–2n1, 64n13, 192, 192n10
Common notions
  peculiar common notions (PCNs), 97n18, 98, 99n22, 111–120, 113n44, 113n45, 114n47, 114n48, 116n49, 159, 209, 209n30, 227n1
  universal common notions (UCNs), 112–116, 113n45, 116n49, 209, 209n30
Compossibility, principle of, 177
Conatus, 162n10, 168n21, 170–174, 171n28, 184, 213–217, 216n39
Conceptualism, 10n27, 72n27
Constructivism, 11, 11n28, 12
Criterion, problem of, 25, 25n2, 26
Curley, Edwin, 1n1, 19, 80n36, 94n10, 97, 98, 98n21, 99n23, 104n33, 110n41, 112, 154n1, 160, 160n9, 178n39, 182n2, 218n41, 221, 233n5

D

Deduction, 11, 64, 99, 123, 136, 141, 143, 169, 195, 197, 212, 212n35, 221, 233, 235n6
Definitions
  and essence, 96n16
  genetic, 64, 64n14, 167–170, 173
  nominal, 108n39
  real, 108n39, 169n24
Della Rocca, Michael, 3n5, 16n35, 23n1, 27–29, 28n4, 41n19, 56n6, 117n54, 167, 168n21, 170, 173
Descartes, René/Cartesian, 2, 6, 7n15, 7n18, 8–10, 8n20, 9n21, 9n22, 9n23, 10n27, 12n31, 13, 16, 18, 19, 23, 23n1, 24, 28, 34–42, 41n19, 42n20, 42n21, 45–47, 47n29, 59n8, 64–65n14, 70–73, 72n26, 76, 81, 84, 89n3, 90n5, 94, 94n10, 97, 98, 98n21, 99n24, 100, 101, 101n26, 103n28, 104n32, 105–106n34, 107, 108n39, 110, 126, 128–131, 128n7, 132n14, 133, 134n18, 135, 144–147, 146n30, 147n31, 147n32, 154n1, 158, 164n11, 165n13, 188n6, 192n9, 197, 198, 212, 212–213n35, 221, 222, 222n46, 227, 232–237, 233n5, 235n6
Determination, 14n34, 15–17, 52, 59, 60, 62, 67, 68, 70, 74, 78, 84, 95n12, 102, 103, 134, 144, 148, 149, 177, 177n36, 178, 228, 231, 237
  figural determinations, 68, 141–143
Duration, 43, 44, 54, 59–61, 140n25, 163–165, 171–175, 171n30, 172n31, 205, 216n39, 219

E

Error, 15n35, 38, 53n1, 100, 104n32, 158, 184, 185, 187, 188, 198–200

Essence
  actual, 154, 163–179, 168n21, 171n30, 216, 216n39
  common, 17, 154–163, 155n1, 155n2, 175, 176, 183, 191–196, 208, 209, 220, 224, 231, 236
  formal, 26, 43, 44, 154, 163–179, 187, 188n6, 191, 216, 216n39
  individual, 17, 154–164, 168n21, 175, 177, 178, 183, 196, 202, 205, 207, 208, 236
  nature or essence, 113, 154
  objective, 26, 34, 165, 188n6
  species, 17, 116, 116n52, 117, 119, 154–163, 155n2, 168n21, 178, 183, 196, 205, 207, 208, 224, 236

Eternity, 3, 137–141, 140n25, 141n26, 143, 174, 205–207, 219n43

Euclid, 164n12, 184, 185n4, 198, 224

Existence
  durational, 44, 154, 171, 173, 174, 188n6, 206
  non-durational, 43, 154, 168n21, 173, 175

Experience, 14, 48, 55, 55n3, 56, 99, 99n23, 99n24, 100, 105n33, 106, 108, 108n38, 117n53, 119, 120, 134–136, 159, 178, 179, 184, 184n3, 195, 207, 224, 228, 229, 232, 233, 237
  sensory, 48, 55, 55n3, 56, 99, 120, 135, 136, 159, 184, 184n3, 228, 229, 232, 233, 237

Experiments, 110n41, 134, 195, 197, 228

Extension, 13–14n34, 14, 35, 43–45, 55, 60, 64n13, 66n15, 70–72, 77, 77n32, 91, 93, 95–97, 96n17, 104–107, 111, 113n45, 115–117, 123, 124, 135, 137, 140n25, 142–147, 146n30, 148n32, 149, 153, 154n1, 157n7, 158–161, 177, 178, 191, 192, 192n9, 201, 202, 202n23, 202n24, 204, 205, 209, 210

F

Falsification/falsificationism, 108n38, 135, 136

Falsity, 1n1, 28

Fiction, 33n12, 53, 54, 62, 65–67, 79, 110n41, 157, 158

Figures
  genetically-conceived, 51, 54, 58, 62–67, 163, 169n24, 209
  geometrical, 6, 8, 14–17, 14n34, 45, 51, 52, 60, 61, 67, 80, 81, 84, 87, 88, 131, 132, 136, 137, 144, 197, 228, 233

Finite body, 8, 13–17, 14n34, 52, 68–84, 87, 95n12, 97, 106, 125, 131, 135, 136, 138, 140–144, 148, 175, 177, 201, 204, 205, 207, 228, 237

Finite modes, *see* Modes

Force, 63n13, 103, 171, 172, 174, 178, 184, 203n25, 204, 213–216

Fourth proportional example/problem, 18, 83, 83n42, 83n43, 183–186, 189, 190, 197–201, 197–198n15, 211, 213, 216, 221, 223n47, 224

Freedom, 3, 103n29, 194, 217, 219

Frege, Gottlob, 60, 60n9

G

Gabbey, Alan, 89n2, 89n3, 94n10, 129, 130n10, 147n31
Galileo, Galilei, 6, 8–10, 9n21, 12–14, 81n40, 84, 107, 232–237
Garrett, Don, 23n1, 43–45, 163, 171, 172, 175, 176, 176n33, 177n38, 178n39, 182n2, 187n5, 188n6, 191n8, 216n39
Gassendi, Pierre, 7n18, 9, 9n23, 9n24, 10, 10n27, 11n28, 81
Geometrical method, 4–8, 6n12, 7n18, 13–17, 14n34, 45, 51, 52, 60, 61, 66n15, 67, 71, 72, 80–84, 87, 88, 95n12, 117n54, 120, 120n57, 131, 132, 136, 137, 140, 144, 164n12, 183, 197–201, 205, 228, 229, 233, 237, 237n8
Geometry, 5, 7, 8, 14, 17, 71, 81, 84, 87, 88, 95n12, 107, 120, 123–149, 153, 233, 236
God, 1n1, 4, 24, 34–39, 64n13, 90, 140n25, 146, 154, 181, 231
Gueroult, Martial, 5, 64n13, 66n15, 114n47, 114–115n48, 194

H

Hegel, Georg Wilhelm Friedrich, 68
Heuristic, 7, 37n15, 45, 82, 169, 170, 228, 229
Historia naturae (History of nature), 90, 99–107, 116n49
Hobbes, Thomas, 9–11, 9n23, 9n24, 10n27, 11n28, 12n31, 61, 90, 90n5, 124n2, 168, 231, 232
Hübner, Karolina, 11n28, 79n35, 155n2, 156, 156n6, 157n7, 159
Hudde, Johannes, 125, 126, 126n4, 130, 131, 131n13
Hyperbolic doubt, 42n21, 101, 101n26

Hypotheses, 17, 37n15, 88, 107, 108n38, 108–109n39, 109–111, 110n41, 116, 119, 120, 140, 162, 169, 204
true-in-form hypotheses, 120, 156, 227n1
Hypothetico-deductive methodology, 17, 108, 108n39, 120n57, 136, 149, 178, 207, 228–230, 232, 233, 236

I

Idea
abstract (*see* Abstraction/abstract)
adequate, 3n5, 15n35, 24, 28, 31, 39, 43, 64n14, 91–93, 98, 99n22, 101n27, 103, 105, 105–106n34, 112, 113n45, 114–116, 117n54, 118–120, 118n55, 123, 144, 159, 168n21, 178, 187–189, 191, 203, 205, 206, 209–211, 220, 222n46, 231, 232, 234–236, 237n8
clear and distinct, 7n15, 33n12, 36–40, 37n15, 46, 47n29, 48, 66, 203n25, 222n46, 235, 236
inadequate, 100, 105n33, 114, 115, 118, 210, 211, 222n46, 234
infinite, 43, 164, 165
innate, 9n23, 105–106n34
mathematical, 4, 5, 16, 23–25, 29–34, 40, 42, 43n22, 44, 45, 47, 48, 232
mutilated and confused, 222n46
true; robustly true, 32, 33, 37n15, 48, 120, 163, 169n24, 209, 211, 232, 236, 237; true-in-form, 33, 34, 43, 83, 120, 120n57, 163, 169n24, 209, 211, 227n1, 228, 231, 232, 236

Idealism, 12n13, 13–14n34
Imagination, 1, 2, 3n5, 7n18, 14, 17, 52–59, 55n3, 63–67, 66n15, 69, 79, 79n35, 87–120, 123, 137, 140n25, 143, 149, 153, 156, 184, 184n3, 186, 198, 200, 219n41
  definition of, 184
Inadequate, *see* Idea; Knowledge
Individuals, 17, 30, 44, 44n25, 57, 60, 73, 74, 74n29, 74n30, 76–80, 77n32, 80n36, 100, 103n29, 111, 113, 114, 114n47, 115n48, 118, 124, 125, 149, 153–164, 168n21, 172n31, 173, 175, 176n33, 177, 178, 183, 193, 196, 202, 204, 205, 207, 208, 216, 236
Infinite modes, *see* Modes
Innate idea, *see* Idea
Instrumentalism, 11, 11n28, 232
Intellect
  finite intellect, 17, 38, 39, 108n38, 116, 158, 163–165, 176–178, 178n39, 193, 195, 207, 208, 229, 234, 235
  God's intellect (divine intellect), 1n1, 29, 39, 48, 165, 234–237
  human intellect, 99, 207, 236, 237
  infinite intellect, 1n1, 38, 39, 116, 158, 165, 176–178, 177n39, 193, 208, 234, 235
Intellectual Love of God, 18, 181, 217–220, 219n41, 223
Intuition, 197, 198, 201n22, 212–217, 212n33, 212n35, 221, 233, 235n6
Intuitive knowledge
  definition of, 182, 184
  as perfection of reason, 181–224
  superiority of, 18, 184, 215, 216
Isoperimetric problem, 198–201, 204, 205, 214, 215, 217

J
Joy, 103, 103n29, 103n30, 117, 117n53, 218–220

K
Kant, Immanuel, 169
Knowledge
  adequate, 17, 64n13, 64–65n14, 79, 87, 101–102n27, 106, 113n45, 149, 182, 187, 188, 191, 201, 204–208, 214, 216, 222, 234, 235, 237
  first kind of (*see* Imagination)
  inadequate, 64n13, 187
  perfect knowledge, 63, 235, 236
  second kind of (*see* Reason)
  third kind of (*see* Intuitive knowledge)
Koyré, Alexandre, 7, 8

L
Lachterman, David R.
Law
  law(s) of nature; conservation of motion, 94, 95; law of inertia, 94; law of reflection, 75, 94, 95, 98, 100
  particular laws (or local laws), 97n18, 111, 112, 116
  physical laws, 148
  universal laws, 94, 96, 97, 97n20, 99, 110, 111
Leibniz, Gottfried, 10n27, 106n34, 131, 132, 135, 135n20, 146n30, 147n31, 177
Locke, John, 7n18, 75

M

Mathematical point, 131, 131n13, 132
Mathematics, 4, 5, 7n15, 8n18, 8n20, 9, 12, 12n30, 12n31, 13, 23–48, 62n12, 95n11, 107, 125, 132, 170n26, 199, 237
Mathematization, 6–19, 7n15, 7n18, 11n28, 13n32, 13n33, 144, 145, 147–149, 233, 236
Measure, 54, 58–61, 62n12, 63, 67, 137, 139, 198
Mechanical point, 131, 131n13, 132
Melamed, Yitzhak Y., 57n7, 60, 62n12, 80, 82n41, 96n16, 160n9
Method
 analysis and synthesis, 90, 90n5
 geometrical (*see* Geometrical method)
 hypothetico-deductive (*see* Hypothetico-deductive method)
 scientific (*see* Scientific method)
Modes
 finite modes, 68, 69, 97n17, 123, 124, 124n1, 138–140, 142, 167, 168, 170, 175, 177–178n39, 178, 179, 188n6, 202
 infinite modes; immediate infinite mode, 77, 97, 111, 123, 124, 160, 161, 176n33, 177, 178, 191, 204, 205; mediate infinite mode, 77, 123, 124, 164, 176n33, 178
Motion, 6, 13n34, 32, 33, 65, 70, 71, 73, 75, 76, 81, 93–95, 94n10, 97–100, 98n21, 104–107, 105n33, 108n38, 109, 110n41, 114, 115, 124n2, 134, 135, 141, 144–147, 146n30, 147n31, 149, 204, 221
motion and rest, 14, 44n25, 73–78, 74n29, 74n30, 76n31, 84, 91, 93–97, 96n17, 113, 113n45, 114, 116, 123, 124, 142, 158, 159, 162, 172–173n31, 175, 176n33, 177, 178, 204, 205, 207
Multiple instantiation, 79, 82, 82n41, 158

N

Nature
 human nature, 80, 113–118, 113n44, 113n45, 114n48, 154, 159, 230, 231
 shared nature, 111, 113, 117, 159
 (*see also* Essence, species)
 See also Essence
Necessitarianism, 177n39, 178n39
Negation, 62, 62n12, 67, 68, 167n17
Nominalism, 10, 10n27, 11n28, 79n34
Numbers, 5, 6, 7n18, 8, 12, 13, 15–17, 44n25, 51, 52, 54, 57n7, 58–60, 60n9, 62n12, 63, 71, 73, 74n29, 78, 82–84, 83n43, 95n12, 101, 137, 144, 146n30, 155, 166, 166n14, 181, 183–186, 187n6, 190, 191, 194, 198, 200, 202n24, 237

O

Oldenburg, Henry, 147, 230
Optics
 optical laws, 97, 141
 optical letters, 132, 133, 136, 197

P

Parallelism (of attributes), 166n14
Particulars, 5, 8, 10, 14, 16, 18, 27, 28n4, 35, 38n16, 40, 42, 43, 45, 48, 51, 54, 59, 62, 74n29, 77n32, 78–80, 80n36, 82, 82n41, 90, 90n4, 93, 97, 97n18, 99, 102n27, 104, 105n34, 106–111, 113, 120, 123–126, 124n2, 133, 135–137, 138n23, 139, 141, 143, 144, 147, 149, 153, 156–158, 160, 162, 162n10, 163, 165, 166, 171, 173n31, 177, 178, 193, 195, 197, 216, 217, 218–219n41, 220, 223n47, 227, 232, 233, 237
Pascal, Blaise, 2, 229, 230, 232
Passivity, 104n32
Physics, 7, 7n15, 7n18, 17, 81, 84, 114n47, 146n30, 147, 147n32, 148, 162
Plato/Platonist, 8–11, 9n21, 52, 72, 72n27, 80, 102
Power, 2, 3, 5, 7n18, 25, 33, 63, 99, 103, 103n30, 106n34, 131n13, 168, 170, 171, 192n9, 195, 203n25, 214–218, 229, 231, 232, 234
Principle of sufficient reason, 16n35, 28, 29
Properties, 5, 8–13, 17, 28, 31, 40, 44, 59, 60, 64, 64n14, 70, 71n25, 72, 73, 75–82, 80n36, 82n41, 84, 87, 90, 91, 93, 95n12, 96, 96n15, 96n16, 98, 99, 101n27, 104n33, 105n34, 107, 109, 113, 114n47, 115n48, 116n51, 119, 124, 124n2, 125, 131–133, 131n13, 135, 136, 140, 141, 141n26, 144, 144n29, 148, 156, 157n7, 158–160, 160n9, 166n14, 167n19, 168, 168n21, 169, 170n26, 172, 178n40, 182n2, 184, 187, 188, 197, 204, 209, 210, 227n1, 228, 229, 232–234

Q

Qualities, primary and secondary, 75, 107, 159
Quantity, 6, 54, 59–61, 76n31, 136–138, 138n24, 141–143, 147, 147n31, 174

R

Rationalism, 194
Realism, 11, 11n28, 51–84, 143, 183, 232
  mathematical realism, 8–11, 51–84, 228
Reason
  and common notions, 79, 91–98, 101n27, 209, 210
  definition of, 188, 208
  interplay of reason and imagination, 118, 143

S

Schliesser, Eric, 12, 94, 108n39, 168n21
Schopenhauer, Arthur, 217
Science
  scientia, 2n1
  Spinozan science, 17, 18, 55, 72, 78, 80, 87–120, 123–149, 153, 197, 198, 224, 232, 233
Scientific method, 2, 7, 12n31, 14, 15, 17, 87–91, 87n1, 89n2, 89n3, 94, 94n10, 95, 95n11, 96n17, 97–100, 99n23, 107, 108n39, 118, 120, 125, 131, 133, 134, 136, 141, 143–145, 148, 159, 194–196, 207, 228, 231, 232, 236

Sensory experience, *see* Experience
Singular thing, 17, 43–45, 44n25, 79, 99, 101n27, 111n42, 141, 153, 154, 160, 161, 164, 165, 171, 174–176, 178, 184n3, 190, 191, 191n8, 193–208, 194n12, 212n33, 215–218, 236
Skepticism, 14, 16, 23–48, 51, 232
Soyarslan, Sanem, 182, 182n2, 210n31, 215n37
Spherical aberration, 129
Steiner, Jakob, 198, 200
Suárez, Francisco, 53n1, 165n13, 188n6
Substance, 4, 18, 19, 37n15, 38, 45n26, 46, 59, 69, 70, 72, 80, 80n36, 82n41, 115, 120, 137–143, 138n23, 139–140n25, 154n1, 160, 160n9, 166–167n17, 167, 170, 202n24, 213, 234

T
Time, 12, 38, 39, 44, 46, 52, 54, 57–61, 62n12, 63, 72, 73, 80, 88, 107, 108n39, 116, 118, 132n14, 137, 138n24, 141, 155, 161, 165, 166n15, 168n21, 169, 172, 174, 185, 189, 196, 203, 215n38, 216, 221, 222, 235

True idea, *see* Idea
Truth
  as correspondence, 32, 35, 40
  form of, 24, 33, 41, 42, 47, 66, 83, 95n12, 136, 237
  intrinsic features of, 24, 42n22, 47
  robust truth, 36, 40, 120n57, 236
Tschirnhaus, Ehrenfried Walther von, 144–146, 147n31, 148, 169n25, 170n26

U
Universals, 8n20, 10, 10n27, 35, 54–58, 63, 67, 71, 79, 79n34, 79n35, 80, 80n36, 82, 89–91, 94–100, 97n20, 106, 107, 110, 111, 116n51, 120, 123–125, 136, 149, 156–158, 162, 178, 184n3, 186, 188, 190, 195, 208, 229

V
Vacuum, 104n32, 105
Viljanen, Valtteri, 5

W
Will, 33, 38, 65–66, 101n26, 156–158
Wonder, 53n1, 102, 103, 103n28

Printed in the United States
by Baker & Taylor Publisher Services